DATE DUE

APR 21 2014	
4-22-15	
	PRINTED IN U.S.A.

SLEEPING
With Your
SMARTPHONE

How to Break the 24/7 Habit
and Change the Way You Work

LESLIE A. PERLOW

Harvard Business Review Press

Boston, Massachusetts

Author's Note:
In due respect to all those who graciously shared their experiences, their names have been changed to protect their identities. To maintain client confidentiality, all client names have also been changed, along with some identifying characteristics.

Library of Congress Cataloging-in-Publication Data

Perlow, Leslie A., 1967–
  Sleeping with your smartphone : how to break the 24/7 habit and change the way you work / Leslie A. Perlow.
     p. cm.
  ISBN 978-1-4221-4404-6 (alk. paper)
  1. Hours of labor.   2. Quality of work life.   3. Time management.   4. Teams in the workplace.   5. Performance.   6. Organizational behavior.   I. Title.
  HD5106.P424 2012
  650.1—dc23

                                                                          2011046408

The paper used in this publication meets the requirements of the American National Standard for Permanence of Paper for Publications and Documents in Libraries and Archives Z39.48-1992.

To Hailey, Talia, and Sasha, who make it all worthwhile.

I love you—Mom.

CONTENTS

Part IV FROM TEAM TO ORGANIZATION

Does It Have to Be This Way?

Go to a Little League game, and you'll see parents watching their kids on the field. Or are they? Their eyes wander back and forth between the game and their smartphones.

That young couple across the restaurant out for a dinner date—one is checking e-mail, the other is wondering, "Are you having dinner with me or your work?"

That person on a quiet beach in the Caribbean, click-clacking away on a laptop—is this really a vacation?

We are all too familiar with the challenges of the "always-connected" age of the smartphone, iPad, Netbook, laptop—or the next big thing that will enable us to be on the golf course, on the beach, on the couch or even in bed, and still be working. We feel overwhelmed, overworked, always interrupted, lacking time to focus; we also feel exhilarated, challenged, rewarded, and freed from the shackles of the office. While being so needed puts a burden on us—and our families, friends, and communities—it can also be fulfilling. Always being on, in fact, is becoming increasingly core to our identities. As one professional said about his smartphone, "I love the thing and I hate it at the same time. The reason I love it is that it *gives* me so much power. And the reason I hate it is that it *has* so much power over me."[1]

The Great Impossibility—Turning Off

Over the last six years as easy access to the Internet was transforming work, I surveyed more than twenty-five hundred managers and professionals in high-pressure, demanding jobs—investment bankers, lawyers, accountants, engineers, and management consultants; people in advertising, marketing, high tech, and nonprofits; people from *Fortune* 500 companies and start-ups; people from eighty-four countries on six continents. I spoke to several hundred of them directly, asking the same questions: How much were they working? How much pure, guilt-free time off did they have? Not the lucky accidental hours away from work with no calls or e-mails, but pre-planned hours, sacrosanct on the calendar when they could disconnect completely from professional responsibilities without experiencing that nagging urge to keep checking their electronic devices. I asked whether they were happy with their current mix of time spent working, spent accessible but not necessarily working, and spent truly off. I asked what could make it better? I also asked them whether they believed change was possible.

While most perked up at the idea of more time *off,* they quickly pointed out how impractical that was in their day-to-day work-lives: if you refrain from e-mailing, colleagues will still e-mail you—and you don't want to let them down. If you stop working long hours and always being accessible, others will likely speed past you on the career ladder. You never know when the client or customer will call, or what the demands of managing across time zones will present. And let's face it: when that phone buzzes, few of us have the mental fortitude to ignore it.

Instead of Self-Help, Group-Help

Plenty of books have been written to help individuals cope with the ever increasing demands of work: how to prioritize work better, how to manage time more effectively across different domains of life, how to survive e-mail overload—even how to beat a BlackBerry addiction.[2] These books share a common premise: your life could be better, richer, fuller; and you could contribute more to your work place if *you* changed how *you* work and live.

Sleeping with Your Smartphone takes a very different approach. Rather than helping you accommodate your life to the pressure of always being connected, I seek to help you alleviate this pressure. I show how this can happen without grand overarching societal change or even bold and costly changes to your organization. It does, however, require that you and those you work with most closely strive, together, to make this change happen. When you do, the changes you make will not only mitigate the pressure you feel to always be connected but will also improve your work process.

It all began with an experiment that my research associate and collaborator, Jessica Porter, and I initiated in order to explore whether one six-person "case team" at one of the world's most elite and demanding professional service firms—The Boston Consulting Group (BCG)—could work together to ensure that they each could truly disconnect from work for a scheduled unit of time each week. This modest experiment generated such powerful results—not just for individuals' work-lives but for the team's work process and ultimately the client—that the experiment was expanded to more and more of BCG's teams. Four years later, over nine hundred BCG teams from thirty countries on five continents had participated.

Sleeping with Your Smartphone shares BCG's story.

It also serves as a guide for anyone who is on a team or leads a team— whether a junior or senior manager, from big organizations or small, in the United States or abroad—and wants to make the impossible possible: turning off more, while improving the work process itself. *Sleeping with Your Smartphone* proposes a way to make exactly that happen: a process tested successfully by BCG teams in North America, South America, Europe, Asia, and Australia. A process I have seen implemented with good and not-so-good managers; on big and small teams, with tight deadlines and less pressing deliverables. A process that I have come to call "PTO"—because at the core, when people work together to create "predictable time off," people, teams, and ultimately the organization all stand to benefit.

To be clear, PTO won't solve all your problems. Nor is it about being always off in a world that is always on. Rather, it is about incremental changes that promise to improve your work-life and your work in ways that make them notably better.

Creating Change Where No One Could Even Imagine It

I chose to conduct the original experiment at The Boston Consulting Group because there was widespread skepticism about the possibility of such hard-charging professionals turning off. "It has to be this way," explained one consultant, echoing many of his colleagues. "It is the nature of the work. Clients pay huge sums of money and expect—and deserve—the highest-quality service." Most consultants simply accepted the resulting demands on their time as the price they had to pay for annual salaries of well over $100,000 for recent business school graduates to millions of dollars for the most senior partners, as well as for unequaled exposure to colleagues and clients of the highest caliber working together to tackle pressing problems faced by the world's leading organizations, not to mention résumé building work experience.[3] Moreover, many actually thrived on the intensity of the work and did not want it to be different. Even those who wanted more time for their personal lives presumed they had no alternative but to leave the firm to achieve it, and many did, including some of BCG's most talented consultants. I figured that if change could be fostered here, it could be made to happen most anywhere.

Imagine my delight then, when four years after we conducted our first experiment at BCG's Boston office, 86 percent of the consulting staff in the firm's Northeast offices—including Boston, New York, and Washington, DC—were on teams engaged in similar PTO experiments. These team members were much more likely than their colleagues on teams not participating in PTO to rate their overall satisfaction with work and work-life positively. For example:

- 51 percent (versus 27 percent) were excited to start work in the morning

- 72 percent (versus 49 percent) were satisfied with their job

- 54 percent (versus 38 percent) were satisfied with their work-life balance

We also discovered that significantly more of those on PTO teams found the work process to be collaborative, efficient, and effective.

- 91 percent (versus 76 percent) rated their team as collaborative

- 65 percent (versus 42 percent) rated their team as doing everything it could to be efficient

- 74 percent (versus 51 percent) rated their team as doing everything it could to be effective

The happy result for BCG was that individuals engaged in PTO experiments were more likely to see themselves at the firm for the long term (58 percent versus 40 percent) and were more likely to perceive that they were providing significant value to their clients (95 percent versus 84 percent). BCG clients reported a range of experiences with PTO teams from neutral (nothing dropped through the cracks) to extremely positive (they reaped significant benefits). According to BCG's CEO, Hans-Paul Bürkner, the process unleashed by these experiments "has proven not only to enhance work-life balance, making careers much more sustainable, but also to improve client value delivery, consultant development, business services team effectiveness, and overall case experience. It is becoming part of the culture—the future of BCG."

The Cycle of Responsiveness: The Root of the 24/7 Habit

The reason PTO can be so effective for both individuals' work-lives and the work itself: busy managers and professionals tend to amplify—through their own actions and interactions—the inevitable pressures of their jobs, making their own and their colleagues' lives more intense, more overwhelming, more demanding, and less fulfilling than they need to be. The result of this vicious cycle is that the work process ends up being less effective and efficient than it could be. The power of PTO is that it breaks this cycle, mitigating the pressure, freeing individuals to spend time in ways that are more desirable for themselves personally and for the work process.

The initial discovery that illuminated all of this emerged from one of the surveys we conducted of sixteen hundred managers and professionals. Of this sample, 92 percent reported putting in fifty or more hours of work a week. A third of this group was working sixty-five or more hours a week. And that doesn't include the twenty to twenty-five hours per week most of them reported monitoring their work while not actually working: 70 percent admitted to checking their smartphone each day within an hour after getting up, and 56 percent did so within an hour before going to bed. Weekends offered no let-up: 48 percent checked over the weekend, even on Friday and Saturday nights. Vacations were no better: 51 percent checked continuously when on vacation. If they lost their wireless device and couldn't replace it for a week, 44 percent of those surveyed said they would experience "a great deal of anxiety." And 26 percent confessed to sleeping with their smartphones.[4] Simply put, people were "on" a great deal.

We defined *on* as the time people spent working plus all the additional time they were available, monitoring their work in case something came

FIGURE I-1

Cycle of responsiveness:
How genuine pressure to be on gets amplified through our own actions

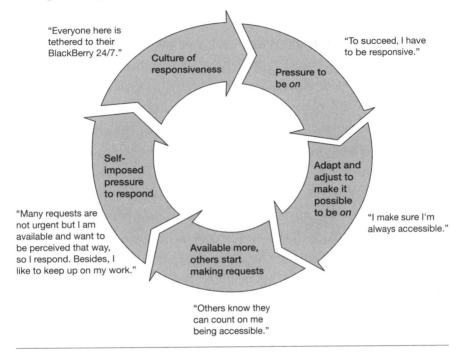

"Everyone here is tethered to their BlackBerry 24/7."

Culture of responsiveness

"To succeed, I have to be responsive."

Pressure to be *on*

Self-imposed pressure to respond

Adapt and adjust to make it possible to be *on*

"Many requests are not urgent but I am available and want to be perceived that way, so I respond. Besides, I like to keep up on my work."

"I make sure I'm always accessible."

Available more, others start making requests

"Others know they can count on me being accessible."

up. And, we discovered that those whose workweek was more unpre-dictable tended to be on more. That was not surprising. What caught our attention was that the more people were on, the more unpredict-able their work time seemed to become. By being constantly connected to work, they seemed to be reinforcing—and worse, amplifying—the very pressures that caused them to need to be available.

Our respondents were caught in what we have come to call the *cycle of responsiveness* (see figure I-1). The pressure to be on usually stems from some seemingly legitimate reason, such as requests from clients or customers or teammates in different time zones. People begin adjust-ing to these demands—adapting the technology they use, altering their daily schedules, the way they work, even the way they live their lives and interact with their families and friends—to be better able to meet the increased demands on their time. Once colleagues experience this increased responsiveness, their own requests expand. Already working long hours, most just accept these additional demands—whether they are urgent or not—and those who don't risk being branded as less committed to their work.

And thus the cycle spins: teammates, superiors and subordinates continue to make more requests, and conscientious employees accept these marginal increases in demands on their time, while their expectations of each other (and themselves) rise accordingly.[5] Eventually, the cycle grows (unintentionally) vicious; most people don't notice that they are spinning their way into a 24/7 workweek. And even if they begin resenting how much their work is spilling into their personal lives, they fail to recognize that they are their own worst enemy, the source of much of the pressure that they attribute to the nature of their business.

Imagine instead that people were not so accommodating and decided to find alternative ways to do the work. Imagine the upside of no longer having to accommodate to all the pressure to be on. Imagine if in the process of making this possible, new ways of working were discovered that were more efficient and effective. Consider the win not just for individuals but also for the organization. The power of PTO is that it makes this all come true—by breaking the cycle of responsiveness.

Breaking the Cycle—Through Small, Doable Changes

In this always-connected age, you cannot break the cycle of responsiveness alone. When you disconnect, everyone else remains connected. That's the reality of today's 24/7 culture. And no individual alone—not even the CEO—can change that reality. But it is also the case that altering the demands of clients or customers is not required. What it takes to break the cycle of responsiveness is for you and your colleagues to strive to do it, together.

Many organizational change initiatives have revolved around empowering employees to change the way they work together. A central tenet of such popular initiatives as Continuous Improvement, Lean, Six Sigma, and Organization Learning is to empower employees to participate in rethinking their work process to improve it. Typically these initiatives entail significant top-level involvement, often creating new programs and more policies that require large upfront investments. Moreover, even in the best cases, when teams succeed, the time gained from team members working smarter gets reinvested in the work itself, with little effect on work schedules and personal lives.

PTO is a radical departure—that benefits both the work process and individuals' work-lives. It is based on a set of small and doable steps that can be executed by a single team:

- Every team member strives to achieve the same goal—an agreed upon unit of predictable time off each week.

- The team meets weekly to discuss how each member is achieving the goal and to discuss the team's work process more generally.

When a team follows these small, simple steps, remarkable things happen—for individuals' work-lives and the work process. In fact, everything about PTO inspires people to give change a shot: because its very purpose is to improve their personal lives without negatively impacting their work, team members are motivated to participate. By starting with one small, doable change—a unit of predictable time off each week—team members discover that challenging the way it is and the way they have presumed it has to be is not as inconceivable as they once believed. And by allotting time to discuss issues—relating to both work and personal lives—the team ends up continually surfacing areas for change and then working together to improve their work process to the benefit of their work-lives and their work. They end up challenging fundamental assumptions about how work is done. They test boundaries, consider options, and discover how to spend more time addressing the most important problems, effectively, and with more control over their work schedules. Individuals, the team, and ultimately the organization all benefit.

Sleeping with Your Smartphone—At a Glance

I have structured the book into two halves, each with two parts: in the first half, I tell the story of what happened when BCG allowed a Harvard Business School professor to explore whether ambitious management consultants could disconnect from work—and reconnect with their personal lives. I also focus on what emerged as the key components of the PTO process, and how together these components benefit individuals' work-lives and their work process. In the second half of the book, I offer guidelines for how you can launch a similar process with your own team (and ultimately organization)—enabling people to disconnect while improving how they work together. Let me quickly add—before you skip directly there—that to understand the value of PTO you have to witness it in action—the struggles, the trial and error, the resistance, the ups and downs that teams at BCG went through to make PTO work. If you're serious about making the PTO process your own and initiating change in your organization, you need to know how BCGers made this happen in theirs. I will bring you into BCG's team rooms, invite you to sit in on their meetings, listen to their skepticism, share their enthusiasm, and watch them struggle as they experiment with making work more manageable and personally engaging while making the work process itself more efficient and effective, increasing the value they deliver their clients.

Part I shares the story of the first experiment at BCG to see whether a collective goal of a scheduled unit of predictable time off could change the way team members approached their work (chapter 1) and describes the core components that propelled the experiment toward success (chapter 2).

Part II elaborates the magic of PTO: the open dialogue that it fosters (chapter 3); the passion and action that arise among team members willing to discuss their successes and failures in trying to achieve the predictable time off goal and get their work done (chapter 4); and the different forms of collective experimentation that teams tried, yielding improvements for their personal lives and their work process (chapter 5). Chapter 6 summarizes the results and describes the continuous learning and improvement that is unleashed at the team level: small, doable steps that focus on achieving personal as well as work goals generate significant benefits for individuals and the team.

Part III translates the BCG tale into practical advice for getting started on your team, describing the essential role of team leadership support (chapter 7) as well as how to identify the team itself and select an appropriate goal (chapter 8). Chapter 9 provides guidelines for the first meeting with the team and for moving forward.

Part IV explores what it takes to diffuse the PTO process from team to organization, deriving lessons from BCG's experience (chapter 10) and highlighting the unique value that facilitators contribute to the process (chapter 11). Chapter 12, the final chapter, distills the power of PTO for the organization: PTO inspires reimagining how work is done, redefining what it means to do good work and be a good worker, and creating a true win-win for individuals and the organization.

For those interested in the research behind this book, I have added a methodological appendix as well as endnotes for each chapter, which report in more detail what I have done, what I have learned, and how it builds on prior research. I have also included a glossary to provide more background on consulting and BCG, in particular.

Whether your workplace is more demanding than BCG's or significantly less so, if you and your team want to break your 24/7 "habit" and markedly improve the way you work, turn the page . . . and meet Mark.

Part I

HOW A TEAM TURNS OFF

1

The Experiment

Mark was exhausted. It was almost 11 p.m., and he had just landed in Boston after a four-hour flight from Indianapolis—and four straight sixteen-hour workdays with a demanding client. He hadn't checked his BlackBerry since takeoff, and his inbox was full of new messages.

He immediately opened the e-mail from Doug, The Boston Consulting Group partner on the case for which Mark was project leader. It contained details about what to expect in two meetings he had set up for the following day. The first was with a Harvard Business School research team to discuss an "experiment" using his team as the guinea pig. Mark had already expressed his reservations that having outsiders hovering around might be too distracting for the team, not to mention their nervous client. Doug, however, was enthusiastic about the HBS project, and tonight's message simply advised, "Keep an open mind—might be helpful for you to develop as a manager."

The advice was hardly comforting. Mark was well aware of his reputation among the BCG partners: outstanding with clients; burns out his teams. The last thing he needed in his quest for partner was a Harvard B-School study shining a light on his inadequacies as a manager.

The second meeting involved a potential client in Boston. That news gave Mark a boost: for the past twelve months he had been traveling to the client's Indianapolis office every Monday morning on the 6 a.m. flight, working with his BCG team until Thursday, and hoping to make the 4 p.m. flight back to Logan. The problem was, he'd made that flight only once. So here he was again, sitting on the tarmac at Logan, long after dark, waiting to exit the plane, checking his BlackBerry to see what he was up against the next day. What a lucky break it would be if Doug and he could sell some local work.

Mark was eager to keep working with Doug. Already a rising star at the firm, Doug had come to BCG straight out of business school and moved quickly through the ranks, recently making partner in his mid-thirties—the same age as Mark. Doug was also the only partner in the Boston office specializing in Mark's area of interest. If Mark was going to get promoted, he knew he would need Doug as his advocate.

The next e-mail was from Lisa, his newest team member, updating him on her day's progress. The client, a large consumer goods company in the Midwest, had acquired one of its major competitors, and BCG had been hired to help integrate the two organizations. The case had recently evolved from a post-merger integration (PMI) to an implementation case. Mark and the people he managed had spent the better part of the last six months devising a reorganization plan; the challenge now was to implement it. At BCG, when the phase changed, so did the junior people. Mark was now leading a new team consisting of two experienced consultants, Charlie and Bob (post-MBA); Lisa, an associate (three years out of college); and Bill, a summer consultant (between first and second year in his MBA program)—all under Doug's watchful eye.

Mark worried about Lisa. She was coming into the project with a spotty record, and he was concerned that mentoring her would take away from the time he needed to spend guiding the others. Mark continued reading and responding to e-mail as he made his way off the plane, through the terminal, and into the taxi line. As his taxi approached the Ted Williams Tunnel, Mark put down the BlackBerry, but the thing continued to beep with answers from the e-mails he had just sent. BCG colleagues tended to be up late responding to messages, trying to get some work done, preparing for the next day. After shooting back another batch of replies, Mark put the BlackBerry down again.

He had been living in Boston for the past two years. After graduating from college, he had spent seven years in the military before going to business school. From there he had tried out consulting for three years, gone to the corporate world for two, and then returned to consulting two years earlier.

His career was going well. He was close to being promoted to principal. He knew he should be excited—it meant more money, more responsibility, and being one step closer to partner. Yet it also meant even more time on the road, more stress, and definitely more scrutiny. He was well aware that the partners, particularly Doug, would be watching him closely and they'd all be asking: Was he committed enough to make partner? Did he have a viable plan to bring in the millions of dollars of annual revenue expected of a partner? Could he both sell work to potential clients and manage a team?

In fact, his last review had made it clear he needed to do a better job of managing his teams. He did not disagree with that criticism: when the client was in crisis, he reverted to his military training, expecting his subordinates to get the job done, no matter what. He knew his teams didn't appreciate his gung-ho approach, and the message from his superiors was clear: if he wanted to make partner, he couldn't keep burning out his teams.

Throughout the past year, he had been getting calls almost weekly from Rachel Levine, the head of the consulting staff in BCG's Boston office, who checked in on a team when anyone's hours went consistently above sixty-five hours per week. And each time she called, he gave her the same answer: "It's a post-merger integration case, the workload is huge, the time line demanding, the number of pieces to be managed endless. What do you want me to do differently?" Mark wasn't trying to be difficult: he genuinely didn't know what else he might do. What he did know, however, was that he had to do *something*.

By the time he got home, it was almost 11:30. His wife had left him a note: "Welcome home, hope it was a good trip." She seemed understanding about how demanding his job was, though he wondered how long that would last. Already, whenever his BlackBerry would buzz in her presence, he could see her bristle. There was also the pressure to start a family. Jenna had begun taking her temperature and talking about "timing windows," and here he was, trudging home totally exhausted after another four-day road-trip. Maybe this weekend, if he wasn't too exhausted, if he didn't have too much work to catch up on—if, if, if.

He climbed into bed and fell asleep instantly.

The Background

The previous year, George Martin, head of BCG's Boston office, had agreed that we could conduct a study of how work was done at BCG. We spent a year in their office, on the road with them, at the client site, observing how they spent their time. We discovered that unpredictability and lack of control over their schedules was a significant driver of discontent with their work-lives, and ultimately had caused many to leave and others to be planning to do so. We proposed a modest experiment to explore the possibility of people getting a small dose of control, a single predictable night off a week. George was reluctant to volunteer any of his teams to participate. He did, however, allow us to wander around the office looking for another partner who might be willing.

Six months later, we finally found Doug. As a young partner with two little kids and a third on the way, he himself was coping daily with the bind between the demands of work and family. Nor was he unaware of the irony of being, as he put it, "a partner in a management consulting firm who couldn't figure out how to get a night off for my team." He seemed genuinely to want to improve things for his people, and also was hoping to help the firm better address work-life issues. Doug was clearly up for our experiment, and we were equally excited about working with him and his team, which, to honor the confidentiality between BCG and its clients, we will refer to as the *Consumer* team.

As eager as we were to proceed, when Mark walked into the room to meet with us that Friday morning, revealing his own ambivalence about participating in this experiment, we were filled with our own ambivalence. Doug and Rachel Levine, head of the consulting staff for the Boston office and our internal liaison at BCG, had each briefed us on Mark's history of working himself and his teams very hard—and his "low upward feedback scores" reflecting his team members' discontent. It was quite possible that Mark might resist getting involved in a project that could expose his weaknesses as a manager; and if he did go along, what were the odds that his struggles managing his team would undermine our experiment? But Doug and Rachel didn't seem to share our concerns; on the contrary, they seemed enthusiastic that the HBS project would help Mark become a better manager. And we were lucky to have found a team willing to try our experiment.

When we presented Mark with our idea of each team member taking a predictable night off each week, his answer surprised us. "I'd be a big fan of blocking out a night off each week so we can't work during that time." He later confided to us that the travel and pressure of this current case had been getting to him. In the military and just afterward, he had been in the best shape of his life. Now he could barely fit in a workout. There never seemed to be any time, even for an early morning run—unless he was willing to do it at 4:30 in the morning so that he could:

Do the prep work for the day in his hotel room by 6 a.m.

in order to

Be at the client's office at 7:30 a.m.

where he'd

Keep working until he grabbed dinner around 8 p.m.

and then

Work until midnight back in the hotel.

He also recounted that during his two-week honeymoon the previous month, he'd been able to totally turn off from work and he and his wife had had a great time together. He realized how lucky he'd been to get a stress-free wedding and honeymoon. He'd heard many stories of colleagues' honeymoons being interrupted by business calls. "My father told me that it took a wedding to actually have a conversation with me," he confessed. His goal going forward was to keep the weekends clear for his wife, but he'd already had to work almost every weekend.

Other team members were also excited. Lisa was applying to graduate school and welcomed the idea of time off to write her applications. Charlie's wife was living in Indianapolis for the summer, so the prospect of spending more time with her appealed to him. Bob, however, was skeptical and resistant. He didn't want a night off in Indianapolis. As he put it, "I would much rather spend the time off with my wife in Boston than in Indianapolis by myself on a Tuesday night."

Team Dynamics

By the time we met with the team, they were four weeks into the new phase of the Consumer case. Doug and Mark's previous team of consultants had spent six months devising plans for going forward. They had discovered the client was "too regional," and that its bottom line would benefit from economies of scale that centralization would bring. The new team faced the daunting challenge of centralizing the organization in Indianapolis—and its interface with distributors across the country.

Pulling this reorganization off would be a huge task for the Consumer team. The work had been divided up into modules, which were assigned to individual team members, who worked on them independently. Mark played puzzle master. He decided what people needed to know in order to do their piece of the work. He saw little need for them to share the big picture. Rather, he considered it his role to "fit the pieces together."

As a result, all his "pieces" were working flat out on their own: Bob had been laying the groundwork for the reorganization for weeks, spending most of his days in meetings with his client contacts, and catching up on his own planning at night. Charlie and Lisa were preparing for visits to distributors where they would spend several weeks interviewing managers. By the time our experiment began, they were planning a six-week "deep dive" at the Chicago location. They were already having frequent meetings and phone calls with their client contacts there as well as in Indianapolis, along with a weekly scheduled client meeting. And then there was the weekly BCG case team meeting, where the team members shared their findings and insights with Mark and Doug.

Such pressure was the way of life at BCG. Under so much stress with their own particular problems and deadlines, these individuals tended to lose focus of the larger issues they faced as a team. At a typical case team meeting, one consultant would make a PowerPoint presentation while the rest of the team checked their BlackBerrys or worked on their own PowerPoint slides. The only people who seemed truly engaged in the discussion were the presenter and Mark and Doug, who listened carefully and asked questions.

To improve the quality of team members' interactions, Lisa had early on encouraged Mark to introduce a tool—the *Pulse Check*—developed by another BCGer to help his team discuss not only how a given project was going but how they really felt about it. The Pulse Check consisted of four questions:

1. How are you feeling?

2. How much value are we delivering to the client?

3. How satisfied are you with your learning?

4. Is the current operating model sustainable for you?

The drill was to go around the room asking each team member to respond to each question using four cartoon faces: smiling, accepting, frowning, or crying.

Mark agreed to give it a try. His team, however, gave quick, superficial responses, sharing little real emotion. "It turned out to be a bit awkward to have everybody sit down and say how you feel," Lisa conceded. "We don't want to seem in any way that we're a slacker on the team."

After a few weeks, Mark dropped the Pulse Check from the weekly meeting, and no one protested. It was right around that time that we turned up with our experiment.

Launching the Experiment

To officially launch the experiment, we had a meeting with the entire Consumer team. It was an opportunity to create a shared sense of what the experiment was about. We had already briefed Doug and Mark about their importance, as the team's leaders, in conveying their support for the experiment.

When the meeting began, Doug stressed his enthusiasm for our project. "If we cannot figure out how to have a night off during the week," he boldly announced, "then I am not sure I want to be at BCG." He saw several opportunities for them to improve their work-lives on this case, and he was excited to have the chance to experiment.

Each member was assigned a person who could cover for him or her. Lisa and Charlie's modules worked well together and lent themselves perfectly to the concept of coverage. Bob's work was more isolated, but Bill, the summer associate, would cover for him—and Mark would help too when Bill was unable to either because of his lower position or because BCG recruiting events for summer associates got in the way. And Bob—with Doug's help, when necessary—was to cover for Mark.

The consultants were initially concerned that having a scheduled night off would mean that all other nights were *on.* Doug and Mark assured them that there was no expectation to work every night—the experiment was simply to explore whether the team could have one *predictable* night *off* each week.

The Predictable Night Off

Though Mark was supportive in the meeting, he confided to us afterward that as the time approached he had become increasingly worried about being able to find time for a regular night off. He characterized his relationship with the client: "We're his eyes, ears, arms, legs—he can't do anything without us. I can push back a little, but I can only go so far, so I'm going to have a hard time personally taking a night off. I just have too much work to do."

We pressed Mark to try it, emphasizing that the team needed to see him do it so that they would feel comfortable taking their own nights off. Mark agreed, reluctantly, for the good of the team. As an experienced team leader, and former military officer, he understood that his participation would convince the team that he genuinely supported the experiment. And he certainly knew Doug wanted him to cooperate. But he still made it clear to us that he resented how it would mess up the rest of his week.

At 6:00 p.m. on his scheduled night off, Mark packed up to leave the office, and made a point of saying goodbye to everyone on the team, joking all the way: "I know you will be lost without me but you'll have to manage."

He later told us that, driving back to the hotel, it occurred to him that he had been staying at this hotel for three nights every week for the past year and a half, but never had he driven there at the end of a day wondering how he would spend his time before bed. He found himself starting to tick through his mental to-do list—e-mails to send, slides to review, meetings to set up for the following day—but then stopped to warn himself, "I'm not supposed to be working." He thought about getting dinner on his way back to his room, but it seemed too early. It was only 6:15, and he was used to working until 8 and then grabbing a quick dinner before getting back online. He wasn't even hungry.

Back at the hotel, he decided to get some exercise. He quickly changed and went to the hotel gym. After twenty minutes on the treadmill, he started to feel a little anxious. He had the urge to check his BlackBerry, which he had brought along. But instead he kept running; and when he finally stopped, he was pleased to find he'd been able to run ten kilometers. He felt great; he couldn't remember the last time he'd had such a good workout while on the road.

After showering and ordering dinner from room service, Mark called his wife. They talked every night, but only briefly. This time, when

Jenna began to hang up, Mark kept talking. As he hung up the phone a half-hour later, he was thinking that there might be something to this night-off experiment. He'd had a great workout, talked to Jenna, and was about to get to bed early—without being distracted by work.

Lisa also found value in her first night off. It was a Thursday, and she'd taken the early flight home so she could work on the plane and land by 6 p.m. Normally, she would have kept the night open to catch up on work, but this time she had made plans to see friends for dinner and a movie. "What a treat to see friends on a weeknight," she told us. "It felt wonderful, though a little strange. It was like that bubbly feeling of slightly guilty happiness when you skipped class in college . . . plus I got a nice night of sleep."

Charlie reported similar satisfaction. He'd specifically asked for Wednesday off: he planned to join some of the guys on the team for nine holes of golf after work and preferred not to have to face more work afterward. "I don't always like the case team events," he explained, "because you end up staying up so late afterward to catch up on work. But this was great. I got to play golf, and since I didn't have to work afterward I even had a couple of beers."

Lisa and Charlie happened to be in the same client meetings every day, and their routine had been to spend evenings each preparing separately for the next day. Now, they started passing this prep work back and forth. They began to check in with each other every morning to determine what needed to be done that day and which of them would do it. Structuring their work this way reassured them that nothing would slip through the cracks on their nights off.

Then there was Bob. He felt that neither Mark nor Doug were giving him enough support to take his nights off, his workload was unaffected, and Bill, who was supposed to cover for him, was so new to the firm that he didn't really understand the work process; moreover, Bill was often called away for BCG social events that were part of recruiting summer MBAs. Bob did concede that his first night off had been useful, because he was nursing a painful sunburn and he'd gone back to his hotel room to take a bath and go to bed early. But as the weeks progressed, Bob began to resent his nights off. Unlike Charlie and Lisa, Bob didn't feel that anyone was supporting him. "I'm working as efficiently as I can. If I'm doing something, it's because that analysis needs to get done. There isn't anything I'm doing that I can just cut out." "Taking a night off," he complained, "is just as I feared. I still have to do the work—and at an even less desirable time."

Bob's growing resentment was a threat to the central purpose of the experiment. The objective of the predictable night off was not just to provide a break but to act as a catalyst that would galvanize the team to collectively engage in challenging current work processes and together find new ways to do their jobs that benefited the client, the firm, and their personal lives. This was not happening. "I was just moving work around" was Bob's description. There was no change in how the team was working together, beyond the small changes Lisa and Charlie had made. They were not rethinking their work practices. As a researcher, I was open to letting the experiment inform me that it might not be possible to create change in such an organization as BCG. But at this point, no one was even exploring the possibility of doing the work differently.

The Discovery

After week 5, Bob's resistance forced us to assemble the team to discuss the experiment and consider whether it should go forward. The meeting began with each team member offering a personal impression about how things were going. Mark led off by saying, "It's nice to end at 6 p.m., get in a workout, and have a real call with my wife that is not rushed because I have to get back to work." Charlie was also positive, noting that he had appreciated the time he had been able to see his wife and friends in Indianapolis.

Lisa voiced similar sentiments: "I like the nights off. I love working with this team, but at a certain point I need some time away, and I like having the night off for that break."

Bob was next, and I braced myself. "Pretty much 100 percent of the time I feel like it is more work for me later," he informed his colleagues as candidly as he had spoken to us in private. "I have had nights I've enjoyed—they are valuable, but they're never as valuable because the time I'm trading is time I'd have off in Boston."

I looked around the room at the reaction—heads nodding sympathetically. And then something unexpected happened. As the other team members discussed Bob's concerns, they came to appreciate that the continuation and ultimate success of the experiment depended not merely on whether *each* was taking (and valuing) his or her own night off, but whether *all* of them were taking (and valuing) their nights off. They also came to understand that to make this happen, they needed to rethink what each of them was doing and how it connected to the team's deliverables. By raising his discontent frankly and persuasively, Bob—the odd man out—had brought the team together. They ended up committed to a shared goal of making this experiment work for all of them.

After that meeting, the Consumer team started acting like, well, a team. Lisa, for example, sent an e-mail reminding the team that it was Mark's night off, which in turn prompted the others to help Mark to get out the door. Mark also called Doug out for e-mailing him on his night off. "It felt a little awkward sending a note that I was off to Doug," Mark later confessed, but then allowed a look of pride to flash across his face. "But I did it."

Most important, the team started to engage with each other to figure out how to get their work done to ensure nights off could happen for all of them each week. For the first time, they were embracing the collective nature of the goal, challenging assumptions about the way things had to be and exploring new ways.

At this point, we decided to reintroduce the Pulse Check. We hoped to encourage the team to continue to speak openly about the issues they were facing. First, though, we made sure Mark and Doug understood the underlying purpose and the importance of their commitment to make the Pulse Check effective this time around. We also underscored to Doug how important it was that he be publicly supportive of Mark. Yes, they both had expressed their commitment to our experiment, and we believed them. But what really mattered was that they convey that commitment *to the team,* through comments, tone of voice, and body language. Candor, we believed, would nurture more candor, and thus open up the kind of dialogue that had been missing in team meetings.

Restoring the Pulse Check

When Mark announced in the case team meeting that they would be using the Pulse Check, he introduced the tool as if the team had never used it before. And, in a sense, they hadn't—at least in an open and productive fashion. He slowly and deliberately put up the slide that listed the four questions, reading each aloud.

"How are you feeling?"

"How much value are we delivering to the client?"

"How satisfied are you with your learning?"

"Is the current operating model sustainable for you?"

Mark explained how everyone would have the chance to identify where they were on each of the questions, using the scale of cartoon faces. He then paused, looked at each of his teammates, and in a tone that showed more compassion than they had ever heard from this military veteran, he said, "Please, be honest in your responses."

Doug echoed Mark's plea for honesty, explaining to the team that the power of this exercise depended on them sharing their thoughts and feelings. "Who would like to get the process started?" asked Mark.

After a few awkward seconds, Lisa timidly volunteered: "I'll try."

Mustering her courage, Lisa began: "I am feeling good, I am a 1 [smiling face]." She continued, "In terms of value, I guess I am a 2 [accepting].

I can't tell what the client will end up doing with our work and if we ultimately will be successful." She reported that she was satisfied with what she was learning and felt that the operating model was sustainable. Then she sat up tall, took a deep breath, and announced something that she had been worried about revealing to her teammates: "I am doing my graduate school applications, and that is taking a lot of time."

Lisa looked around the room, anxious to see the reactions. Doug and Mark were both smiling and nodding. Lisa's revelation came as no big surprise to them: after a few years at BCG, associates tended to apply to graduate school. Seeing that her bosses were not distressed by her news, Lisa let out a sigh of relief.

I was also relieved: it was a good, honest start to the meeting.

Mark suggested he go next. From my point of view, Mark's performance would be a make-or-break step for the Pulse Check—and maybe even the experiment. He had begged his team for honesty, and now they were waiting to see how he answered the questions. Would honesty prevail or would the team slip back to the feckless responses that had made the Pulse Check such a waste of time in the past?

Mark sat up, looked for a split second at the screen, as if to remind himself—and his audience—what the questions were; then he turned to the team and gave his answers: "The team is doing well, and I know if we were not here [working with this client], this project would not be going forward. We are forcing change management and that is really important." But he also shared his concern about who in the company would take over once the BCG team left. And he admitted that he was not learning as much as he would like in terms of case content, but he noted: "I am learning about working effectively with the team."

Mark had never discussed with his team his ongoing struggle to be a better manager; even to open up this much was progress.

Doug went next. He echoed Mark's concerns about who would take ownership of their work. Team members would later remark how much they appreciated hearing both Mark and Doug express concerns over something that they, too, were worried about. It was reassuring to learn that they were all on the same page.

Doug also lamented that the case was not pushing him to learn new things, perhaps because he had been with the client for so long. This also was a revelation to the team: It was the first time that most of them had realized that learning and development were not just a junior person's concern but also something project leaders and even partners worried about.

Our effort to persuade the team's leaders to talk candidly seemed to be paying off. Suddenly, Doug revealed surprisingly personal details: he informed his colleagues that his wife was pregnant with their third child, and that he was looking forward to taking a three-week paternity leave. The team knew he was expecting a child, but they had rarely heard him mention it—or the implications for his work.

Charlie and then Bob went next. Their responses were cautious, but everyone could hear a willingness to try sharing some details of what was going on for them, both at work and at home.

At one point, as the trust was building, Doug revealed some sensitive information regarding the client. He cautioned them not to let this news leave the room: the senior client overseeing a portion of their work might be removed. (After the meeting, several members of the team reported how useful knowing this possibility would be to their work. It was also important to them that Doug had shown this level of confidence in the team.)

The Pulse Check had functioned perfectly. When Mark ended it, he noted cheerfully, "I think we'll try this again next week." There were lots of smiles and nods. Even Bob, who had emerged as the experiment's reality check, had turned hopeful and later conceded, "I was skeptical going in because I couldn't picture Mark or Doug really talking about their feelings. I was pleasantly surprised."

Legitimating Dialogue

In the twenty weeks that followed, the team members continued to hold the Pulse Check in their weekly case team meetings. They also always made sure to discuss their nights off. For each meeting, there was now a chart that listed each team member's answers to the three questions:

1. Did you take the night off as planned?

2. What time did you leave work?

3. How much time did you work after leaving?

The chart showed that everyone was taking a night off. And then, just a few weeks later, next to one team member's name the answer to question 1 was *no*. Surprisingly, it was Charlie, who had embraced the experiment from the start. Early in the afternoon of Charlie's night off, his client contact scheduled a meeting for 5 p.m. Charlie did not even stop to question whether the meeting had to occur or whether he was the only team member who could be there. Charlie had simply reverted to the team's prior default position: when the client called, the consultant jumped.

In their team meeting later in the week, the team reflected on what had happened. They talked about how Bob or Mark could have covered the client meeting. They discussed how they needed to shift from their BCG mindset and try to find alternatives to situations that threatened to disrupt the predictable-time-off experiment. They also talked about the importance of no longer assuming that each of them had to solve such problems unilaterally; that instead they should reach out to each other for help.

As this kind of candid give-and-take continued over the next few weeks, people felt increasingly comfortable speaking up about what was on their minds. As Lisa noted, "I was intimidated by Mark in the beginning. Between his military background and demeanor, I couldn't really read him, and I never knew what was okay to say. He was always so gruff. But that has really changed. He is much more receptive than I expected him to be."

One afternoon, Charlie, a huge sports fan, sent an e-mail to the whole team, including Mark and Doug, that read, "If the Red Sox can pull out the ALCS [American League Championship Series], I'm hoping to shift my night off next week to Wednesday night. Otherwise, I may have to bring my laptop with me to Fenway." Before, he would have feared that his colleagues might think that he actually believed that a baseball game was more important than serving the client. Now he knew that they would make no such judgment; moreover, they would do what they could to make it possible for him to get to the Red Sox game.

Once the space had opened up to talk, Bob, who had hesitated to state his reluctance to spend so much time on the road, ventured to mention his complaint and gauge the reaction. It turned out that the others were receptive, which gave him the courage to bring it up again in a future meeting—and finally to ask, "Do we all need to be traveling to the client four days a week, every week?"

Mark reflected, "We ended up having a constant conversation, in our meetings but also informally, about what should be done, what was important, what work the consultants could share, and what someone could cover so their teammate could take the night off. The responsibility shifted. It was no longer just a burden on me as the project leader; it put the burden on the team."

The Transformation

As people spoke up more about their issues and concerns, and received positive reinforcement for doing so, trust and respect for each other grew. They shared more. They came to know each other in new, more personal ways. They cared more about each other as people. They ended up feeling more connected both as a work group and also as people with full, rich lives both inside and outside of work. As Lisa put it: "It made people pay attention to their teammates' lives and to try to work together to find ways to protect what matters to each of us. So often we compartmentalize, but this made everyone aware of key elements of people's lives, so our interactions were more genuine."

Of course, team members couldn't always accommodate each other's requests, but they were committed to trying. According to Mark, "The experiment created a good opportunity to bring up issues the team might like to work on, like, 'Can we travel less?' It also taught us how to work together to actually make these changes."

The Consumer team came to appreciate just how much they could change if they were willing to try. On one particularly hectic week, Mark e-mailed us, that he, Lisa, and Charlie would all need to switch their nights off to accommodate their work. Our response: "If you really need to do all of these shifts, of course you should. However, it will be a total blow-up, so if there is any way to avoid some of the changes you should try to do that. Bottom line: make the changes that you need to, but we are really hoping they won't all be necessary."

Mark noted that our e-mail pushing back had "forced us to plan work and prioritize." They arranged to transfer work between Lisa and Charlie so they could keep their scheduled nights, though Mark did change his night off because of a rescheduled meeting with high-level clients. Still, this was an important moment for the team. Their first instinct had been to jettison all the nights off to accommodate the work. All it took was a simple prompt; they realized that they could still do the work and keep to the nights-off schedule if they set priorities and planned for it.

Charlie later reflected: "I think the experiment is helping us prioritize better, like we did last week." He added, "Before, we would have just canceled the night off and done all of the work, but [sticking to the experiment] forced us to sit down and think about what we needed to do, what was most important, and how we could make things happen differently."

Bob, too, was beginning to appreciate the implications of the experiment. "It has led to explicit conversations in our case team meetings about 'What's the priority? What is the scope? How can we alter this? What do we need to do about it?' as opposed to just sort of being implicit that this is the work and we have to do it regardless of how long it takes. It forces discussions to happen. How much we are working and why has become a very explicit part of everything we talk about in our case team meetings."

Eventually, the team was even able to tackle Bob's preference to travel less. They experimented with staggering travel schedules so the client would always have team members present, but each team member would only work from Indianapolis three rather than four days a week.

The case team meetings themselves took on a different flavor. As Doug described it:

> The case team meetings started out using the Pulse Check to discuss "How are you feeling?" But the conversation would morph into "I'm concerned about the client for this, that and the other reason," and all of a sudden the whole team is concerned about market valuation of the client as an organizational issue in week 6 or 7 of the case . . . Usually you don't see the Cs [consultants] and As [associates] owning the big picture, but these guys are talking about the case in a completely different way now, at a much higher level . . . It was interesting and very thrilling to see.

We also felt we were watching a very different group than the one we had first met just a few months earlier. We were watching a team discussing their work openly, and not only taking predictable nights off each week and helping each other pull it off but also striving together to satisfy additional work-life goals—while improving the work process itself. We had been warned endlessly that management consultants would never be able to turn off. Our experiment set out to test this conventional wisdom. We discovered that simply was not the case, and moreover, the process that the experiment had unleashed improved not only people's work-lives but made BCG a more productive player in one of the world's most competitive businesses.

2

The Winning Formula

The predictable-time-off experiment had succeeded beyond everyone's wildest expectations, mine included. The Consumer team had taken 98 percent of its scheduled nights off. Only 12 percent of the nights off were rescheduled within the week due to work reasons, and three-quarters of those were rescheduled with at least two days' notice. Moreover, team members were not simply shifting their work to other times in order to take time off. Their weekly work hours *actually decreased*. The team had worked an average of 65 hours per week before the experiment, by the end of the project, the average was down to 58 hours. The group reported that they were able to find alternative ways to do the work on 94 percent of their nights off—65 percent of the time eliminating all the work that they would have done had they worked that night and 29 percent of the time eliminating most of it.

The Consumer team had also quickly evolved from ensuring that everyone had a single predictable night off to addressing a much broader range of personal needs and desires. As Bob (the original skeptic) reported, "The experiment created an open culture where the biggest value wasn't the fact that I was getting a Tuesday night off, it was that we were a team trying to address work-life issues."

The workweek was more predictable, and the control that each team member had over the work had improved. Better still, the case team's work process had also improved. According to Doug, the executing partner, "The team looked for ways to team better and support each other, which was great; and it raised the level of dialogue . . . to a higher level than I've seen other teams get to." His conclusion about the experiment was certainly music to my ears: "It was really helpful for the project, and ultimately for the client."

The managing partner of BCG's Boston office also recognized the transformative effects of the experiment. George Martin had only reluctantly allowed us to proceed with our experiment, even once Doug and his Consumer team had agreed to be our guinea pig. George had remained highly cautious, not at all convinced that we could make a dent in the firm's always-on culture. To our surprise, after hearing about the Consumer experiment results, he shared an idea: "What if we make next year the year of predictability in the Boston office?"

At that time, more than the usual number of star performers were choosing to leave the firm (what some companies refer to as having "regrettable losses"). And high on the list of reasons they gave for leaving was that the work was just too unpredictable. George had no solution, until we showed him the Consumer team results. Suddenly, he saw an opportunity to address one of the Boston office's most nagging problems, and decided to seize it.

An entire day at the next all-office Boston staff meeting was devoted to sharing the results from the Consumer team and encouraging other teams to engage in a similar experiment. The day ended with a senior partner's assertion: "Today is a declaration of public intent by the Boston leadership. What this means is that in the future we will either have a hanging date or a celebration date, because this is out there now and there's no going back." Still, there was much skepticism. An office-wide survey showed only 36 percent of BCG's consulting staff was even slightly optimistic change was possible. A project manager explained, "I think [the ability to take time off] would be a really nice thing to have, but it will never happen because it would require such a deep level of cultural change."

Over the next few months, ten teams signed up to take part in what came to be referred to as PTO—originally for *predictable time off*. As we came to recognize that PTO was about so much more than just predictable time off, however, we renamed the effort *predictability, teaming, and open communication*. Now that we have come to appreciate both its components and its expansive power, PTO has come to stand for a process where *predictable time off*—when embraced collectively and complemented with structured dialogue—markedly improves people, their teams, and ultimately the organization.

PTO:	Collective goal of predictable time off	+	Structured dialogue	=	Better work and better lives

To oversee the expansion of PTO, early on George Martin created the PTO Rollout Team, which included himself in the lead, joined by Paul Schwartz, another senior partner in the Boston office, and Rachel Levine our internal liaison at BCG, whom we introduced in chapter 1. Within a few months, the PTO Rollout Team also included two of the office's top veteran consultants, who were pulled from client work and assigned as *facilitators* to help teams execute the experiment.

We stayed involved not only as members of the PTO Rollout Team helping to guide the initiative forward, but also as academics studying how the initiative unfolded. The core of the book is based on the results of PTO's implementation by the Consumer team and then the ten teams that followed. As BCG diffused PTO to its offices around the globe, we remained involved. What we learned over the next three years also informed the book. I have included an appendix that catalogs our involvement throughout the process and the data we collected at each stage.

A Goal Is Not Enough—Adding Structured Dialogue

As often happens in inductive research, the struggles to keep the experiment with the Consumer team alive gave us insight into the prime variable that really powered it toward success. We came to realize that the collective goal of a weekly predictable night off was not enough to make the experiment work. As noted in chapter 1, when Bob's discontent almost forced us to end the experiment after only five weeks, we reintroduced the Pulse Check—and an amazing thing happened: not only did the entire team, including its leaders, start reaping personal benefits from the experiment, but the work process benefited and ultimately, so did the client. This insight was confirmed over and over as more teams participated.

Before the experiment, Consumer team members had been asked to use the Pulse Check to speak candidly about their work. The effort failed; they continued to keep even their most constructive criticism to themselves and focus on their own work modules. However, when we added the Pulse Check back after the experiment with the night off was under way, team members started talking to each other. Opening up in small ways at first, they began taking risks and exploring how these risks were received. This built some trust, and in turn they kept on conversing about work and personal issues. Eventually, when they raised issues, they questioned whether the status quo had to be the way it was and worked together to explore alternatives.

I soon realized that for the experiment to work, it needed a forced-talk component—*structured dialogue*. Frankly, it took me way too long to realize the power of the combination of a *collective goal* and *structured dialogue*. When I finally did, it was definitely a slap-hand-to-forehead, why-didn't-I-think-of-this-earlier moment. Others, myself included, had long been experimenting with a collective goal as the catalyst to get a group to rethink work and find new ways that improved both their work and their work-lives.[1] In my own earlier research, I had tried to create blocks of "quiet time" within the normal workday for engineers who complained of their daily interruptions.[2] But, my results were quickly squelched by the reigning culture.

The Consumer team's experience made me realize that we had all been so focused on creating a collective goal to inspire change that we had failed to recognize the importance of also engaging in open dialogue. In retrospect, I of all people should have seen this connection more quickly. *Dialogue* and *openness* have been buzzwords in the corporate world for years; thousands of books have been written to nurture communication in organizations.[3] And most ironic, I myself had written one such book: *When You Say Yes but Mean No* focused on the costs of silence and affirmed the value of speaking up.

What we all had been missing was the power of the *combination* of the action orientation of the collective goal and the emphasis on open dialogue.[4] These two components are the essence of PTO, what we have come to call the PTO rules of engagement.

Rule 1: A Collective Goal of Predictable Time Off

It all begins with a goal that is personal, collective, aspirational—yet doable: at BCG this meant a weekly predictable night off. It meant that one could say with conviction, "Next Wednesday I'll be off." It meant that the team planned for time off far in advance—often months, certainly weeks.

What made the goal of a predictable night off, in particular, so powerful at BCG was that it was: (1) personally valued by everyone, (2) doable but still a stretch, (3) a collective and shared endeavor, (4) required integrative thinking, and (5) a means, not just an end.

Personally Valued by Everyone

The goal of predictable time off was fundamentally about providing a benefit to individuals for their lives outside of work. People recognized and accepted that intent. However, not everyone wanted a night off, especially on the road. As one consultant noted, "I could see if I were on a case in New York, a night off might be fun. But I'm in a small town in the Midwest for the next four months. What am I going to do with a night off?" Some people wanted to work hard during the week to preserve their weekends for family and friends; others preferred more frequent, smaller chunks of time off during the day for exercise, or if on a local case, during the early evening so they could have dinner with their families. But even to those people the idea of a night off symbolized that ultimately the experiment was focused on improving a significant issue in their work-lives—reducing the unpredictability they experienced— and not on the organization's bottom line.

Doable but Still a Stretch

The goal of taking a predicable night off was designed as a stretch. It was aspirational. Before the experiment, "I don't make plans" was a constant refrain from BCGers at every level. While the goal was not perceived as impossible, no one thought it would be easy, either. After all, the default position at BCG was to be accessible and ready to work at any time of the day or week. "I try to go to some of my kids' events," said one partner, "but they make fun of me because I'll be watching the lacrosse game from my car while I'm on the phone with my client." Such hyperresponsiveness also worked its way down the hierarchy. As one project leader put it, "I take my BlackBerry to my daughter's Saturday-morning soccer game because the partner often e-mails me questions at that time."

Even though it was meant to create collective change and needed to be a stretch for this to occur, the goal was also perceived as doable. Too often, when companies know that there has to be systemic change, they set some huge, overarching goal or grand plan. With PTO, the goal was small and doable at the team level.

Collective and Shared

To encourage people to take time off—in a culture that didn't value do- ing so—the goal needed to be a collective, shared one. If team members were left to choose their own goals—time to exercise during the day or put their kids to bed at night—two problems would likely have emerged: (1) in a culture where work is the priority, people would have an incen- tive to minimize their personal goals and be inclined to "blow-up" those goals as soon as the pressure hit; and (2) the cheaters would disparage those who continued to take their time off as "entitled." One consultant described the inevitable company response: "Look, I am paying you this amazing salary, this is a wonderful company, why do you feel so entitled to do X, Y, Z?" If the goal was not collective, the always-on culture would smack down the effort to alter it.

People also needed to feel compelled to help each other achieve the goal. If fundamental change was to be made in how they worked together, teams had to share together in this change process. When one consultant didn't initially take his night off, teammates reminded him that he should have worked around his PTO night better, and moreover that they were there to help him. Having a shared goal—one that all team members were expected to help each other achieve—gave people the incentive to work together to make changes in the work practices that no team member alone could make.

Moreover, if the goal was not shared, management's fear that people would feel entitled to the goal could become a reality. This happened in Professor Lotte Bailyn's experiment to give nurses more control over their shifts. The goal in this case empowered nurses to choose their own schedules. The problem was that many nurses wanted the same shifts, leaving blocks for which no one signed up. Without any provision for working together to figure out how to best meet each other's needs, while ensuring 24/7 coverage for patients, nurses started complaining when they didn't get their first choice. They were unable to resolve their differences, and the experiment had to be ended.[5]

Requires Integrative Thinking

While it is essential that people share the responsibility to ensure everyone achieves the goal, they must also do so without undermining (and ideally enhancing) the work. This requires *integrative thinking*, which is the capacity to consider two opposing ideas and produce a synthesis that is superior to either.[6] Work and work-life goals must be held in mind at once, and the possibility explored of new ways of working that improve on both.

In practice, BCGers needed to find ways that ensured people took their nights off but without any negative effect on their clients. One structural change that BCG teams made upfront was to set up a system for handling a client request on someone's night off. On any given project, consultants are specialists, not generalists. Still, each team member was assigned another team member to cover for on that person's night off. That didn't mean the coverage partner could necessarily do the work. Rather, the person covering was responsible for deciding whether the issue could wait until the next day or if not, what needed to be done to satisfy the client. The person who was off could be contacted, but only as a last resort.

A Means, Not Just an End

While teams were to do whatever possible to achieve the night off—without undermining their work—the intent underlying the collective goal was much more than helping individuals get a unit of time off. Rather, its primary intent was to encourage people to engage in challenging the status quo by rethinking work—collectively—in ways that would benefit their work-lives without undermining their work. What mattered was ultimately not just achieving the goal but that they learned to all strive together to achieve it, for themselves and each other.

The predictable night off served as a way to "force" people to experience the process and benefits of challenging the status quo. Some of the most resistant people, convinced they were workaholics, also learned that they valued the time off.

Rule 2: Space for Structured Dialogue

The Consumer team proved how important it was to combine the collective goal with a specific time for team members to discuss how their predictable nights off were working and more generally how their work was proceeding. All future experiments included a requirement for such structured dialogue, which was introduced in a kickoff meeting and practiced in weekly meetings throughout the team's duration.[7]

Kickoff Meeting

Launching PTO on a team began with a kickoff meeting purposefully designed to engage people in structured dialogue and to model the desired openness. The meeting included a discussion of the work process and what it meant to engage in the experiment—and be designated a *PTO case*. Teams discussed the collective goal, its purpose, and how they would work together to achieve it.

Over time, the kickoff meeting also became an opportunity to discuss what the team's norms would be: the group would create explicit expectations about where they would be working, how much travel would be necessary, when people were to be accessible online during the week and weekends, and how they were going to handle time away from work (e.g., vacation, or training and recruiting commitments). They also discussed how they wanted to work together—alone at carrels, in a team room, in the hotel in the early morning or late at night, or from home when not traveling; whether they wanted team dinners or other social activities, and how often. Conversations included discussion of work styles—how each person, for example, preferred to give and receive feedback. Another important topic was people's individual preferences for times that they wanted to protect for personal activities. For example, on one team, members' desires included: go for a run in the mornings, do yoga at night, be home as many days as possible to join the family for dinner, work hard during the week but preserve weekends off.

For many BCGers, this was the first time they were on a team that took the time up front to make their norms explicit and agree on what they would be. Even if they had had such conversations in the past, this was often the first time they resulted in more than lip service.

Weekly Meetings

BCG teams had always had weekly meetings, but not everyone viewed attendance as a high priority. For PTO teams, attending a weekly meeting was mandatory. Some preferred to hold thirty-minute weekly meetings devoted exclusively to discussing the PTO process, but most added time to their weekly case team meeting. In either case, there were two parts to the PTO discussion. First, members addressed the calendar of nights off, reviewing how they had done in the past week as well as what was coming up in the week ahead. This fostered discussion about how they could have worked together differently as well as what they could do going forward to enable them to work together more effectively and to take their time off.

Second, teams engaged in the four-question Pulse Check (see chapter 1). The Pulse Check turned out to be an effective way for structuring a discussion about the work process and work content as well as individuals' work-lives. "There is enough there to get at everything but not so much that teams get into minutia or trivia," commented one project leader. "They don't get into things not worth discussing but they do hit everything and surface all the major issues. And everything relates to how much they are learning, value to client, or their work-life balance. You pretty much get at the entire agenda from the case team meeting through this tool."

The Pulse Check also obliged everyone to participate. More-reserved team members reported appreciating being forced to take some airtime. And the team benefited from everyone being engaged and knowing where everyone stood. Nevertheless, a wide-open Pulse Check was a countercultural process at BCG. As one partner put it, "I'm not a touchy-feely person, and I don't really look forward to the Pulse Checks. But I do them because they are so useful. We end up jumping all around and sometimes it takes a while, but in the end we've had a great discussion with the full team engaged."

At times, however, even individuals on teams using the Pulse Check effectively found it hard to raise certain issues in front of the full team. There was a second tool used by some teams to encourage their members to express their concerns—from specific situations ("I am worried I won't get the data on time.") to more general issues ("How will the client manage this project once we're gone?"). The tool was labeled *Tummy*

Rumbles. Many didn't like that name but, as one principal explained, "It sounds stupid at first, but it does accurately get to what we need to be thinking about. What are the issues that are starting to gnaw at your gut, and how can we deal with them before they turn into the kind of thing that will keep you up at night?"

With Tummy Rumbles, a designated team member would e-mail everyone with a request for their tummy rumbles, usually a day or two before the case team meeting. The responses were aggregated onto a slide—without any names attached—and presented for discussion during the PTO check-in. Consultants often used Tummy Rumbles as a way to raise specific issues they wanted leadership to consider but preferred not to bring up directly. Interestingly, people tended to reveal themselves in the meeting, but even this thin veil of anonymity turned out to be beneficial for helping people raise issues.

The Win-Win Combo: Collective Goal Plus Structured Dialogue

The combination of striving for a collective goal of predictable time off and having space to say what was on their minds paid impressive dividends for BCG case teams (see figure 2-1). Consultants on the first ten PTO teams were far more likely (70 percent) to say that they would be at BCG for the long term than those on non-PTO teams (49 percent). For George Martin, this was the most important comparison of all. He had hoped this effort would help remedy his retention problem, and it appeared that PTO was delivering. We heard from a number of PTO participants who had changed their minds about leaving the firm. According to one, "Confidentially, before I started this case I was seriously considering leaving BCG. But having boundaries—not feeling like I have to respond to e-mails 24/7—is making a world of difference. Even if just every second project was a PTO project, I would be more than twice as likely to stay here." As the head of BCG's Americas region summed it up: "In a world where retaining our top talent is our single-most important priority to sustain the long-term growth of the business, I think we

FIGURE 2-1

Comparison of initial ten PTO teams to non-PTO teams

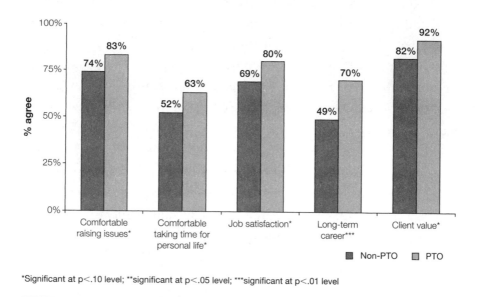

*Significant at p<.10 level; **significant at p<.05 level; ***significant at p<.01 level

now are seeing that PTO really makes a difference in the BCG experience and people's desire to make it work for the long term."

Team members on PTO teams were also more likely to recognize the benefits not only for their lives, but for the client: 92 percent agreed that they were delivering significant insights to their clients—compared with 82 percent of those on non-PTO teams. These were numbers that the firm's partners could not ignore. "I was a skeptic heading into this," admitted one, "but I have really come around on it. I now see it makes a big difference in the quality of the team work and in the quality of the experience overall . . . Before PTO, the client kept giving us feedback that they wanted a broader perspective. With PTO, we started having a broader conversation in our internal meetings, and that led us to provide the broader product our client wanted. That was the real value of PTO."

By the end of the first year, 189 consultants had participated on PTO teams—mostly staffed from across the Boston and New York offices. By the end of the second year, 833 BCG consultants had been exposed to

Three Years Later

Based on survey results three years after the PTO initiative was launched in Boston, we grouped teams into three overarching categories—teams that embraced both the goal and the dialogue (Embrace PTO—37 percent), teams that embraced either the goal or the dialogue but not both (Partial PTO—49 percent), and teams that embraced neither the goal nor the dialogue (Dismiss PTO—14 percent).

We found that the Partial PTO teams were almost entirely composed of teams that embraced the dialogue and not the goal—97 percent. For all intents and purposes, therefore, teams either don't adhere to either of the rules of engagement, they embraced the practices of structured dialogue but not those of the collective goal, or they embraced both. As our observations showed—and the literature on open dialogue would predict—having open dialogue improves the work and work-life dynamics on the team. Our real contribution, however, is that if you further add a collective goal, the team improves significantly more on both work and work-life dimensions. As the charts show, the Embrace PTO teams do significantly better than the Partial PTO teams, who do significantly better than the Dismiss PTO teams on all the work and work-life dimensions we measured (see figure 2-2).

at least one PTO team. BCG offices in Washington, DC, the West Coast (which included Los Angeles and San Francisco), and London had all launched their own PTO teams. By the end of the third year, nearly 1,400 consultants had been involved, and offices that had launched PTO teams included: Chicago, Detroit, Atlanta, Houston, and Dallas as well as offices in Latin America, Europe, and Asia—São Paulo, Rome, Milan, Brussels, Helsinki, Moscow, Zurich, and Tokyo.

What we discovered is that by combining the collective goal with structured dialogue PTO provided team members the safety and inspiration to raise more work and personal issues that went far beyond the initial goal of predictable time off, and better yet they worked collectively to

FIGURE 2-2

Three years later—Boston, New York, and Washington, DC

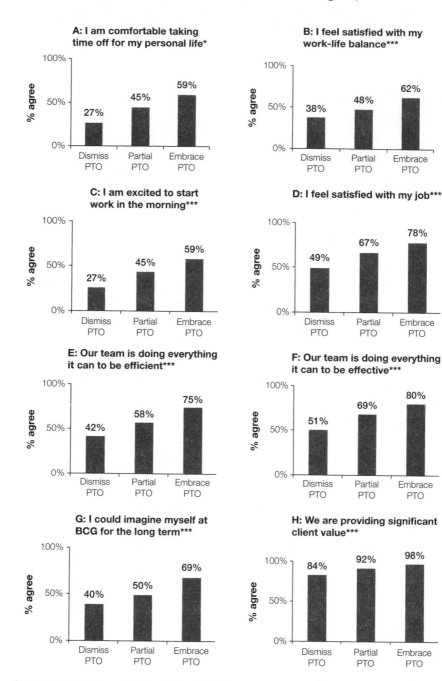

A: I am comfortable taking time off for my personal life*

- Dismiss PTO: 27%
- Partial PTO: 45%
- Embrace PTO: 59%

B: I feel satisfied with my work-life balance***

- Dismiss PTO: 38%
- Partial PTO: 48%
- Embrace PTO: 62%

C: I am excited to start work in the morning***

- Dismiss PTO: 27%
- Partial PTO: 45%
- Embrace PTO: 59%

D: I feel satisfied with my job***

- Dismiss PTO: 49%
- Partial PTO: 67%
- Embrace PTO: 78%

E: Our team is doing everything it can to be efficient***

- Dismiss PTO: 42%
- Partial PTO: 58%
- Embrace PTO: 75%

F: Our team is doing everything it can to be effective***

- Dismiss PTO: 51%
- Partial PTO: 69%
- Embrace PTO: 80%

G: I could imagine myself at BCG for the long term***

- Dismiss PTO: 40%
- Partial PTO: 50%
- Embrace PTO: 69%

H: We are providing significant client value***

- Dismiss PTO: 84%
- Partial PTO: 92%
- Embrace PTO: 98%

Questions were asked on a 7-point scale (1=strongly disagree; 7=strongly agree). The graphs compare respondents who answered 5 and above.

*Significant at the $p < .10$ level; **significant at the $p < .05$ level; ***significant at the $p < .01$ level address these issues. A process of continual learning, adaptation, and improvement emerged.[8]

In the face of mounting competition, organizations around the globe strive to achieve a culture where employees are continually surfacing and addressing issues. Yet, while such ongoing learning and improvement is clearly a desirable aspiration, it has proven difficult to achieve.[9] The power of PTO: it provides a small, straightforward, concrete way to achieve this highly desirable result. And it is noteworthy that teams that embraced the combination of the collective goal and structured dialogue outperformed all other teams. We saw that in the first experiment with the Consumer team, and again on the next ten teams. And we continued to see this combination delivering impressive results for BCG over the next three years. (See "Three Years Later.")

Part II explores precisely how these two simple rules of engagement brought about such fundamental change.

Part II

THE MAGIC OF
THE PROCESS

Speaking Openly

As the power of combining the collective goal and structured dialogue became increasingly clear, I kept flashing back to the year we had spent observing BCG before proposing the experiment. We had studied a full range of BCGers, from the newest, most junior members to the most senior partners. We had watched them draft proposals and make presentations. We had ridden with them in their taxis, traveled with them on their flights, stayed at the same hotels. And we had sat quietly observing them interact with each other and with their clients.

We witnessed team after team grappling with sixty-plus-hour workweeks, almost constant travel, and the persistent demands of clients and their own team leaders, while neglecting their families and their health. Yet almost all of them seemed mired in the 24/7 mystique of management consulting; work demands ultimately trumped every well-intentioned effort to change that ruinous dynamic. As much as BCGers wanted openness and were eager to change the culture—and many seemed to secretly harbor that desire—they kept insisting, "It has to be this way." How was PTO able to challenge this deeply held belief?

Two Teams: A Study in Contrasts

Too often before introducing PTO, we had heard leaders talk a great game about improving the personal lives of their team members—"traveling less," "working less," "eating well," "exercising more"—and then set up schedules that made all of that impossible. The following cases contrast the fortunes of two teams: one that followed this pattern of good intentions/same old schedule and another that successfully practiced PTO.

The Metal Team—Same Old, Same Old

A BCG team was launching a new project with a first-time client in Ohio—let's call it the *Metal* team. Their objective was to research potential markets, customers, and competitors to determine the best strategy for the Metal Company to grow and increase its return for investors. Five out of the seven team members were filling new roles, and thus had something to prove: a recently promoted partner, a new principal, a consultant who was acting as the project leader, another consultant on his first case, and two associates.

The senior partner wanted to assemble the whole team to discuss what would be the team's dynamics, a fairly unusual discussion to have on a BCG team. That week, the meeting was postponed three times for "more pressing" matters. When the team finally met at 3 p.m. on Friday afternoon, the senior partner put forth a proposal to ensure positive team dynamics: "So often we are so focused on what we're doing for the client that we end up putting our own discussions on the back burner. We need to make time to talk about how things are going and how we can iron things out when we have issues. And, in the end, that just helps us do a better job for the client." He suggested that in this meeting and then again at regular intervals that the team address the five questions BCGers typically asked at the end of a case: (1) What worked well? (2) What didn't work well? (3) How well was the case managed? (4) Did we create value for the client? and (5) Did we achieve appropriate work-life balance?

Everyone agreed enthusiastically, and they all practiced answering the questions in this meeting. They talked about their hopes for "camaraderie," desires for "clear deadlines and deliverables," and "time for working out and eating meals."

As the meeting progressed, however, cracks started to show. This meeting had been pushed to the last possible moment; the weekend was fast approaching, and they still had to discuss what needed to get done the following week. The more junior partner started glancing at his watch with increasing frequency, and more than once interjected, "Can we move on?" Sensing the strain between the two partners, team members began to visibly tense up and limit their engagement.

Soon the meeting shifted to the next week's work plan, and despite the senior partner's plan to talk about how things were going and iron out issues, no such attempts were made during the rest of the twelve-week case. Nor did the team ever again raise issues about the effect of the work process on their work-lives. People had expressed desires to limit travel, cap work hours, go to the gym. But nothing changed. And no one ever mentioned it.

The Tech Team—PTO Makes a Difference

Tech Operations A—for simplicity, the *Tech* team—was one of the original ten PTO teams.[1] Their objective was to help a technology company bring down costs by reconfiguring global operations. To avoid any distractions or client meetings to compete with their focus at the PTO kick-off, the senior partner decided to hold the meeting in BCG's Boston office rather than at the client site, even though it was a Monday. Travel schedules were changed, and the senior partner made sure he was there in person. As the principal later said, "I was impressed that the partners wanted to change their travel schedules around to accommodate the kickoff meeting. When they did that, and both showed up, it convinced me they were genuinely supportive and not just paying lip service." An associate agreed: "I couldn't believe Keith [the senior partner] actually spent three hours with the team in that meeting—it was the first time I'd ever seen him since starting to work for him, and it really made me pay attention."

The kickoff meeting involved twelve members of the larger Tech team (two different teams were working concurrently to address different issues for the Tech Company).[2] At the beginning, a detailed description of the PTO experiment and its rules of engagement were introduced, followed by a discussion of team norms. A consultant raised the issue of traveling on Mondays, and the project leader agreed that she found that an exhausting way to begin a week; another team member said he had no problem with Monday travel and was more concerned about working late during the week and not getting a healthy dinner. Hearing all the personal desires openly expressed for the first time, the senior partner sat back and asked, "Does everyone really need to be there early on Monday?" The consensus was no—a few members could fly in to handle any early morning meetings, while the others could arrange their travel according to their personal preferences and work schedules.

As for dinner, some wanted to work late and be done; others preferred to eat early or go to the gym and return to work. The senior partner interrupted again: "You're all acting like I expect you to be in the team room every night, but I don't. I just expect you to get your work done. I don't care where or when you do that."

The Tech team's conversation continued, and the candor increased. The principal confessed sheepishly, "I have to admit, sometimes I imply I have early phone calls keeping me in the hotel, but really I just can work so much more effectively there."

The senior partner turned to the principal and said, "Tell me truthfully, how well are you able to work in the morning? Because now I'm worried I distract you. I see you online at 5:30 and I start instant messaging you, and I really appreciate being able to do that, but I don't want to do it if you don't like it." The principal again looked a little sheepish: "To tell you the truth, most of the time it's fine, but if I'm really cranking on something and I see you are online, I will sometimes turn off my IM so you don't interrupt me." His teammates looked anxiously at the senior partner, who surprised them all by laughing and encouraging the principal to keep doing that.

And so the meeting went: the team discussed travel, late nights, time for workouts, priorities, the head guy's expectations—much, in fact, that the Metal team had discussed in their own opening meeting. But Tech's leaders sent a very different signal about the importance of the discussion and their intentions to foster openness and encourage change.

Within the first week of the Tech team's case, the principal was assigned to spend only 10 percent of his time working with one of the subteams. That left the responsibility of managing the subteam (two consultants and an associate) and its relationship to the supervising partner pretty much in the hands of the project leader, in her debut in this leadership position. Typical of a new project leader, eager to impress the partners on the case, she was anxious to have materials perfect for every meeting. Before the first case team meeting, she started making requests that the consultants on her subteam felt were unnecessary.

When one consultant found the courage to raise the issue with the project leader about all the slides she was requesting, the project leader explained her strategy in detail and how she thought the process would help them to refine their thinking. The consultant later conceded, "That gave me a view into how she was thinking. She did have a clear idea and, as we were all new, we got a sense of where it all fit into her strategy." The project leader reflected, "I would never, ever have questioned my project leader in a case team meeting . . . But there I was, having to explain to them what was going on in my head. My explanation made me realize a few things . . . It made me articulate what they were doing and forced me to be very clear and focused. It also helped them understand why they were doing what they were doing and how it all was to come together in the end."

The consultants felt encouraged by this interaction and continued to raise issues, sometimes in the PTO check-ins, sometimes in other group settings, sometimes one-on-one. At one point, the team members felt that they were working inefficiently: they would have little to do in the morning, and then at 3 or 4 in the afternoon the project leader would give them assignments, requiring them to work until 10 or 11 at night, only to repeat the same pattern the next day. After a few days of this and mounting frustration, they approached the project leader and asked if there was anything they could do to alleviate the situation. Once she learned the effects of her late-afternoon demands, she made an effort to even out the day's assignments. "And we didn't have late nights any-more," reflected one of the consultants.

The Tech team's project leader willingly stuck with the experiment, even when she became the target of the team's increased candor, and it made a difference. She noted, "I would describe open communication on this case to be extreme. I really don't think it could have been any more open. People always said what they thought on this case, but they were good about being constructive." She added, "Once open commu-nication started, everyone took it very seriously, and it flourished, and so did the team."

Extreme Communication

The power of PTO was that it made it okay for people to speak openly about the work process and their work-lives. This was a big deal. It is typically difficult to create an environment where people will take the risk associated with speaking openly. It was as if PTO was assuming that burden, and giving everyone the courage to speak up. And, once they did they were able to create team cultures where "there was no taboo," as one consultant described it. "You could talk about anything. They [more senior members of the team] did not always agree, but it was okay to bring anything up."

This "extreme" communication was not typical at BCG, where, as several members of the Tech team noted, personal issues rarely came up, especially as part of a team's discussions about how best to do the work. "We don't tend to ask about personal lives. Normally, we stay professional and just ask about work." And it was not just work, but work content, to which conversation tended to be limited.

Senior people echoed the benefit of being able to bring up whatever was on their mind in team meetings. One partner observed, "Whether it is job-related stuff, training or recruiting, or personal stuff, like 'Oh, I'm having a baby,' you have to be able to bring that up, and the real value was helping people do so." According to another:

> I saw PTO as a very simple, straightforward mechanism for getting the team to engage in a dialogue that we want to have but don't always have, that if you cornered any partner, they'd say, "Of course the consultant ought to be surfacing these issues"; but they don't, and we don't know that they don't . . . PTO is a mechanism for making it culturally okay to say, "Listen I need some help over here," or "I think this is coming unwound," or "There is an issue in my personal life."

BCGers at every level became more comfortable expressing preferences about where and when they worked (e.g., early morning versus late night, weekdays versus weekends, home versus on road, breaking for meals versus working through meals). They also were more comfortable sharing personal commitments they hoped to keep (e.g., ballet tickets, comedy club, child's concert) as well as things they cared about on a more regular basis (e.g., coaching Little League, being home for dinner, a subscription to the theater). They were also more willing to talk about issues, struggles, even mistakes they had made in their work.

Central to PTO's success was this ability to foster open dialogue. After all, there are shelves of books in stores and libraries on how to foster openness in organizations—and few examples of success.[3] What was different about PTO? First, the rules of engagement established at the outset of the experiment put an emphasis on openness about personal as well as work issues. Second, there was a concrete, actionable, measurable, and achievable goal that was both personal and collective. That goal provided an opportunity for team members to take a small risk, raise issues around achieving it, and see how it was received. If the response was positive, they would take a slightly larger risk, and see how that was received. The Pulse Check also provided an ongoing opportunity to start small and see how the issues played out. Positive responses built trust, and people were able to raise increasingly large issues—both work and personal. And, as people continued to share, stronger connections and deeper trust were built, which further increased everyone's willingness to speak openly. One partner summed it up this way: "You think you're being open until you try PTO."

Handling Bumps in the Road

The path was not always smooth. Not everyone spoke up openly and constructively all the time. What mattered, though, was that people were committed to trying. And once team members embraced PTO's rules of engagement, they realized it could bail them out of the kind of conflicts and workaholic behavior that had destroyed the best-intentions to change things in the past. A good example of this was the *Healthcare Lean II* team, which was helping a major healthcare company operate more cost effectively according to a strategy an earlier team (*Healthcare Lean I*) had created for this client.[4]

Members of the Healthcare Lean II team immediately embraced the concept of open dialogue and freely discussed personal priorities regarding travel, work hours, and visits to the gym; they clearly felt empowered to try to meet their personal objectives. Several consultants adopted a routine of leaving most days at 4:30 p.m. to make a 5:15 p.m. exercise class, after which they continued their work for several hours. The client had commended the team's work several times—without a word about the afternoon absences.

However, the early departures irked the principal. This was his first case since the birth of his twins. Exhausted but still trying to work flat out, he was troubled by how this would look to the client yet also felt it would be a violation of the PTO experiment to mention his concerns.

So he said nothing, at least for a while. Then, one day, as the consultants were packing up at 4:30 p.m., he blurted out, "You shouldn't be doing this!" The consultants were stunned. They had no idea there was an issue: the work was getting done, the client was happy, and they were feeling energized by their workouts. In the face of their superior's outburst, they stood speechless.

One of the other consultants jumped to their defense: "I don't understand; if I were to get up and leave early every day at 3:00 p.m. to go across the campus to a meeting with the client, you wouldn't care. How is this any different? To me, the bottom line is that you don't trust that we're actually getting the work done." For the next hour, the team debated their differences about what "delivering client value" meant. Yes, their job was about providing value in their work, the principal conceded, but in the end theirs was a client-service business and perceptions were important. Agreeing that it was important to keep talking about this issue, the team went out to dinner to try to get past their differences.

The principal had let his concerns fester. If he had raised them in a constructive way when he had first become aware of them, it is unlikely that the team would have been as shocked and defensive. Instead, what became known as the *blowup* occurred.

Neither the principal nor the partner gave up on PTO, however. They renewed their commitment to the practices of structured dialogue. They became adamant about the weekly check-ins to discuss how the project was going. One consultant told us, "I was genuinely impressed that they continued to push for openness after the blowup. I would have given up. It clearly could get ugly with people getting emotional. But they kept pushing for openness. This was an example of their tremendous commitment to PTO. Because of this, I still felt comfortable to speak up."

Another consultant reflected: "[After the blowup], we had some really productive discussions . . . we were doing our best to keep it constructive instead of being negative." In fact, she noted it was in this period that [the principal] started opening up more about his own stress levels. She valued this: "It is easy to get so focused on the work that we don't always see each other as people."

In the end, everyone on the team felt that open dialogue had been a key benefit of PTO. The partners were proud of the work that the team delivered, and the team members were pleased with the client's positive response—they also felt like their demanding work schedule was made more manageable as a result of PTO.

The Process at Work

People need to share their reactions, frankly but respectfully. PTO inspires people to open up in a variety of ways. The goal is not to make everyone happy or meet everyone's needs but to understand each other's concerns. There is no guarantee everyone will get what they want, but as long as people dedicate themselves to seeking mutual understanding even when confronting misunderstandings and raw emotions, progress can be made.

Sparks Sharing Personal Issues

With PTO, the collective goal and structured dialogue, working independently as well as together, created the expectation that people could talk about issues without getting burned for speaking their minds.

Before PTO, a partner didn't feel right admitting to her team that she couldn't travel because her daughter was starting kindergarten. Instead she implied that she had some sort of work conflict. With PTO, in contrast, a partner explained to his team that he could not travel to an important client meeting because his wife was traveling that week and he needed to be home to get his kids to school. Another partner, whose client was local, told the team that he planned to leave the client each day by 6 p.m. so he could be home for dinner with his family. One partner revealed that he really struggled with work-life issues and was trying to set stricter boundaries around work. On one team, a partner with a newborn began sharing stories about spending time with his daughter.

More junior staff started speaking openly about their personal lives as well. To provide some context for why she'd appreciate working out ways for the team to travel less, one consultant shared that she'd like time to ride her horse. Another was married to a medical resident, and described how frustrating it could be to get their schedules to align. These were the kind of details rarely shared before PTO. With PTO, however, from partners to associates, people began to open up about personal events—such as family visits, anniversary and birthday celebrations, and sporting events or concerts they wished to attend.

This is not to say that people at BCG knew nothing about each others' personal lives before PTO. That is far from the case. People had friends and acquaintances. They shared taxis and rental cars, they flew and stayed in hotels together, they had case team dinners. Such events provided opportunities to talk about non-work-related parts of their lives. But these conversations were relegated to time spent not "really" working. When these conversations occurred, they did so outside work, not in any forum that was meant to impact how the work itself was done.

With PTO, what was different was personal issues were shared broadly with the team in conversations about how the work itself was to be done—issues that hadn't previously factored into the discussion of work itself. One senior partner reflected on the difference, noting that prior to PTO his team was running so smoothly that he wondered what the benefits of PTO could possibly be:

> As we went forward with it, the team started to talk about what the intense travel schedule was doing to their personal lives, which frankly we hadn't even considered. We always looked at client value—that was always out there, and everyone was happy with it, but what I hadn't realized was not just people were unhappy, but that people hadn't felt they could express it . . . The PTO process helped the consultants to have more open dialogue in public without having to feel like they were the bad guys who were raising the issues.

He went on to explain that once they did, this triggered the team to work together to change how they were doing their work.

Surfaces Issues About Work Processes

Not only did PTO legitimate people raising personal issues and then working together to address them, but it legitimated raising issues with the work process that one would previously not have felt comfortable raising. One such example occurred on one team where the partners' work styles were not aligned. As one consultant described the problem:

> The partners had opposite work styles and never sat in the same room together. So there was no coordination in their input. The more junior partner was continually asking us to expand and add things so we would end up with forty- to sixty-page slide decks at the weekly meetings. The senior partner would wonder why we were all in the red zone [working more than sixty-five hours per week] and say, "Why do you have all this stuff?' . . . One partner was up late and would send you changes at 11 p.m., and the other was up early sending e-mails at 6 a.m. . . . We were getting it on both ends.

This consultant credited PTO with enabling the project leader to raise this issue: "This request for alignment from the partners would never ever have happened without PTO because it is too politically sensitive. PTO forced the discussion of why we were all in the red zone and enabled us to bring partner behavior up as one of the reasons."

Compare that to a similar situation on the Metal team (introduced at the beginning of the chapter). At a critical point, the partners differed about how to prioritize the work. The team decided to go in one direction, but when one of the partners got sick and missed a few days, the other suddenly decided to switch the team back to his preferred path. The principal, next in the team's hierarchy, simply acquiesced, despite his concern that the switch was not in the team's best interest and his realization that the other partner was likely to overrule it as soon as he returned. The principal, however, had recently been promoted and wanted a good review. His attitude was, "Partners like hearing 'yes' more than they like hearing 'no,' and I'm trying to give them what they want."

Other team members had similar misgivings, but they also elected not to speak up. They simply executed on the new orders, while complaining to one another. The associate most affected by the change complained to the project leader about the principal's reluctance to stand up to the partner: "We agreed a few weeks ago we weren't going to do it this way." The project leader confirmed that this had been agreed, but he too was unwilling to challenge the decision.

PTO created space and legitimation for conversations about the work process itself to occur. A consultant explained, "It was not just someone standing up at the end of the meeting and asking, pro forma, 'Any questions?' 'Any issues?' 'Anything anyone wants to raise?' Rather, there was a very formal time set aside within the meeting for the discussion. And, beyond creating time for the discussion, there was an expectation that we would speak."

Challenges People to Speak Up

It was a shared perception that people felt pushed, expected, compelled to speak. While the pressure itself was sometimes implicit, other times it was quite explicit. We found lots of evidence that the experiment encouraged even the shyest junior consultants to speak their minds. "If you are quiet," explained one partner, "your natural tendency will be to not say anything. And then we go around the room and you have to say something. All of a sudden now you get that wallflower type to speak." Suddenly people who were not used to speaking were adding value.

Engenders the Confidence to Push Back

As openness grew on a PTO team, so did people's confidence in standing up for what they now saw as the essence of PTO: high-quality work and high-quality time for life outside of work. A consultant recounted pushing back on his project leader at noon one busy day to ensure his night off. "It is my PTO night," he informed his project leader, "and I was hoping to make plans tonight with my fiancée."

The project leader suggested discussing it again at 4 p.m. But the consultant insisted that she make the decision: "If the point of the PTO night is predictability and the ability to make plans," he argued, "I need to know now if I can make plans with my fiancée." He added, "I am fine with whatever your decision is, but I want to uphold the standard." Hearing this, the project leader paused and then said with conviction "OK, you are going to take it." The consultant later reflected, "When I put it that way, in terms of the value of PTO, she got it, and we worked together to make it happen."

Consultants participating in the PTO process felt empowered to question requests that would make them change plans or work late. In turn, managers at every level were forced to ask themselves whether the work they were delegating was really urgent. Some partners had worried that there would be a problem of entitlement among the PTO teams—if team members could challenge the immediacy or the purpose of their work, they would be less willing to do it. In fact, to the contrary, on all but a few struggling PTO teams that lacked leadership support and failed to embrace the rules of engagement (we will discuss this rare circumstance further in chapter 7), team members gained so much from the opportunity to question work demands that when a project leader explained the request adequately, they performed the task with a renewed sense of commitment, because they now understood more clearly why it had to be done.

Enables Hearing More from Others

When people open up in public, it encourages others to do the same. One young associate described her reaction when a partner acknowledged that he had so many projects pulling him in different directions that he was marking himself with "threes across the board"—the second-lowest cartoon face on the Pulse Check. "That made me think," the associate recalled, "if a partner is comfortable enough admitting that he is a three, we should all be honest and open."

A consultant described how, at the PTO kickoff meeting, the executing partner talked about how important work was to him and how he spent most of his waking hours working. But he then suddenly confessed that work was not the most important thing in his life, and that he didn't "want to be embarrassed to say that." His candor was a revelation to that consultant: "I found that statement very liberating. I have never heard a partner say that before. While work is very important to me, it is not the most important thing in my life, either. Hearing him say that made me feel comfortable admitting that too."

A clear sense emerged that the participants felt more comfortable responding candidly when others, particularly superiors, modeled the desired openness. And this sense of comfort with speaking up tended to build on itself.

The Cycle of Transparency

As effective as the process was in getting people to speak their minds, to get the process started required some gumption. As one partner explained, "It takes consultants being willing to say I have ten things on my plate and in order to meet my night-off goal, I can do five of them. I think these are the right five; what do you think? People need to have the courage to say these things." The support and legitimacy surrounding PTO helped make this happen, and once people spoke up and found the response positive, they spoke up again and again.[5]

PTO's power was that it gave people something around which they could take a small leap of faith—to try speaking up and see how it went. Once people took that initial risk, they learned more about each other and each others' expectations as they clarified, explored, tested, and negotiated their expectations. In turn, as they built mutual expectations they created more trust, more willingness to speak up, and deeper and richer understandings of each other.[6] Transparency bred more transparency or, as one consultant summed it up: "The real triumph in the end was being able to talk about anything that was an issue."

This willingness to talk openly, in turn, unleashed more forces inside those meeting rooms that changed BCG teams—and the firm—in ways that they had not believed possible.

Passion and Action

As team members participating in the experiment began sharing more—and listening to their colleagues share more—they began to care more about each other, both as teammates at work but also as people who had personal lives outside of work—just as they did. Numerous stories emerged about how embracing the rules of engagement was inspiring people to help each other meet their personal needs. For example, one associate revealed to his colleagues that his girlfriend, who lived in Japan, was scheduled to be in town—on what happened to be the very last Friday of the case. Everyone was well aware how important that Friday was likely to be: their final chance to put finishing touches on their recommendations to the client. When the project leader heard about the dilemma, he suggested that the associate take the day off and spend the time with his girlfriend. The associate was incredulous: "I asked him more than once, 'Are you sure?' But he was determined to make it work out for me and it absolutely worked. I was really impressed."

So was I. During our original year shadowing teams in the Boston office, team members had often confided to us about missing events, even those they had long scheduled. And they had to cancel plans so often that they tended to give up bothering to make them at all. But they did all of this without letting their teammates know. When one associate's parents invited her to join a family trip to Africa between Christmas and New Years, she told them she could not go. She feared that her parents would spend a great deal of money on her airline ticket only to have her back out at the last minute. She never mentioned the potential trip to her teammates or superiors; she just assumed it was best to say no. What makes this example so noteworthy was that the case she was working on wasn't particularly intense, nor was anything expected to pop up during the time she would be gone. To her, working for BCG meant being ready for something to happen, anytime, and while she was willing to suffer that craziness, she did not want to expose her parents to it. The firm was full of similar stories of people resigned to missing out on what mattered to them personally.

Engaged in the PTO experiment, people started to share more. Opening up started about nights off but soon was about travel time, exercise breaks, work demands, even that commitment to spend time with a girlfriend on the busiest day of the case. Importantly, what was different with PTO was individuals were not just sharing issues with the team but, in turn, sharing the responsibility to address these issues.

It is one thing to *know* about your employees' personal lives—which most of us like to at least believe we do—and quite another for the team to *own responsibility* for addressing each others' personal issues as part of figuring out how to best do the work. PTO inspired the latter. Because of their involvement in PTO, people came to recognize the possibility for and value of striving together to find new ways of working. At the same time, as they came to know each other better, they cared more about each other as people. In turn, they became more passionate about helping to meet each other's needs and about making their team the best it could be. This newfound passion, combined with their new appreciation for the power that came from working together to change the way they worked, inspired people to join efforts to improve their world for themselves and each other.

Dealing with a Deadline—Pre- Versus with PTO

Time pressure was pervasive in the life of BCGers. Their work revolved around a set of deadlines to deliver updates and ultimately the final presentation to the client. Consider how PTO affected the team's way of handling major deadlines. The following anecdote comes from the Metal team, the pre-PTO team we met at the beginning of chapter 3.

It was 8 p.m. The Metal team's three senior members—two partners and principal—were camped out in the conference room in the client's offices, putting together the deck for a major presentation. Five day-long steering committee meetings with the client had been scheduled throughout the project, and the fourth was taking place the next morning, when the team would share a financial analysis that had turned out to be more complicated than anticipated and was bound to be confusing, possibly overwhelming, to the client. The client was already nervous about the direction BCG was planning to take the rest of the case.

Down the hall from the conference room housing their senior leaders, the team's four consultants sat in a temporary workspace fashioned out of stacks of desks and chairs once populated by employees the client had recently laid off. The consultants waited and wondered where the presentation stood, what its overarching goals were, and what remained to be done. They were nine weeks into a twelve-week case, and this seemed to be part of the drill: consultants trying to read their leaders' minds, late into the night. For them, working on the case meant doing the best they could on their own distinct deliverables. They had no broader understanding of the overarching connections that would be important to the client.

Having no clues about how they could be helpful, the consultants began to discuss dinner. When they checked with the principal holed up in the conference room, he told them to get something to eat and come back. The implication was, grab a quick bite and hurry back. But those words were never said.

The senior partner decided to go to dinner, too. He had just flown in a few hours earlier and hadn't eaten all day. The most senior consultant opted to stay behind in case the remaining team leaders needed any help. Too hungry and jet-lagged to pay attention to where they were going, the senior partner soon found himself joining the consultants at one of the nicest restaurants in town, not the place around the corner from the client's offices where he'd assumed they would eat. They ordered appetizers, entrees, several bottles of wine, and dessert. And they enjoyed their meal—no word was spoken about hurrying back to support the trio still cranking away on the slide presentation. In fact, during that two-and-a-half-hour dinner, no one even suggested ordering take-out to bring back to their colleagues.

When the dinner group returned, the senior partner slipped back into the conference room to see what had been accomplished in his absence. The rest of the group returned to their desks and continued to wait for updates and requests. The more junior partner, who had, in the meantime, been left to carry the weight of the presentation, later told us behind closed doors, "I felt like we were on the *Titanic* and we had been left to drown."

Two and a half years later, the Tech team, the PTO team that was compared with the Metal team in chapter 3, was also looking at a long night preparing the deck for a big presentation the next morning. It also happened to be their project leader's night off. When she announced that she was not planning to leave, the two consultants and associate on her team "ganged up on her." They told her, "You have to leave; you have to believe in PTO. This is great for PTO. This is great for our development."

"I had long decided I was not going to take the night off," the project leader later recounted. "But at 5:30 p.m. the team started pushing, and the consultants promised to stay and finish the slides. I decided to leave."

According to one of the consultants, "We checked things four times instead of two to make sure all the ends were meeting up. It was such a positive experience. She got to take her night off, and we got to be the ones to directly deliver the deck. We were given the responsibility to make sure it was right. It was a good learning experience for us. It made us work to a higher level." The principal added, "I think it was just fantastic that she [the project leader] took the night off. She falls into the workaholic, super-control, can't-let-go type. It was just great to see the team tell her 'No, we can handle it; it is time to go.' And they did a great job."

The fundamental difference between the Tech and Metal teams' behavior under similar circumstances was how much they understood what was going on and how much they cared about each other, as well as their motivation to take charge of their world. The Metal team consultants had been left to focus on their discrete tasks, shielded from their leaders' discussions about the big picture. As a result, when the final crunch came, they were in no position to help, and, worse, lacked any real desire to do so.

The members of the Tech team, in contrast, felt that they owned the larger client problem and were eager to step up and deliver—for the good of the whole project and their leader. The project leader did not see herself as the puzzle master integrating all the pieces. From the start, she had empowered her team to deliver without her constantly looking over their shoulders. "I wanted them to get comfortable owning their work and thinking about what to do, so they wouldn't always have to come to me," she explained. "I asked them to debrief each other about what they were doing. They checked each other's slides, they shared what they were doing, what their best practices had been. They became comfortable giving each other suggestions and feedback. That way, they were able to think even more effectively about what they were each doing themselves, and they also understood the whole project."

Doling out responsibilities and letting her people run allowed the project leader to focus on other aspects of the case. And she pulled this off in spite of the challenges of being a new project leader. As she reflected, "You want to show the partners and principal that you're doing a good job, that you're adding value. I would have to force myself to be quiet in a meeting and let the consultants do all of the talking, so they would present their materials to the partner or principal themselves.

But they did a good job, and they could see that I trusted them, which helped them feel more ownership over the project." And, in the end, the partner in charge reflected: "It was a true example of the team being better than the individuals . . . the whole ship was running so well . . . the client was super happy."

The contrast between how these two teams operated carried over to their personal lives as well. When the Metal team's principal wanted to attend his daughter's performance in a school production on a Thursday morning, he flew home for a "personal commitment." No one pressed him for any details, and he never mentioned where he was going to anyone on the team. Ironically, if he had bothered to level with them, he would have found out that his colleagues had plenty going on in their personal lives, too, and would likely have appreciated having the chance to share. One consultant was planning her wedding—and never raised that rather significant fact to most of her teammates; the new partner had recently become engaged, but no one did anything to celebrate, and most didn't even know. Their sole focus was getting the work done.

In contrast, members of the Tech team were very much aware of each others' personal lives—and made an effort to accommodate them. One consultant worked from Minnesota remotely on two Fridays because of family commitments; two others took time off to go to concerts; one consultant's family paid a visit, and he took some extra time with them. The project leader herself tried to set a good example by working from Boston to be with her family, who were visiting from Europe, while the team was in Texas. And, when it was her night off before a major deliverable, the team made sure she took it.

Of course, the Tech team could not address every issue, but all issues were welcomed into the work-related conversations. Here's how one of the Tech team's consultants described it: "I felt 100 percent comfortable telling the project leader if I had plans even on a non-PTO night. I would tell her and emphasize [that] if I couldn't make them, it was completely OK. I just wanted her to know in case it worked. Sometimes it worked. Sometimes it didn't. But I never had to worry that I'd be labeled 'the guy wanting to be out of work.'"

The Benefits of Openness

When we launched the original experiments, we were focused on addressing unpredictability in the work. We hadn't recognized the power that focusing on a personal issue could have far beyond that issue, if combined with structured dialogue. As a culture of openness emerged on PTO teams, people came to better know what the others were doing at work and what mattered to them outside of work. They came to care more about each other and the team.

Gaining New Understanding

As a result of being part of PTO, leaders reported that they had a richer sense of what was going on in their team's personal and work-lives, which enabled them to make changes on the work front that enhanced the team's day-to-day performance. As one partner noted, "I felt like I had a much better handle on how hard people were working, what issues they were facing, how they were dealing with them, what they were hearing from the clients, and so forth. It facilitated my ability to better manage the team, the projects, and the client."

On the other end of the hierarchy, junior team members came to better understand their superiors and their expectations. "We learned how partners think, how they are structuring our work, and what the expectations are coming from the client," explained one associate. "It helped me better understand what the client wanted out of my piece, and to better understand how I could contribute."

Feeling Heard

The amount of change and insight into the work process that PTO was racking up among teams was impressive. Even when nothing changed or no one gained any new understanding, being able to speak up was a big deal for the people who did so. Simply knowing that their perspective was on the table mattered. "It really helped the team feel like they were being heard," said one partner. A project leader was even more blunt: "It allows everyone to voice concerns—and not by saying 'this sucks.' It is a constructive outlet where people can feel heard and speak to particular concerns." In an associate's view, "It does wonders for team morale if your project leader is able to just acknowledge that you are in a miserable situation, and you are all in it together."

Connecting with Something Larger

One project leader, well able to communicate with his team members one-on-one, summed up the added value of the experiment: "The single biggest benefit of PTO was that it opened up this communication with the team. It enabled the whole team to discuss things that previously I would have heard about privately. By discussing them as a group, the team felt better because they realized we are all having similar experiences, they learned we are all in this together."

Feeling part of a team seemed to generate a range of positive emotions; participants in the experiment reported how "uplifting" it was to be part of a team with a common purpose, and leaders noted that the discussions seemed to leave people feeling happier in their day-to-day work. "[Now], when you are in a team meeting, you are more engaged because you know what everyone else is doing," explained one associate. "You can help each other out and contribute ideas on the whole project."

Taking the Human Factor into Account

As a result of the increased openness and understanding, team members began viewing each other all the more as humans with lives both at work and beyond. One associate noted that she looked forward to hearing the weekly check-in of the partner overseeing her case "because it made him seem like a real person."

From one partner's point of view, "If you just work with someone, you get to know them on a very uni-dimensional level. You don't know about their life, if their father is ill, if they have children." He found that getting to know team members better on a personal level actually improved working relationships: "It helps you manage them better. It helps them feel better about working with you." A consultant summed it up this way: "PTO brought the team together as humans."

We witnessed an important shift among team members in the experiment: from focusing on themselves, and sometimes a few others with whom they had created bonds, to focusing on the team as a group of people who shared a common goal at work and had lives beyond work that mattered to them too.[1]

A Passion for Change

It started with a newfound openness about what needed to occur to make their PTO nights possible. As people opened up about their issues, they came to care more about each other. That is not so surprising: the research on self-disclosure suggests when individuals get to know personal information about each other, they like each other more. And the more they like each other, the more they are willing to disclose.[2] However, what we further discovered was that the positive reinforcing loop of liking and disclosure combined with the action orientation resulting from striving to achieve the collective goal, amounted to teams focused not only on raising but also striving to address issues. Here's how the Tech team's project leader summed up what she called "the dramatic change in my attitude toward work": "PTO really forced me to think and solve so many situations. I was continually asking myself, 'Can we make this work?'"

Another project leader gave a similar type of example: "When forced to talk, people will tell each other things that they care about. Maybe you learn that someone likes ballet, or just went to an art exhibit or stand-up comedy. Just knowing that breeds some level of care for those around you. Maybe you end up asking the person, 'Did you manage to go to the comedy show on Thursday?' And if the person says no, you are more motivated to brainstorm how to make it happen next time."

A consultant reported how his team "wanted to make sure that everyone felt the workload was sustainable. Even if we were working hard we were still looking out for each other to make sure that people were not getting burned out. People would be up late sending each other messages saying, 'Why are you up? Go to bed.'"

This newfound caring became the motor for change, creating in teams the passion to take action to improve their work process to the benefit of themselves, their teammates, and the team's deliverables.[3] As one BCG consultant explained: "Someone would say that they were feeling stressed and others would immediately find out what they could do to help."[4]

As BCGers' passion to improve their world grew, so did their optimism about actually making change happen. That optimism was fueled by the real and measurable fact that their work processes were improving, as was the predictability of and control over their work schedules.

Learning to make the one night off a week a reality was having a profound effect. BCGers came to appreciate just how much *could* change.[5]

Experimenting with Change—Together

At the outset of our experiment, even those who longed for change never thought it would happen. So ingrained was the notion that the nature of management consulting was unpredictable and therefore required a 24/7, always-on work ethic, that those who could not sustain that lifestyle assumed that they had no alternative but to leave the consulting industry.

Within six months after PTO became a Boston office initiative, when ten case teams had participated and five more were starting up, team members we interviewed about their experiences kept echoing one word: *change*. PTO had changed their attitude toward work, toward their managers. It had changed not just the way they were doing their work—where, when, and how they were interacting with each other—but it was also changing their mindset. It was changing what they believed was possible.

PTO inspired efforts to experiment in small ways toward solving problems that seemed to bother BCG teams but were generally accepted as the way it had to be in management consulting—four days a week on the road, last-minute meetings that resulted in late-night or weekend work, and team members focused on perfecting their individual deliverables. PTO engaged people in a process that perpetually chipped away at these "givens." This led to a profound realization: *the status quo could change.* And more changes followed.

As a result, people on PTO teams were no longer willing to acquiesce to the status quo but were constantly questioning the way they did things and assessing whether better alternatives could be created—alternatives that would benefit both the work and their personal lives. One consultant summed it up beautifully: "The officers really made it clear from the start that we were to take this seriously. And once we took it seriously, we came to realize there weren't many instances where we couldn't make change happen." It is one thing to raise issues and quite another to act on them. Stanford professors Jeffrey Pffefer and Robert Sutton have labeled this the *knowing-doing gap.*[1] PTO inspired people to close this gap, investing a great deal of effort, working together, to discover and try out new ways of working.

Collective Experimentation

The simple goal of predictable time off inspired individuals to find their own more productive ways of working. As one consultant explained, "PTO caused me to think about what needs to be done for today and is this important for me to do." Without question, it made individuals more efficient.

The real value, however, was that it did so much more than that, because individuals worked together to make changes beyond those that anyone alone could make. On PTO teams, members engaged in what I call *collective experimentation,* which has two defining characteristics: (1) multiple members of the team are experimenting together, and (2) in the process, they are challenging the status quo. As one BCG partner explained: "People are talking and thinking about what needs to be done and then working together to achieve the end result, rather than executing individually in a suboptimal fashion."

By framing PTO teams as engaged in an experiment—there is an explicit emphasis on trial and error, and a tolerance of failure. While technically only the Consumer team was an experiment, later teams were called experiments to continue to foster the mindset that PTO is not a set process but rather a mindset to be lived—a continuous openness to challenging old ways and exploring new ones.

The resulting changes need not be big to have a significant impact; indeed, they can be the most micro adaptations in work practices. In the words of Tom Peters and Robert Waterman, "There is absolutely no magic in the experiment. It is simply a tiny completed action, a manageable test that helps you learn something, just as in high school chemistry."[2]

Having a discussion about what should be the work location or travel schedule or weekend practices around e-mail, or how to make a single night off happen on a given date, and then acting to make these changes, results in micro adjustments to the work process. These micro adjustments provide a platform for further changes, and create new work practices. Over time, groups revisit these work practices and continue to tweak them. Each micro change is an incidence of *collective experimentation*. As small as they may seem, each fundamentally challenges how work is done, work practice by work practice. By building on each other, these small changes unleash deep and significant change in the team's, and ultimately organization's, culture.

Engaging in such ongoing micro adjustments has been PTO's core outcome—and the reason the experiments at BCG have been so successful.

Experimenting, Experimenting, Experimenting

Before PTO, teams tended to focus on plowing through the work. The typical result: having not used their time as efficiently or effectively as they might have, they ended up overwhelmed by the work. Engaging in PTO has led teams to recognize these issues, and, in turn, prepared them to be more able to address them.

One consultant described how PTO helped his team iterate less—pulling them out of the rut of working on the same deck over and over: "Once the issue was raised, the principal simply changed the way he reviewed the team's slides . . . It helped me realize what was core to PTO, which is having the confidence to say it's not going great, if that is what you think." He paused and continued, "Then you work to fix it."

A partner on a different case reflected, "I think what really happens when we do PTO well is it creates a conversation among the team around how to structure the work, and it gets us to think about things earlier that will hopefully allow us to have less repeated cycles and less redundant work and actually get the output faster. So I found it very useful to have those early conversations as a way to make the work move more smoothly."

A senior partner told a similar story:

I will give you an example where PTO worked really well. I was on a multifaceted transformation effort. The team was big and we were getting off to a very intense start. One of the things I realized very early on because of PTO was the fact that the team was working crazy long hours, some of that was driven by the client, but some of that was driven by preparations for meetings with me. So what was happening was multiple iterations of documents from the project leader to the principal to the partner in preparation for meetings with me. And while I appreciated the hard work and the effort, it was causing an enormous amount of stress on the team. And within a week and a half, because of PTO, we were able to surface that, and reduce dramatically the number of iterations and frustrations on the team. I think on a typical effort, even with the right intentions and the right listening skills, it could have taken as much as a month to diagnose that. So for me, PTO is a tool to enhance communication and to surface issues quickly. And I think the quicker we surface issues and can resolve them, the better we all are.

Another chronic problem teams faced was the lack of alignment between partners, each pressing team members to pursue contradictory objectives—a problem we saw vividly in chapter 3. Once this problem surfaced on PTO teams, they agreed to new review cycles and new ways to include partners in the meetings. This led to fewer iterations and a reduced workload.

PTO also forced team leaders to prioritize. According to one partner, "PTO was very helpful at surfacing trade-offs that needed to be made. People would now say things such as, realistically, we cannot do everything so what are the key parts that we want to make sure to do." A consultant described a PTO meeting at which the team decided that it was realistic to complete only the first three points of her five-point work plan. "I did that, and the client was extremely happy," she reported. "Focusing on just these three points rather than all five made the work better and the project better overall."

Sometimes what surfaced was a need to reallocate resources or seek additional resources; at other times it took going to the client and discussing, one more time, what had to get done.

The changes that occurred in the BCG case teams can be grouped into several categories. Their common denominator is that individuals worked together to challenge the status quo, experimenting with alternative ways of doing their work, and discovering new ways of doing things that enhanced both their own and each others' work-lives and the efficiency and effectiveness of their work process.

Travel

When working on a case that required travel, BCG teams spent up to four days a week working away from home. Many partners chose to have their teams be at the client site as much as possible in order to build deep client relationships, be available if the client wanted anything, help the client take ownership of the work they were doing, and be on the lookout for additional problems the client might need help in addressing (i.e., new lines of work for BCG).

Team members, however, tended to prefer to work from the firm's office whenever possible. So it was not surprising that once PTO teams built enough trust one of the most common areas for experimentation was the travel schedule. Previously, teams would frequently fly out of Boston on the 6 a.m. flight Monday morning, which meant that people would have to leave for the airport at 4:30 or 5:00 a.m.—and then spend the rest of the week at the client site trying to catch up on sleep. Teams began to experiment with leaving on Sunday night, taking flights later during the week, or not going at all. There were frank discussions about who needed to be at the client site when and for what purpose. Supporting the client, getting their buy-in, making sure they ultimately took ownership of the work, and being on the lookout for new projects continued to be important reasons for BCG's onsite presence. Teams realized, however, that not everyone needed to be there all the time, even for these purposes. The new norm became traveling only when there was a reason, and moreover trying to minimize these reasons. Team leaders kept saying, "Make it happen; don't be at the client when it isn't necessary; schedule your client meetings accordingly."

E-mail Overload

BCGers would frequently find themselves exchanging e-mails late at night. It was not unusual for an e-mail chain to rally back and forth a half-dozen even a dozen times on a given evening. I myself came to recognize that if I wanted a response from Rachel Levine, our key contact at BCG, I should just log on at 10 p.m., and she would engage.

But this norm led to all sorts of bad behavior. Time was wasted going back and forth when a quick conversation the next morning would have been much more efficient. And people felt pressure to always be *on* to receive these messages. A consultant described, "I usually don't go to bed until around midnight because the partner often sends me e-mails late at night." The partner tended to travel to a different city every day, and when he would land, often around 11 p.m., he would send all the e-mails he had written on the flight.

One partner related, "I'm a morning riser, so I do e-mails early in the morning." He added, "I started noticing that consultants started answering them, and I'm like, 'Are you a morning riser too?' and they're like, 'No, but you usually send out e-mails,' and my response was, 'Oh my god.'"

PTO teams would often set norms about when they could send e-mails. On one team, a consultant wrote a program within Microsoft Outlook that enabled the team to hold any e-mail after a certain hour in the evening and automatically send it the next morning. Later, BCG's global IT unit got involved and developed a tool that automated the batching of e-mails to reduce the amount of late-night and weekend traffic.

Teams would set explicit times when e-mail response was not required, such as after 8 p.m. and on weekends, and program these times into Outlook. Someone who tried to send an e-mail during off hours would get a reminder that it was outside of normal e-mail hours. A series of prompts would offer the choice of holding the e-mail until 6 or 7 a.m. the next morning, sending it immediately with an urgent subject line, or sending it immediately with a non-urgent subject line. A consultant explained, "Both my principal and my project leader were really good about not pressuring us to engage over the weekend. If they sent an e-mail over the weekend, the title would be something like 'for Monday' so I knew I didn't need to stop what I was doing and read it."

Many teams found managing e-mail not only helped reduce the amount of evening and weekend e-mail traffic, but also reduced inefficient e-mails overall. A project leader described the e-mail batching as "a total lifesaver from my perspective. We went from having forty-two e-mails being sent back and forth at night to turning that into a conversation in the morning . . . It does more than shift e-mail times, it also reduces the cycles of e-mail. So many things can be solved in person instead."

Constraining Work Time

Teams made other innovations around work time as well. Some team leaders would make it a point to leave the team room in the evening, even if they intended to keep working later that night. A principal elaborated, "I noticed that even though I would encourage people to leave at a reasonable hour, no one wanted to take a break until I did. Now I try to leave early at least one day a week, to set an example that they don't need to stay in the team room at night."

Another way time was saved to the benefit of the team was tinkering with who did what work. A project leader who felt swamped by client meetings realized that while he couldn't send consultants and associates in his place, because his seniority was required, he could bring a consultant or associate as an extra set of ears. He began to bring a junior member of the team to each client meeting, and assigned that person to write up notes and to-dos from the meeting. That allowed the project leader to save time capturing the key takeaways, and provided the junior team with more context and exposure to clients.

Time was also saved by constraining how much work was done. One team set a goal of never showing more than five slides to the client at a time. This goal was originally set to help the project leader prioritize her time in what she showed the partner, but then realized it would also be better for the client, because it would make the team's recommendations more actionable. The partner later noted he'd asked previous teams to share only five slides with him, but they never had. He thought setting this goal in the context of PTO helped the team realize he was serious: "PTO made it legitimate that I cared enough about the team to have this dialogue with them and set the five-slide goal."

Several teams established a recurring meeting every Thursday or Friday to review deliverables and set priorities going into the weekend, with the explicit goal of avoiding weekend work. When weekend work was necessary, they would use this time to set expectations and schedules so that people could protect important personal events.

Meeting Effectiveness

One of the most impressive challenges to the status quo was the effect PTO had on the nature of team meetings themselves. Previously, during case team meetings, team members tended to remain in the room physically, but unless it was their turn to present, they tuned out. Often they would focus on their own work modules, preparing their own decks of slides, for example, or attending to their e-mail, rather than listening to colleagues present their findings to the team leaders.

On PTO cases, team meetings became much more focused on overall client issues. There might still be portions dedicated to an update from a consultant, but instead of being aimed at the senior members, the updates became full discussions about the case. Consultants participating in the experiment reached the point where they were continuously and confidently raising struggles, seeking help, and experimenting with new solutions that they would have previously felt too risky to raise. Consultants also commented on each other's slides, making suggestions and sharing relevant information from their own client contacts and work assignments.

This process built on itself: the more engaged team members were, the more context they each had, and the better able they were to converse about their work. As one project leader described the change, "Case team meetings are no longer just a read-out of each module's progress. I now structure case team meetings around core client issues and can leverage the collective intelligence of the team."

Free-flowing discussions emerged in response to the first question on the Pulse Check, "How are you feeling?" Someone might note that he was feeling a little discouraged because he hadn't been able to set up a meeting he needed, which would prompt a teammate to share a similar experience, which would prompt the rest of the team to reflect on whether this was a pattern indicating that the client was disengaging from BCG's intervention; a half-hour later, the team would have hammered out a plan for getting the client to buy into what BCG had been hired to do.

The new process was a win from top to bottom: junior members felt good about their contributions to the discussions; the senior people appreciated that the more junior members were stepping up and taking more responsibility for the project, which relieved time and stress for those senior members, who had previously been the ones tasked with all the integration and oversight. Positive reinforcement encouraged people to engage all the more in the next meeting.

Meeting Times

Another nagging issue for teams was the scheduling of meetings. A 5 p.m. meeting erased any hope of getting home in time for family dinner. A Friday meeting for a Monday client presentation would mean weekend work. A Monday team meeting would likely amount to weekend preparation.

Despite the adverse impact of these meeting times, BCG teams had tended to give little thought to when meetings were scheduled. PTO changed that. As a result of more open dialogue, team members were able to express their frustrations. And the leadership responded. When a case team meeting was scheduled for late Friday afternoon, a consultant asked that it be changed—and the project leader did so. As that consultant put it, "Before, I would never ever have asked a project leader to do something like move a case team meeting to accommodate my personal life."

New Ways of Sharing Information

Some teams established a team blog, a shared website where team members could post comments to share information about client meetings and analysis. Daily reminders on each member's calendar prompted them to submit an update for that day. There were no requirements as to the content of the updates—they could post something as simple as "No update today," or as detailed as summaries of every meeting they had had that day and the analyses they had done. They would then e-mail their updates to the blog, which posted them automatically.

On one of the earliest PTO teams, when a principal first suggested the use of a blog, the team was reluctant to try it. After the principal pushed on this for a week, the team agreed to see what he had in mind, and he set it up for them. Within less than a week of implementation, the team was elated—the process of daily posts helped them organize their own work better and also gave them useful insight into the rest of the project. Rather than feeling like overhead, the act of writing the updates was helpful, as it caused the team to reflect on what was important and how to prioritize their work the next day. As one consultant put it, "It helped me think about what I was doing during the day and made me question whether what I was doing was value added, and plan accordingly." An associate agreed: "Knowing I'm going to write down what I did during the day makes me think twice about what I'm doing. As I'd go through my day, I'd ask myself whether what I was doing was important. It really helped me focus on the key things."

Further, at the end of the day, the team could read through the blog entries to get a sense of what had happened in client meetings that day, learn about hallway conversations, and get an update on current analyses. The partners and principals found tremendous value in reading the blog entries, as well. As a partner noted, "I'm only at the client one day a week, but with the blog, it was like I was there every day. By reading the blog, I could walk into a meeting with a senior client and really know what was going on."

Where Work Gets Done

Another prime area for experimentation was where the consultants physically worked when they were on the road: in a team room, in their own cubicles, from the hotel. Most teams had never discussed this very basic issue.

PTO enabled team members to raise their preferences and figure out ways that worked best for all of them. One team, for example, had felt compelled to work in their team room—even though it turned out that most of them found it distracting and inefficient. But that revelation came only after the team began to engage in PTO. The principal's response once the problem was raised: "I don't care where you work, as long as you are getting the work done. Cubicles, the hotel room, whatever works for you."

Performance Issues

Sometimes experimentation did not revolve so much around team members' preferences or work processes but rather around how they dealt with certain other team members—particularly those branded as underperformers. Participants tended to question whether poor performers should even be allowed to participate in an experiment centered around taking time off. Yet the PTO process turned out to be very powerful for teams perceived to have such members, precisely because it enabled discussion of these performance issues.

All too often, managers don't understand what exactly causes certain mistakes or missed deadlines or lack of results. They jump to conclusions and identify the person involved as a weak link on the team. Even if the manager has not made this explicit, people who fail to deliver assume that the leader or colleagues are blaming them, which amplifies performance anxiety. Soon the person who has not met expectations is struggling harder to avoid issues in the future, while others are now scrutinizing the work, looking for mistakes. The more others look, the more anxious the person becomes, the more mistakes are likely to happen, and the more they are likely to be noticed.

It is not that poor performers don't exist or mistakes don't happen. But all too often a mistake by a perfectly adequate performer takes on a life of its own, and the person spirals into a *performance trap* where mistakes lead to performance anxiety, more mistakes, more anxiety, more mistakes, and so on, in a vicious spiral. What the PTO process does is help break such spirals of negativity before they spin alleged underperformers into a performance trap, undermining their ability to succeed or their ability to be fully useful to the team. When mistakes happen, as they inevitably do, PTO offers the team a chance to explore why they occurred and what can be done differently going forward. As one partner explained, "People worry that PTO is hard with underperformers, but I completely disagree. With PTO, you actually shine the light earlier on issues than you would without PTO. By shining the light, you force adjustment and corrective action earlier in the case, before a weakness or hiccup becomes a real problem."

Consider Rick and Peter, a consultant and an associate on one of the more recent PTO teams. They were tasked with analyzing data the client was to provide. The data was received late and, worse yet, not in the form that the team had requested. Already under a tight deadline, the pair had to spend a great deal of extra time to produce an interim set of numbers for the team's senior members to review in preparation for a client meeting.

When Rick and Peter handed the numbers to their project leader for review, she found multiple errors, which raised questions in her mind about the pair's competence. Both Rick and Peter were relatively new, and she wondered if the errors were the result of carelessness or a sign of a bigger issue.

Meantime, the data from the client did not improve; nor did Rick and Peter have the time they needed to be more careful while producing all the expected analyses. The only thing that changed was their stress level, which increased by the day. And the more they worried about the data, the less they were able to focus on the big picture of understanding what was driving the numbers, and the more they failed to do so, the more concerned their project leader became.

When it came time for the PTO check-in, they all showed up with concerns. The project leader expressed—in the spirit of PTO's quest for openness—that she wanted to be kept better informed about what was happening. Suddenly, Rick and Peter came to understand that they could have done a better job of communicating with her.

Being part of a PTO team, and responding to the project leader's openness, Rick looked the project leader in the eye and said, "I'm embarrassed about this," and she felt that his *mea culpa* went a long way toward helping address the issue. For his part, Rick was relieved to address the issues in the open, and noted that, without PTO, he never would have felt comfortable bringing them up. Rick also reported that the experience had provided him a valuable opportunity to learn from his mistakes in a way that would help him handle similar problems on future case teams. The partner was impressed with how well Rick and Peter were able to turn the situation around, as was the project leader. She explained, "They really improved and got out of [the negative spiral]. I think they learned a lot, and they each started thinking about the work proactively . . . not just about executing a given task but about what that task meant for the whole project." In the end, the partner felt

strongly enough about Rick and Peter's performance that he requested
to staff them on his next project.

Without PTO to encourage such open conversation, it's easy to imagine a different scenario: Rick and Peter would have kept struggling, the
project leader would have ended up working more to bail them out or
even cover for them with the partner, who was known to label a project leader weak if there was a struggling consultant on the team. The
project leader and her not-so-dynamic duo would have kept working
harder and getting more and more frustrated, each thinking less of the
other's abilities. Worse yet, the duo would likely have gone to their next
case under a cloud of incompetence; under more pressure than ever
to deliver, they would have been all the more likely to make mistakes.
Instead, they learned PTO's most valuable lesson: change was possible.

Achieving the Unimaginable: Change

The power of PTO is twofold: work and personal issues are brought to
the forefront, and teams are further motivated to explore ways to address these issues. Over and over, in small ways, assumptions about how
the work is to be done are challenged. As we have seen in this chapter,
by altering travel times, meeting locations and schedules, team interactions, 24/7 demands to always make work the first priority, and tendencies to jump to conclusions rather than explore performance issues,
PTO chipped away at the status quo. New ways of working evolved,
with profound benefits for individuals and the organization.

6

Small Steps, Big Results

Four years after the Consumer team embarked on the PTO experiment, 88 percent of BCG's Boston office consulting staff were engaging in the PTO process on their current team, and 95 percent of them wanted their next team to be engaged in PTO. By this point, 72 percent of individuals felt that their colleagues were considerate of their personal lives, compared with 55 percent before the initiative began; 59 percent felt they had sufficient control over their work schedule, compared with 43 percent before the initiative began; and 81 percent derived a sense of personal accomplishment from their work, compared with 71 percent at the start.

The work itself was also believed to be benefiting. More individuals felt it was safe to speak up and express opinions (74 percent versus 58 percent) and more felt they were collaborating well (71 percent versus 39 percent). As a result, the client was also thought to be better off: 91 percent versus 83 percent of the consulting staff felt their teams were delivering significant value to their clients.[1]

FIGURE 6-1

The first three years of PTO (Boston office)

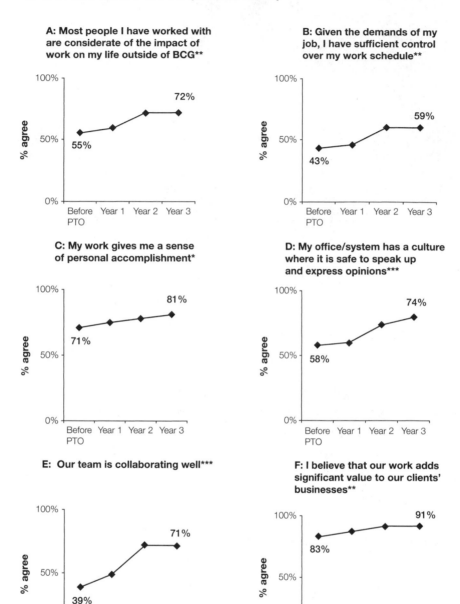

A: Most people I have worked with are considerate of the impact of work on my life outside of BCG**

B: Given the demands of my job, I have sufficient control over my work schedule**

C: My work gives me a sense of personal accomplishment*

D: My office/system has a culture where it is safe to speak up and express opinions***

E: Our team is collaborating well***

F: I believe that our work adds significant value to our clients' businesses**

*Significant at p<.10 level; **significant at p<.05 level; ***significant at p<.01 level

The data in figures A–D and F was provided by Towers Watson.

Eliminating Bad Intensity

It happened step-by-step, one change at a time. Team members tackled the bad intensity—the wheel spinning; unnecessary iterations; lack of communication and alignment; last-minute, late-night changes; and weekend "emergencies" that result in that never-ending pressure to be *on* and get in the way of people doing their best at work and having time for life outside of work. Eliminating the bad intensity energized people and gave them a greater sense of control and personal accomplishment. Not all bad intensity was eradicated. But the bad stuff served as a catalyst for rethinking the work process in constructive ways and making changes wherever possible.

As one BCGer had confided back in the days before PTO, "I thrive on the adrenaline rush that comes from working hard to deliver high-value work to the client. What I don't like is never being able to make a plan." What PTO did is make these two desires synergistic; it used people's desire for more control over their work-lives as a catalyst to improve the work process in ways that focused their attention on the more engaging aspects of the work while making it more manageable.

Recall how the Tech team members made it possible for their project leader to take the night off, even though it was the night before a major client presentation (see chapter 4). Team members were gratified by the opportunity to step up their responsibilities and work together in new ways, while the project leader glowed with pride at her team's accomplishments. The partner, too, was delighted, and the client was pleased with the final deliverable. A clear win all around.

In fact, eliminating bad intensity was a recurring event on the Tech team. When the project leader doled out assignments in the late afternoons, causing team members to stay until 10 or 11 at night, they spoke up and worked with her to solve the problem (see chapter 3). When they didn't understand why she was making a request, they asked. Sometimes things changed. Sometimes nothing changed. But by raising problems to a project leader who was willing to discuss them, team members better understood why they were doing what they were doing. In the end, they came to feel a greater sense of personal accomplishment associated with their work because they felt that what they were doing had value—whether the value was created through the PTO process or came to be understood as a result of being part of PTO. And when changes in the work process resulted, the benefits extended to giving people more control over their work-lives.

Too often we see teams that strive to be more efficient succeed in making changes—only to find themselves being asked to do more. With PTO it was different. Through open dialogue and the trust it nurtured, teams discovered new ways of working and then shared in the benefits.

Creating a True Win-Win

As the initiative expanded to more BCG offices, the benefits of the process never ceased to surprise PTO skeptics as well as its fans—or me. I had begun with modest expectations, hoping to determine whether a single team of BCGers could take predictable time off—despite their belief to the contrary—and without any negative (and ideally with some positive) impact on the work process itself. One of PTO's biggest surprises as the process spread throughout the firm was that its influence reached far beyond the particular issue of being able to take a unit of time off—benefiting over and over the work process and people's work-lives.

PTO had a positive impact on people's work-lives along two core dimensions—control over the work schedule and a sense of accomplishment from doing the work itself. I describe those who experience high control over their work schedule and a high sense of fulfillment in their work as living the *Dream*.[2] Those at the other end of both spectrums— with low control and low fulfillment are caught in the *Grind*. The power of PTO is that by eliminating the bad intensity, it helps people move from Grind to Dream. And when it does, morale is significantly higher (90 percent versus 13 percent), and people are much more likely to see themselves at BCG in a year (87 percent versus 47 percent). (See "The Grind and the Dream.")

The Grind and the Dream

The *Grind* perpetually works hard but feels that his work is out of control—and he's deeply demoralized by it. Despite endless effort, there is always more to do, and little of it feels meaningful. Whatever feelings of energy or satisfaction the Grind got from this job at the outset are long gone. Instead, he faces the frustration of having to work in seemingly unproductive ways—attending too many meetings that last far too long, scrambling to respond to last-minute requests, making unnecessary changes to the document for the nth time. Resentful, the Grind is constantly wondering: To what end am I working? Is it really worth it?

The scenarios

	Low	High
Control over work / High	**The Employee:** It may be doable, but to what end? My schedule is manageable, but my work is uninspiring.	**The Dream:** ★ I am thriving, and it's doable. Work is a gigantic source of fulfillment for me—and I have enough control I can have a personal life, too.
Control over work / Low	**The Grind:** I am overwhelmed, and it's just not worth it. Why am I doing this job? I run hard, but see little positive impact as a result of my work—and my life is totally out of control.	**The Junkie:** I find my work exhilarating, but is it sustainable? I love the work—but don't know how long I (or my family/friends) can stand it.

Fulfillment from work

Two other types of workers "have it all" along one dimension but are sorely lacking on the other. The *Junkie* finds work fulfilling but is so addicted that he has absolutely no control over how much he works.[3] He

(continued)

(*continued*)

adores his work and everything that comes with it—the long hours, the travel, the thrill of being indispensable, the exhilaration of meeting tight deadlines. But this mental rush bears a high price tag: he can't make dinner plans, can't see his kids awake during the week, and hasn't gotten to the gym in ages. For a while, the Junkie is satisfied—but he may well end up jeopardizing many other valuable aspects of his life if he doesn't change his behavior. By contrast, the *Employee* has a high degree of control and is grateful to have a personal life, but he has little attachment to his work, which he finds unsatisfying. He's not learning, not being pushed, not achieving any real sense of accomplishment; he's just punching the clock and collecting a paycheck, all the while wondering if there shouldn't be something more to work.

The *Dream,* in contrast, is in an enviable situation—he's got control over his schedule without having to give up the thrill of a challenging job. He thrives on the adrenaline of responding to a tough client question, of working on deadline, of being pushed and taking on new responsibilities—that exciting new project with a highly visible client. Yet he still has enough control to enjoy his personal life. The career isn't perfect, and it is never easy, but life overall feels positive, energizing, upbeat.

Making Good Managers Better

PTO clearly helps managers reduce the bad intensity undermining their teams, improving the work process and moving individuals closer to the sweet spot of the Dream. But what about teams that do not suffer from as much bad intensity? We are often asked whether PTO still adds value for even the best managers, who already foster dialogue, collaboration, and care for their team's personal lives. What about teams where there are already fewer last-minute requests, fewer late nights, less unnecessary travel, less time spent on nonessential work, and fewer unproductive meetings?

Some of BCG's top managers certainly viewed PTO as an unnecessary intervention, which, given their success, was understandable. For example, Ron, a partner in Boston, had twice won the firm's prestigious Northeast Award, given annually to 10 to 12 percent of BCG partners worldwide for outstanding performance along two dimensions: revenue generation and upward feedback scores. His teams already had kickoff meetings where they discussed work styles, preferences, and personal needs. "Personal information makes a difference in how you manage the case," he explained. "I know your mom is sick, or that you have a training next week . . . that personal piece is part of the equation, always." Ron went so far as to call PTO "a step backward" for managers like himself.

As PTO evolved, we periodically had conversations with Ron, wanting to understand his persistent reservations. Unlike most of his colleagues, Ron did not believe that it was the nature of client service that required teams to be on all the time. "I do not feel that I am required to be available to work 24/7. I do feel that some others feel this way and have little regard for people's personal lives—but I do not feel this way myself, and I do not think our clients expect this either. I have never had to cancel a vacation, and I have never asked one of my team members to cancel a vacation."

What Ron thought BCG really needed to do was change its training and incentive systems to encourage managers to care about their teams and treat them well. "There is plenty of incentive for partners *not* to care about the work-life balance of their teams," he noted, adding: "If BCG is serious about creating change, it needs to be built into compensation and promotion decisions—with incentives for those who learn to manage well."

In the eyes of many BCGers, the fact that someone as well known for caring about his people as Ron was resisting PTO was a mark against it. Over time, however, the consensus shifted to "What is wrong with Ron? If he's so concerned with his team's well-being, why won't he support PTO?" It reached the point, according to Ron, "People would come up to me, junior people, and suggest I was a bad person for not doing PTO."

Despite the pressure, Ron held out, convinced that PTO would not be valuable to his teams. Then, eleven months after we launched the PTO initiative in Boston, Ron found himself working with a large group of partners supporting a major change effort at one of his key clients. The senior partner wanted everyone to engage in PTO. Ron had little choice but to oblige, and he soon reached the conclusion that by playing an active role he could at least help shape how PTO was implemented on his team.

It was not long before Ron concluded that he had underestimated PTO. "For a good manager, PTO is a formalization of things they are already doing," he conceded. "It's a reminder to keep doing those things, instead of getting lazy when times get tough. Having that weekly discussion is a reminder that each and every week I better be focused on this."

Ron also observed that PTO check-ins helped create trust for a practice he had long encouraged—speaking openly. Moreover, after team members reported being overwhelmed by the sheer volume of e-mail, they were able to address the issue by setting guidelines and clear expectations for e-mail use. "It was a huge benefit," Ron later told us.

But the real power of PTO for Ron was that regardless of how involved he was with any of his teams day to day, he could be assured that team members were still engaging with each other in the open way that he—as a major advocate for training and rewarding good managers—believed was so important. Because team members now had a true voice, they began to speak up about issues that they wouldn't previously have raised, including how the team itself was working together and how the managers were managing the process. Ron explained, "Managers get feedback that they otherwise wouldn't get, and those feedback loops are an important part of how we learn."

When we went back to speak with Ron two years after his first reluctant experience with PTO, we found him convinced that PTO was doing just what he had claimed it could not do—changing partner behavior. "There are still some partners who drive their teams very hard," he said, "but it's happening a lot less now. It has shifted, partner behavior has shifted, and now people are much more thoughtful about team members' personal lives." We could not help but smile at how far Ron—indeed, all of us—had come. PTO had proved that not only could

BCG's best managers learn from their teams and become even better managers, but in the process PTO had changed what it means to be a good manager.

As another Boston partner who had used PTO on over fifteen cases and had worked with nine principals and project leaders using PTO put it: "The good managers could do it individually, talk to the team members one-on-one about issues that were troubling them, but it would have been considered almost a violation of the group to bring it into the team, whereas this actually makes group conversation the norm." Another senior partner simply said, "It is an enabler and performance improver for nearly everyone."

What the Clients Said

Given the improvements that PTO triggered in the work process, one would expect clients to be enthusiastic about PTO as well. And many were. Others, however, less familiar with the ins and outs of BCG's day-to-day work, were less aware of the benefits but still clear that they had experienced no costs.

It was difficult to have clients assess the benefits of PTO because most didn't even know it was going on. Indeed, for the most part, PTO teams were intentionally set up to have no impact on the client, with a coverage system in place for those times when the client needed something on someone's night off. One of the times that the client knew about the existence of PTO, however, was when we set the collective goal as an entire day off a week rather than just a night off. In that case, each of the five BCG team members was assigned a client contact with whom they worked closely, meeting on a near-daily basis. Given the depth of those relationships and that each of the BCGers would now be gone a full day a week, the probability that the client might be affected greatly increased. The senior executive managing the relationship from the client end was notified about the plan and assured that if there were ever a problem, the experiment would be halted immediately. That never happened. At the end of the case, we interviewed the five key client contacts to understand the impact of the experiment on them. (See the appendix for a detailed description of the day-off experiment.)

One client contact told us. "If I needed to get something done, it always got done." Another added, "I never had to worry about which of them [different members of the BCG team] was doing something or that the other would not have full information about what had been done."

While two of the five client contacts focused more on how the day-off-a-week goal had no negative impact, the other three stressed the benefits of PTO. "It was a big advantage . . . [my BCG contact] was much more informed about what else was going on with other modules, and it was easier to get answers and people were more informed about the whole project." A second client added, "This holistic view really enhanced what was going on." And the third summed up the trio's experience: "There are no cons, only pros."

The client contacts in this case also expressed genuine interest in PTO and a tinge of envy that BCGers were engaged in an initiative to provide them time off. One put it simply, "I think it's great. I wonder if we could do something like that here?"

There was a shared sense within BCG that PTO was having no negative effects on clients and in many cases was having profound positive effects because of the improvements made to the work process itself. However, by the end of year 3 of the initiative, we thought it prudent to interview a few clients who had been involved in PTO cases with a predictable night off as the collective goal to make sure they shared this sentiment. These clients had no knowledge of PTO before the interview request was made. Part of the interview involved revealing to them what had been going on with their BCG teams.

Most striking was the similarity of the clients' responses—whether the team they were working with was engaged in an experiment around a predictable day off or a predictable night off. First and foremost, everyone noted that nothing dropped through the cracks, and they were pleasantly surprised to learn that BCG was involved in this process. One senior client we interviewed reviewed in our presence every e-mail he had sent the BCG team to confirm his sense that he had always gotten a response within a few hours. Sometimes that response was simply to inform him what preparing an answer would entail and when he should expect it. But he made clear, "That is what matters most to me. Most of all, I want to have a sense of when I will get what I need."

One client admitted how surprised she was when she noticed (not having been aware of the formal PTO initiative) that team members were taking nights off. But she had also been impressed by how well BCGers covered for each other. "Nothing ever suffered," she recalled. "Never a beat missed." She added, "I remember thinking that they have time off, and that was a pleasant surprise."

Another client was particularly thoughtful about the experiment and its consequences: "We are paying so much money and we expect a response from the firm. But I don't want to be a jerk. I get to know the guys personally, and I want them to be able to live their lives . . . Besides, I don't want to work with machines. When someone was covering for [his key contact] I remember thinking to myself, 'Oh good, he has a night off and that is a positive thing. It shows people are people.'" Told that PTO was the reason for this time off, this client turned into a big fan of the process: "You have cracked it. You have found a way to deal with the inconsistency. You have found a way of enabling individuals to have a life, but I still get the response I need . . . You have found a way to reconcile that I have different expectations of the firm and expectations of the individuals who make up the firm. That is ideal."

And not only was there appreciation for the fact that people were getting their time off while still meeting the client's expectations; there was also a sense that by having to cover for each other in each other's absence—even if for only a night off rather than a day off—the client was getting more minds focused on solving their problems. Several acknowledged this benefit. And clients were happy to learn that BCGers were engaged in their own learning process. As one client put it, "I had no idea. I am intrigued. It is great that they practice what they preach. They don't have an attitude that they know everything, but rather have a willingness to learn."

The Starting Point: Learning to Turn Off

At the most basic level, PTO provided BCG consultants some predictable time off and thus a chance to learn how to disconnect and experience its benefits. Many reported that simply being "forced" to take time off made them experience something that was not only unusual but also made them uncomfortable; something they would not have tried on their own. "The value of PTO," noted one of the firm's principals, "is we didn't have a choice. My wife really appreciated that while I was on this case, on my night off I really checked out of work and wasn't always checking my BlackBerry. I could probably have done that on past cases in terms of what the work required, but I never would have felt like it was OK. But because I was forced to . . . I could really check out and that made a huge difference."

Being able to "really check out," people discovered they felt more rested, more energetic, and thus more positive about their work. As one associate described it, "While you are still working a lot, the nights off put the team in a better mood—people are more relaxed and have fresh eyes. Even if all PTO means is that you get eight hours' sleep, it helps the case overall." According to a consultant, "I am exhausted on Mondays [after getting up early to travel to the client site], and it was so good to get out at night, since I get so tired at 4:30 or 5 p.m. on Mondays. I had a nice quiet dinner and went to bed early. It made me more productive on Tuesday." A project leader agreed: "It's really valuable to have a break in the middle of the week. I would take my time off and come back refreshed and ready to go. I know I was more effective on the day after my night off, because my head was clear, I was rested, and I felt so excited to be back at work."

A regular night off also improved people's personal lives, particularly their relations with family and friends. "I finally made it to one of my child's parent nights and am no longer the negligent parent," said one BCG principal. A consultant explained: "I didn't do anything special on those nights. But I would have a wonderful evening with my husband— we would go for a run together and have dinner."

The time off also had a positive effect on people's weekends. For some, it was simply having time to rest during the week; for others, it was using the time to get chores done that they would otherwise have had to leave until the weekend. A principal echoed the responses of many to a midweek night off: "In the past I have needed the weekend to decompress, but now I can do that on my night off. It has really changed the tone of my weekends for the better."

Small, *Doable* Changes—Collective but Personal

The real value of the night off, however, went far beyond the free time itself. It was a vehicle for learning that it was possible to disconnect and how to make that happen. We often compare the experiment to tying your right hand behind your back so you are forced to learn to write with your left. Once people learned how to turn off, and experienced the benefits of doing so, they took this learning far beyond just a night off. As we saw in chapter 5, the work process itself was continuously being questioned, challenged, and improved.

There is a long line of theorists who have espoused the idea that, since workers know their own work processes best, they should be the source of such change. Mary Parker Follett first noted the benefits of drawing on participants' intelligence nearly a century ago. More recent theories that fall under the rubric of continual improvement also suggest the power of drawing insights from the workers themselves to reduce waste and increase efficiency—Lean manufacturing, Six Sigma, and *kaizen,* to name but a few.[4] Similarly, advocates of encouraging team learning and creating learning organizations aim to create conditions that allow individuals, teams, and the organization to raise issues and learn from one another in the service of continuous personal and organizational development.[5]

The persistent problem with these proposals is that they tend to be big ideas that, to succeed, require a big vision, a big leadership commitment, a big investment, and ultimately a big—and equally daunting—change in the organization's work practices and culture. And any gains are reinvested into the work.

There is another unrelated body of work that, rather than changing the way work is done, focuses on how to help individuals cope better with all the demands they face by providing more options (part-time work, job sharing, telecommuting, leaves of absence, etc.). Much of the field of human resources and certainly work-life is devoted to helping people better manage, given the demands of their jobs.

However, all of this advice addresses only one side of the equation or the other. It is either about improving the work process—but with little attention to the personal needs of employees—or it's about helping individuals accommodate the organization's demands—with no attention given to challenging the demands themselves (and thereby changing the way work is done).

What's unique about PTO is that individuals' desire for more predictability and control continually sparks innovation in how work is done.[6] Usually, employees work hard to push aside personal needs, thinking at best they should strive to accommodate these needs. With PTO, in contrast, a desire for more predictable time off inspired people to experiment together with ways of working they had never before imagined possible—eliminating the bad intensity and improving both their work-lives and the work process.

By legitimizing the discussion of personal time as well as the collective act of experimentation, PTO unlocks a more pervasive openness about surfacing work-related and work-life issues. It also fosters people's innate desire to work together to address these issues, and a shared sense that change is possible. Addressing personal issues in turn comes to

FIGURE 6-2

The PTO process

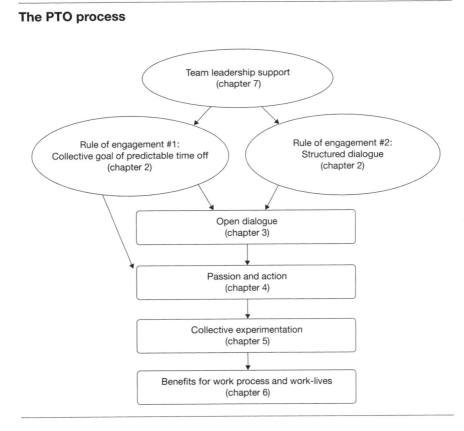

serve as both a desirable end goal as well as an ongoing catalyst for collective experimentation, which continues to improve the work process itself.[7] Small doable changes amount to big results. (See figure 6-2 for a schematic of the PTO process in full.)

There is one critical component that I have yet to address. In chapter 2, I laid out PTO's two core rules of engagement: (1) the collective goal of predictable time off and (2) structured dialogue. Chapters 3 through 6 have described the results: open dialogue (chapter 3), passion and action (chapter 4), collective experimentation (chapter 5) and ultimately the benefits for individuals and their teams (this chapter). However, the BCG experiment taught us that none of the above is likely to happen without the support of the team leader. As one BCG partner put it: "We have learned that team leadership commitment can make or break PTO." That is the subject of the next chapter.

Four Great Assets of PTO

1. *Teams are motivated by the personal*—personal issues are legitimate to discuss in the context of the work and trigger rethinking the work process in new, innovative ways that are meant to benefit individuals' personal lives.

2. *PTO creates a true win–win*—not only do individuals benefit but so does the work process, as the team rethinks and improves the work process, week after week.

3. *PTO is about small, doable change*—not some large organization mandate. This is not top-down change that requires large investment. This is change that the team owns, bounded only by the team's imagination and willingness to engage.

4. *Small change can fundamentally transform the organization's culture in a big way* —step by step. At BCG, the process began on a single team within a single office; four years later there was substantial change at the office and even firm level.

Part III

GETTING STARTED ON YOUR TEAM

1

The Team Leader's Crucial Role

While it evolves through small, doable change, the PTO process still requires people to say and do things that are at odds with the culture. For people to open up and take risks requires that they perceive it safe to do so—safe to speak about their concerns about how the work is proceeding or, worse, mistakes they have made, and safe to take their time off regardless of what pressures at work might arise. That sense of safety depends heavily on the team's leadership.[1] Without team leadership support, PTO does not work well.

The Need for Support

We saw the importance of team leadership support play out over and over at BCG. The *Healthcare Lean I* team provides a perfect study in contrasts. This began with two subteams working on a "Lean" strategy to make the Healthcare Company's core processes more cost-effective. The team's project leaders were two of BCG's top performers, Jim and

Sam. Jim had been a project leader for the past year. He was married and eager to spend more time with his wife if he could, but most of all, like so many of his colleagues at BCG, he was eager to do whatever it took to succeed at the firm. Sam, on the other hand, was only a second-year consultant, but on the cusp of being promoted to project leader, and was playing the role of project leader for the first time on his sub-team. With a young child at home and in the process of buying a house, Sam was considering leaving BCG if he could not make it work from a work-life perspective. On his previous case, he had joined a PTO team very late in the project, but those few weeks provided him a taste of what a high-functioning PTO team had to offer, and he had become a champion of the process.

The third player who is important to this story is Tom, the executing partner on the Healthcare Lean I team. Tom was a hard-charging, newly promoted partner, who took it for granted that working long, hard, and unpredictable hours was a requirement of the job—and he expected the same of those he managed. Tom did not seem to care that his workaholic style was hardly in line with the spirit of the experiment. As Sam bluntly put it, "Tom's actions really undermined PTO. I remember when we were setting it up. Tom had joked that he would take Friday night off, but then he said he usually ends up working Friday nights." Tom even called into the case team meeting from vacation. Sam was not shy about telling Tom that he was sending the wrong message to the team, and Tom had confessed the obvious: he had "a work-life balance problem but didn't know how to fix it."

That Tom's first priority always seemed to be work signaled to Jim that Tom's commitment to PTO was simply lip service. Sam started off more optimistic, but soon decided that questioning the priority of work was a losing proposition on this team. Both Jim and Sam resigned themselves that they were not going to change Tom's attitude toward PTO.

Still, Jim and Sam's own leadership of their subordinates differed substantially on this team. Jim made no effort to engage with the two consultants working for him to make their time off happen; inevitably it became for them "extremely difficult," as one of them put it, to get a night off. "The option exists if I want it," she explained. "But it always translates into more weekend work because nothing comes off my plate." Jim concurred, noting, "I hope my consultants get their nights off, but we cancel it if something important is coming up." For Jim's teammates, demands at work trumped the night-off goal—and the result was that nothing changed in how his team executed their work.

In contrast, Sam, trying to maintain his commitment to PTO, worked with his subordinate, Nancy, to ensure that she could take her nights off. And even though at a lower level than Jim's subordinates—an associate to Jim's subordinates consultant status—Nancy was able to work with Sam so closely that she could even cover for him, both at night when the client was unlikely to call but also often during the day. When, for example, the closing on Sam's house was scheduled for the same day as a client meeting, Sam was perfectly comfortable sending Nancy. And one week when Sam's wife was not feeling well, he flew back to Boston to be with her and their young son, while Nancy covered for him in that week's client meetings. "I was so grateful, and impressed," Sam said, "I knew the work was completely fine in her hands." The mere fact that a young associate was covering on her own for a project leader in meetings with client contacts was a clear example of how PTO challenged assumptions about how work got done at BCG. It's also important to note that the client never mentioned Nancy's rank. Rather, the client benefited from having two minds rather than one, and Nancy benefited because the arrangement proved a powerful developmental opportunity. Nancy reported, "I think I had the best experience of anyone on the team due to Sam's buy-in." She added, "He was so adamant about making it work and getting the time off. The experience of PTO is completely dependent on whether the person one layer above you supports it."

The difference between Sam and Jim as leaders was Sam's willingness to challenge old ways and explore new ones, while Jim was convinced that change was not possible. In a crunch, Jim was not willing to risk being perceived as less committed for taking a night off. As a result, he never had to rely on the consultants he was working with and never discovered whether they could have covered for him. Sam, on the other hand, used the night off as a forcing function to find new ways to work with Nancy. Both Sam and Nancy felt that their personal lives and their work had benefited from their new ways of working together.

The results from the Healthcare Lean I team taught us just how much a team, or even just a *teamlet*,[2] could benefit when the leader—even if he was junior himself—was supportive. In the end, Jim and Sam both delivered to the client and their manager and continued to have highly successful careers at BCG. Sam, however, received higher upward feedback scores on the Healthcare Lean I case. He also got to spend more time with his family and continued to be a big proponent of the benefits of PTO for his work and personal life. Jim ultimately became a believer, though more gradually: after seeing Sam's success and finding himself with more supportive senior leaders on subsequent cases, Jim eventually found the courage to take more risks. And one of the most important lessons Jim came to appreciate about PTO was that when it works well it can seem at first like a great deal of overhead for the manager, but in the end it helps those very managers do their job better, relieves stress, and reduces their workload; the manager's job is made easier, not harder.

Managing Up

The most successful PTO teams at BCG had support from the top as well as the middle. As one project leader explained, "It is the project leader or principal, the most senior person on site everyday, who keeps driving the message in order to make PTO work." But support at the partner level was also invaluable for the process to live up to its potential. Still, you may well find yourself, as Sam did, supportive himself but without the support of his superior, or so he thought. That's no reason to give up, though. As the example shows, Sam still reaped benefits. Moreover, you may be able to generate a surprising amount of more support than you expect, through your actions.

Consider what happened with Tom. After Healthcare Lean I completed its case, BCG sold the client the follow-up project, Healthcare Lean II, with Tom continuing as the executing partner aided by two consultants who had also worked on the original case, but with a new principal. You might recall that we already met the Healthcare Lean II team, back in Chapter 3; that's the team that experienced the *blowup* after several team members were leaving most afternoons for an exercise class.

After the blowup, the new principal, Carl, learned to embrace the tough conversations, even opening up about his own struggles as a new parent to twin boys. Tom had never experienced this level of openness, which began to enter into the team's PTO check-in meetings. "I realized the only reason I was learning that we didn't have enough resources was because of the PTO discussion," Tom later reported. "I was shocked. You end up taking it very personally, like, 'Wow, people must be scared of working with me.'"

Tom began to realize that his direct reports on previous cases had been filtering their comments for fear of his responses. Heavily affected by the blowup and Carl's response, Tom started to open up too. As Tom and Carl opened up, the rest of the team felt encouraged to do so as well. The value of open dialogue became increasingly clear to Tom, who started to encourage his team to be even more open, explaining, "Now when I get an answer to a question, I try to probe a bit deeper and to find a way to learn more. I'm also trying to have one-on-one breakfasts with each team member. I wouldn't have done that before PTO, and I'm finding it quite helpful. And, in those times, we don't talk about the content of the case, but more about the dynamics, what they're getting out of the case, what should I be working on in terms of relationships, those type of questions." Tom further explained how he had come to realize that fostering the well-being of his people paid impressive dividends: "The trick is understanding what is important to them. Working once in a while on a weekend may not be a big deal; what might be more of a big deal to someone is to be on site all the time, realizing you have no contact with the client, and working on things that seem marginally interesting. PTO helps me better understand what matters to people and how to address it." Tom concluded, "I am finding it a win-win."

Tom had changed. Whereas the Healthcare Lean I team had expressed a great deal of skepticism about Tom's support and behavior, the Healthcare Lean II team credited Tom for making PTO a success and helping them overcome the blowup. One consultant told how, now when Tom sent e-mails over the weekend, he advised the team that they didn't have to respond right away. According to another consultant, "It reached the point I was getting scolded rather than getting points for doing stuff, and that was a big change." A third member of the team added, "I was so skeptical in the beginning, but now it is clicking so well that I am scared to ever be on another case. It all comes from the top, with the sincerity of the partner. You can easily tell when it is not sincere, but Tom has sincerity, which empowers all of us to follow PTO's broader ideals."

Note just how much Tom evolved over the course of a year—and that the impetus for this change came from his subordinate. Over thirty years ago, John Gabarro and John Kotter wrote a now-classic article, "Managing Your Boss."[3] In it, they note that people tend to focus much of their attention on how their managers manage them—whether effectively or not. But it turns out we can do a great deal to bring out the best in our bosses too. That is exactly what Carl was able to do with Tom.

It is also interesting to note the different impact that Carl had on Tom versus Sam, the project leader who led the very successful teamlet with Nancy, but had much less impact on Tom. Carl brought the conversation into the team room, where Tom heard it. Sam created a cocoon around himself and Nancy, effectively using PTO for the two of them, but having much less impact on the whole team and on his boss—and as a result diminishing his own opportunities to really act differently with his manager.

It is important to recognize the power and significant role you play in managing your team but also to recognize how both through your words and actions you may further be able to affect your boss.

Leadership Support Begets More Support

Just as we saw with Tom, as other leaders became increasingly supportive of PTO, they too saw more benefits emerging from PTO and became all the more supportive. "Once I started realizing the value of PTO, and open communication in particular," explained one partner, "I started pushing people more to invite them to share issues. I find myself spending more time on the soft side of managing than typical project management." PTO's positive effects in turn engaged him more and that led to more positive effects—what he described as a "reinforcing loop" of open and probing discussions that further engaged him in the experiment.

A different partner confessed that he used to go to his team's weekly case meetings when he could fit them into the rest of his schedule, but the experiment changed that. "My feeling is that these meetings are a really good use of time, and they are more rewarding and I enjoy being a part of them . . . The case team experience itself has changed with PTO." Another partner added: "Because PTO forces a forum in which we are all forced to talk, things come out that wouldn't otherwise. I benefit because I learn things about what is going on in the team process—it resensitizes me to things I've gotten too distant from and makes me more empathetic."

A positive reinforcing cycle emerged: the more rewarding partners found these meetings, the more likely they were to attend and support the open dialogue, which increased the team's inclination to speak their minds, and the benefits partners reaped from participating.

The Perils of Resistant Leaders

As leaders with an open mind engaged in the PTO process, they tended to experience positive benefits, and their commitment grew in a virtuous cycle. In contrast, in the rare BCG teams where leaders were outright resistant at the start, the process quickly spiraled negative.

Consider what happened to the *Healthcare HR* team. The project leader, Jay, had recently been promoted and was struggling in his first job as a manager. He was not happy about participating in PTO. "I was not approached, but told 'You're doing this case, and it is PTO.' I didn't have a choice. I also had the sense that the partner wanted to say he was leading a PTO case." While never explicit and perhaps not even at a conscious level, Jay's anxiety about making PTO work was expressed in various ploys to make the experiment fail. After all, if PTO failed, then Jay avoided the possibility that he might fail at PTO.

Jay pushed for a goal that was bigger than the predictable night off—his team decided to focus on a night off in their home city, thus reducing time spent at the client site. Instead of traveling four days a week, Jay's team was striving to travel only three and to take their nights off when they got home. This required them to leave the client site at 2 p.m. so they could catch the 4 p.m. shuttle and be on the ground by 6 p.m., reducing time spent at the client site from four to two-and-a-half days per week.

The partners viewed that goal as inappropriate and concluded that Jay and his team were acting "entitled." The executing partner recalled his reaction: "This was my first exposure to PTO, and I think to a certain extent the team may have abused it." It was as if by spending so little time at the client, Jay's team was using PTO as what the executing partner called, "an excuse to create a lifestyle that was incongruent with the kind of work we needed to do and the kind of relationships we needed to build."

The senior partner on the case had a bigger dilemma. He happened to be George Martin, the head of the Boston office who led the PTO Rollout Team, and was now participating in the PTO process himself for the first time. On the one hand, George was eager to promote PTO, but on the other, he was now wondering whether the experiment was simply creating too much entitlement on his own team.

This led to tension and heated debates between Jay and George, in front of the team. George felt that the team was not serving the client adequately; Jay countered that it was impossible to have it both ways—three days with the client *and* PTO. "I said, 'Well, what do you want me to do?'" recalled Jay. "'Would you have me throw the PTO night away? Just tell me be here three nights a week. I will tell you I am not happy, but I will do it. But it can't be PTO because you can't have a night at home and make it work.' I wanted George to admit that if we had to be on site three full days, that this meant throwing the PTO night away."

When a leader is essentially out to prove the experiment cannot work, there may well be little anyone can do to change his mind—at least until the naysayer has seen the positive effects for other teams. And without the support of the entire leadership team—the principal and/ or project leader as well as the partners—PTO doesn't stand a chance of achieving its potential.

The people on Jay's team, for example, did not focus on helping each other achieve the goal of a night off. Indeed, they were not even really focused on anyone achieving the goal. And, there was no sense among the team members that they could be open and honest. According to one of them, "There was one instance where I clearly made a mistake of being open during a PTO check-in. I basically was just honest and said that the PTO schedule was not working for me. I had been up until 3 a.m. the night before because the project leader had not given me directions about what he wanted until 1 a.m. I had asked for directions earlier, but he had written back that he was too busy and would get to me when he had time. He then sent me an example of what he was looking for at 1 a.m., and it was not at all what we had discussed." She recalled raising the issue of this middle-of-the-night work at the next feedback meeting, when George was present, and Jay later warned her to be very careful what she said to the senior partner in case he took it literally. "This was so frustrating to me, because what I said was true," she recalled. "Jay implied that he didn't want George thinking it was like this all the time, but midnight e-mails were totally normal on this case." She felt that Jay hammered her for the rest of the case for that one comment, and simply threw up her hands in frustration, concluding, "If I am going to get smacked down for being honest, I might as well keep to my PTO nights off. My mentality was, 'Forget it! I am going to just do my thing.' I figured I was going to get a terrible review on this case, so why make an effort?"

This turned out to be an instance of a rare case where those fears that PTO would encourage team members to feel entitled to a night off actually had some merit. We learned that if any member of the leadership team was outright resistant—whether project leader, principal, or partner—then it was better for the whole team not to participate in PTO. It was still OK for a principal or project leader managing his or her own team, as we saw earlier with Sam's teamlet. It was also OK if a leader was not convinced—as long as he or she was not outright resistant—as we later saw with Tom. The issue arises when outright resistant leaders are expected to be involved but they don't make any effort to deliver on this expectation.

Over and over, team leadership support turned out to be a necessary—although not sufficient—condition for a PTO team to succeed. It further mattered how the team was structured and the rules of engagement defined and carried out. In the next two chapters, I outline the critical design choices that need to be made to effectively launch a PTO team: (1) team membership; (2) the forum for structured dialogue, and (3) the collective goal. I further suggest how to think about making these choices to best suit your unique context.

Leading a PTO Team

If you are the team leader, whether the head of a project team or a unit or even the CEO, here are some guidelines to keep in mind:

- Every team member must commit to the process—in particular, striving to attain the predictable time off goal to which you all agree. The only way that your team members will take this leap of faith is if they believe that you, their leader, are behind the experiment.

- Outright leadership resistance is sure to be a game-ender. Teams respond to resistant leaders by performing worse than teams that don't participate in the PTO process at all. The prospect of trying something different raises the team's hopes (and fears). As soon as they detect any lack of commitment on the part of the leader, they feel let down, and issues of entitlement and frustration are likely to emerge.

- "Leadership support" does not mean that you must be convinced PTO will work, but only that you are genuinely willing to invest the time and effort to engage in the experiment. And team members must sense your commitment.

- Beware of how you are coming across. You may think you're modeling the process perfectly, but how your team members *interpret* your behavior is what matters and what affects the risks people will take in what they say and what they do. As one BCG associate complained, "The partners explicitly said during the case team meeting check-in that we should be taking our nights off. However, they were not exhibiting that through their actions." And, you certainly do not want to be described in the way one BCG consultant sized up her principal: "He said he was supportive, but I don't believe he was totally committed."

- Being supportive does not mean you necessarily agree with every problem or complaint your team members raise or must take action. You do, however, need to be willing to try to understand their problems, explain your responses, and invite others to push back if they don't understand you. Team members must feel that you are listening to them and understand why you are taking the team in one direction or another.

- Mistakes are bound to surface, and they too need to be addressed constructively. The true test of leadership is to turn a mistake or a problem that makes others uncomfortable into a learning opportunity. Punishing someone for an error is likely to silence the whole team for a long time.

- Actions speak louder than words. Make sure you participate in achieving the PTO goal whenever possible and let others know you are doing it. When a partner talked about having a date with his wife to watch *Mad Men* during the week, the team took notice. The project leader noted, "I love hearing that a partner has a date with his wife during the week, not to mention the idea of a partner actually sitting down and watching TV during the week. It's nice to hear that he can be honest about it."

- Encourage others to take their time off. People respond very positively when their leaders explicitly tell them, "Stop working"; "Turn off"; "Go home"—and mean it. A principal described the effect his partner had on him: "Ultimately, everything is top-down. My PTO night was Thursday, and I would sit in bed and check my e-mail. My partner would respond to me in all caps saying STOP DOING E-MAIL, YOU ARE ON PTO." This principal admitted that if the partner had not chastised him, he would have finessed his night off. An associate further noted, "I was impressed—my project leader even stopped by my office to make sure I had left early [for my PTO night]. I was still there because I was chatting with another associate, and I had to show him my computer was already packed away!"

- Call out those who don't take their time off. In one meeting, a project leader openly chided an associate who had failed to take his night off: "I firmly think you could have made it work if you had prioritized your work better. This is something I can help you with, but I expect you to plan ahead and make it work." The rest of the team got the message: finding a way to take their nights off was very important, and if it was going to be a problem, they needed to speak up. As one consultant on the team reflected, "That really made it clear we had to take this seriously."

- Call out those who aren't being open. When the junior members of one PTO team began their first check-in after a difficult week, they tried to appear candid without saying what was on their

minds—"I love the work"; "I don't mind"; "I know it will get better." The project leader finally interrupted with a dose of candor:
"It will not get better," he announced. "The only way it will get
better is if you tell me it is not sustainable, and we work together
to make it better." When a project leader speaks up and tells a
team to express their concerns, it makes an impression. They may
still shy away from absolute candor the next week, but gradually
they begin to open up, and this candor continues to evolve.

- Be open yourself. Participate in the Pulse Checks. Share anticipated challenges and concerns. As one senior partner advised
  other partners engaging in PTO, "Talk about the issues you are
  facing, that you think the team is facing, and that you think the
  team needs to address, but go in with an open mind. Also, ensure
  that you are just as open with your comments and conversation
  about the team as the team is because it enables the team to feel
  more comfortable in raising issues."

- Don't pretend to be heroic. Make yourself human. Talk about your
  personal life. Admit when things are tough. Share your triumphs
  and concerns. As one BCG project leader advised, "If you come
  across as being someone [who never has] a bad day, never admits
  to having a meeting that didn't go well, or can't share a personal tummy rumble—that portrayal of being invincible actually
  undermines your team and [keeps] them [from] sharing their
  own feelings. Being honest in the PTO meetings, being open and
  sharing something yourself creates an environment where everyone can share." As one consultant explained about the partners
  on his team, "They would describe what they were anxious about
  going into the next week. It was so interesting. I forgot how much
  their reputation and career depend on the ability to deliver really
  long-term value to the client. It really meant a great deal that the
  partners were honest about what was keeping them up at night."

Defining the Team and the Goal

I hope at this point you are excited to try PTO on your own team. Before gathering your team to launch PTO, however, a few critical decisions must be made: (1) Who will be involved? (2) In what forum will you meet? And (3) What will be your collective goal of predictable time off?

The Team

The PTO team's membership may be obvious. Or it may be a bit more complicated and require a careful selection process. At BCG, the choice was clear: BCG consultants—from the newest associate all the way up to the level just below partner—are typically staffed full-time as part of a single case team. In many fields, however, individuals are part of multiple teams at the same time. For instance, lawyers and investment bankers often work simultaneously on cases for several different clients; engineers may be staffed on design teams working on multiple products; scientists may be exploring the effects of several promising drugs; staffers of nonprofit organizations, such as philanthropic foundations or think tanks, tend to work across projects within their program areas.

If, in your situation, the team members are accountable to leaders of more than one team, this section is meant to help lay out a set of decisions that must be made. If, however, team members are accountable to a single team leadership, as tended to be the case at BCG, the experimental unit should be clear, and you should feel free to skip ahead to the next section—"the forum for structured dialogue." And if it is further clear when your group will meet, most likely because you already have weekly meetings and you can add the structured dialogue component to those meetings, skip that section too, picking up on the following section—"the collective goal of predictable time off."

If in your world, team members work with other teams in a larger group or practice area and thus have allegiances to multiple team leaders, either all teams in the larger group or practice area must be included in the experiment, or at a minimum other leaders in the group or practice area must be on board before launching the experiment. Why is this so important? Imagine that one team member, John, is scheduled to take Wednesday night off. However, John is simultaneously working on another team up against a major deadline that week—and the leader of that other team expects John to work on Wednesday night. Now what? In cultures that value work as one's first priority, it is easy to imagine that John will be inclined to bow to the pressure from the other leader—and fail to attempt to achieve the experimental goal.

To make the experiment possible, the leader from John's other team must be supportive. If, for instance, John is part of the Real Estate area of a major law firm that consists of four partners and fifteen associates, one can imagine the entire Real Estate group doing the initial experiment. However, if John is part of the Corporate area with fifty partners and three hundred associates, then it will be necessary to find a different way to get John's other masters on board. Too large a group is simply going to be unwieldy for the experiment, especially if there is to be constructive, structured dialogue as part of the process.

In the latter scenario, what's needed is to get the support of the other leaders such that they will treat the experiment as they would any major demand a member of the group were to face. If, for example, team members were suddenly under immense pressure to deliver to the client of the experimental team, the other leaders to whom that team member reports would have to understand that the team member would be temporarily away from other work; the other leaders not directly involved in the experiment must be willing to give the collective goal that same level of priority.

While an admittedly larger hurdle to getting started, experimenting with a team that is part of a group that includes other teams has an upside: the early buy-in of the other team leaders will bestow on the experiment the kind of wider commitment and visibility that increases the odds for benefitting more people in your organization, sooner.

Once the team is defined, the next step is to consider the forum in which you will gather for regular discussions.

The Forum for Structured Dialogue

If the chosen group already gets together on a regular—ideally weekly—basis, then the best meeting time will likely be within the already existing meeting, although that meeting may need to be elongated to accommodate the additional practices associated with the structured dialogue component of PTO—namely, the time spent discussing the team's achievement of the goal and also more generally their work process (i.e., using the Pulse Check). If, however, the chosen group currently meets infrequently or not at all, it will be essential to create a forum to meet. For instance, recall the example of John, if he is in Real Estate and the chosen group is all four partners in Real Estate, it is unlikely that the whole Real Estate Group gets together frequently enough and additional meetings will have to be scheduled. It will be important to put these on the calendar and stress their importance doing everything possible to ensure attendance. Without these meetings, the structured dialogue and more generally PTO will not be effective.

Initially these meetings should be held once a week, if at all possible. Over time, they can become less frequent, as both the willingness to raise issues and the proclivity to work together as a team to address these issues solidifies. But, no matter how effective the team becomes, these meetings cannot be dispensed with altogether; they are crucial for reinvigorating the experiment periodically. At the outset, most BCG teams engage in structured dialogue once a week. Three or four weeks into the process, as the practices become more ingrained and team members feel more comfortable about opening up about their feelings, leaders sometimes choose to transition structured dialogue meetings to every two or even three weeks. But this decision must be made thoughtfully. We have found no benefit, only cost, in rushing to reduce the frequency of these meetings.

The Collective Goal of Predictable Time Off

Beyond defining the team and their forum for meeting, it is important to consider what will be the goal of predictable time off that everyone on the team will commit to trying to achieve. Keep in mind that the primary purpose of the goal is to be a forcing function to get people to challenge their beliefs about what the work requires as well as to cause people to actually make changes in how they do their work. At BCG, having consultants at every level take a predictable night off challenged the dogma that they must always be available to serve the client—and pushed them to change what work they did, where they did it, when they did it, and how they interacted while doing it.

When defining a goal, make sure it meets the following criteria: (1) personally valued, (2) a stretch but doable, (3) collective and shared, and, (4) concrete and measurable.

Ensure the Goal Is of Personal Value

The goal you choose must address a manifestation of the always-on problem as it is experienced by all members of the experimental group. That doesn't mean the entire group must agree that it addresses the biggest manifestation in each of their work-lives or even that it is the best way of addressing the problem identified. But they do need to agree that the selected goal will help them address a nontrivial manifestation of the always-on problem.

At BCG, we discovered early on that the always-on problem manifests itself as an inability to make plans. Nevertheless, not everyone at BCG ranked the inability to make a plan the most vexing issue with their work schedule. Plenty were more bothered by the long hours and punishing travel. And the number of BCGers who did not want a night off, in particular, was quite sizable (especially before they tried it). Still, no one questioned that the inability to make a plan was a major problem at the firm or that the predictable night off was aimed at anything other than helping to solve this problem.

The always-on problem manifests itself in different ways in different organizations. Other goals that might be effective in your setting include:

- Hard stops—constraining the work day. This might be a night off, but also could be a more significant chunk of time off; it might start at 3 p.m. or 4 p.m. on a given day, or less significant chunks starting at 8 p.m. or 9 p.m.

- No work on weekends

- Call schedules (as in the medical world where doctors are on, off, and on-call)

- E-mail blackouts—times when no e-mails are sent

- Meeting moratoriums—times when meetings cannot occur

Whether one of these goals or a different one is best suited to your situation depends on the manifestation of the always-on problem that your group faces. On BCG teams where the work demands were particularly intense, for example on due diligence cases, a predictable unit of time off might need to be the weekend or a portion of it. When BCG first launched PTO in their Tokyo office where it is typical to work until midnight every week night, they used one night a week as their goal—but the night didn't start until 9 p.m.

In a commercial goods company focused on keeping a major customer stocked, team members worked long and often unpredictable hours in case the customer called. In reality, the customer rarely called. A suitable goal in this case might be an on-call schedule so that, like doctors, the employees would know when they were "on" "off" and "on call." This would likely be an effective way for challenging team members to rethink their assumptions around how best to do their work to their own and their company's benefit.

At a nonprofit think tank focused on youth development, to take another example, team members tended to specialize in different program areas—health, media/Internet, and leadership development. The main concern was the quantity of e-mails sent and the expectation for an immediate response. A reasonable collective goal here might be certain hours of the day when one couldn't send e-mails. It might be seven nights a week, no e-mail. Or, all nights after 7 p.m., no e-mail. The goal needs to be chosen to be a stretch but doable, in the particular setting. Once the goal is set, any violations would be discussed at the following week's check-in, forcing the team to explore how they might work differently to avoid having to send such e-mails in the future.

At a high-tech start-up, the problem was that half the team was based in the United States and the rest were halfway around the globe, in South Korea. The thirteen-hour time difference meant that team meetings were either really early for one group or really late for the other, who often found themselves on the phone for four straight hours. A possible goal in this case would be no meetings before 8 a.m./p.m. or after 10 a.m./p.m. This change would cut down the late-night work and force the team to rethink how best to use the meeting times as well as what needs to be addressed when and by whom.

Though different according to the specific circumstances, each of these goals is intended to break the cycle of responsiveness, challenging assumptions around what it means to do good work and be a good worker. To this end, the goal needs to force team members to rethink the work itself—e.g., why do we do what we do and are there other ways that would be more efficient and effective? Having a personal goal that feels beneficial to individuals motivates them to engage in the process;

and a personal goal further legitimates the discussion of personal issues. When coupled with the structured dialogue, such a goal provides a vehicle for ongoing reflection and improvement of the work process that positively affects individuals' work-lives and the work itself.

Choose a Goal That's a Stretch—but Doable

At BCG, a predictable night off was a seemingly small goal, but in the context of the firm's 24/7 culture, it was a stretch. Had we set the goal there as weekends off, for instance, it would not have been demanding enough for most teams, which were rarely forced to work weekends. Some BCG teams, however, were involved in such short, intense cases that having time off on the weekend was a real stretch; for them—as mentioned above—a weekend off was an appropriate goal.

At first, the goal may seem complex to identify, given the ingrained assumptions that teams already have—the very assumptions that will have to be challenged in an effort to usher in change. When we initially suggested a weekly night off to the Consumer team, for example, they countered that the client might call and "that is outside of [our] group's control." From their perspective, the problem—an unpredictable workweek—was driven by the nature of their client-service business. They saw a predictable night off as much more than a stretch—in the context of BCG, it struck them as an unrealistic and therefore impossible goal. It was only when we pushed them to review the sources of this pressure that they began to recognize that it wasn't the client that called them most but their own teammates. Only then did the predictable night off goal seem more plausible.

The key is to choose a goal that is significant enough to push the team to challenge its assumptions but not so large and daunting that it will be perceived as unachievable and therefore not worth trying. Keep in mind that it is easy for teams to shy from goals, and insist they are impossible. Challenge that "impossibility."

Ensure That the Goal Is Collective and Shared

Everyone on the team has to strive to achieve the goal, which makes it a *collective* goal. That doesn't mean everyone will necessarily achieve it, but everyone needs to make the same investment in trying every week. Moreover, every team member has to try to make it possible for every other team member to achieve the goal. It is therefore a *shared* responsibility. Otherwise, there would be no incentive to work together to rethink work practices.

In Lotte Bailyn's study of nurses (see chapter 2), the goal was to get the nurses involved in scheduling their own work shifts according to their personal needs. The problem was that the nurses became so focused on their own preferences that the scheduling process became a classic example of pure self-interest; the group never engaged to figure out how to optimize the process for everyone, and the experiment had to be halted. In this case the goal was collective, but the individuals did not *share* responsibility to make it work out for each other.

The experience of the PTO teams at BCG suggests that if the nurses had shared responsibility to make the goal work, they might well have found ways to maximize their individual interests while ensuring that there were nurses on the ward at all times. Without the shared aspect of the collective goal however, people ended up looking out only for themselves. In the case of the nurses, the problem that reared its head was entitlement; in other cases, group members might shy away from trying to achieve the goal at all because they are afraid of being perceived as deviant and are worried about the implications for their careers.

In the end, the goal needs to have a dual property: that individuals want it for themselves *and* accept the responsibility to make it happen for each other. Only then will the goal motivate people to be part of the process and provide the desired forcing function to have them work *together* to rethink their current work practices.

Set a Goal That's Concrete and Measurable

There is nothing abstract about whether a team member took a night off or not. It's a simple, concrete goal that can be easily measured: you either took the entire night off, or part of it, or kept working. End of story. And that tally can easily be integrated into the weekly check-in discussion about who was unable to meet that goal last week and what it might take to make sure that it will be met this week—using achievement going forward (and lack of it in the past) as a way to shine a light on existing problems with the work process and surface opportunities for change.

Concreteness and measurability are essential to whatever goal you choose. If the goal is not concrete, people can more easily evade it; if it is not small or doable in finite time increments, it will not facilitate ongoing action and discussion; and if it is not measurable, the team cannot keep track of the efforts to achieve the goal, know when people are failing, and decide what needs to be done to remedy the situation.

Remember—This Is an Experiment

Keep in mind the purpose of the goal is most of all a means to a larger end—to unleash openness, passion, and collective experimentation that benefits both individuals' work-lives and work processes—and that it's fine, even desirable, for the team to work together to choose the goal. This is all meant to be one big *experiment*. With PTO, the ongoing intent is for the team to be experimenting with new ways of working. Along the way, you may well need to experiment with getting the goal right.

For example, you may discover that the goal you choose may not be enough of a stretch in your particular situation, and you need to make it more so. Some of our teams at BCG added travel requirements to the predictable night off goal—such as having the night off in their home city or reducing travel to three days a week. Other teams found that given the intensity of their cases, they couldn't fit in a night off, and they relaxed the goal to taking certain hours off over the weekend.

What's important to recognize is that finding the right goal may take some trial and error, and such floundering is part of the learning and discovery process. As long as the team works together to figure out the goal, there will be much benefit accrued along the way.

The Power of Small Wins

As you embark on this process, keep in mind the fundamental idea underlying PTO: small change can ultimately amount to big results. If you start by asking people to challenge the status quo, they are inclined to perceive that as substantial change; they are likely to claim to be too busy and too consumed with their work to even consider the benefits of such change. Small change, in contrast, encourages people to give it a go, and can still make a profound difference.

At BCG, they had long touted to potential recruits the firm's individualistic approach to designing work modules so that each consultant would have his or her own, distinct responsibilities whenever possible. Team members harbored a strong preference for this approach, wanting to "own" their work and be evaluated for what they did.

On some of the earliest PTO teams, in order to facilitate achieving the goal, the leadership team proactively tried to shift work interactions to a more shared, and therefore more flexible system, dividing work among team members so that their responsibilities overlapped more than usual. We called this way of allocating work responsibilities *teaming*. Instead of consultant A being responsible for module 1 and consultant B being responsible for module 2, for instance, managers would allocate work so that A became responsible for 80 percent of module 1 and 20 percent of module 2, while B took charge of 20 percent of module 1 and 80 percent of module 2. It was still clear who had primary and secondary responsibility for the module; the difference was that shared responsibility was designed into the work.

As my own earlier work had led me to expect, the more teammates filled in for each other, the more they came to understand each other's work, and therefore the more versatility they each developed at work and the more flexibility they had about when they worked.[1] The biggest cost of people having overlapping work assignments was the investment of two people in a particular part of the work rather than one. There were also concerns about evaluating individuals involved in joint work, and some individuals were not so sure they wanted to share work. Among those who actually tried teaming, however, there was unanimous support for this new way of working, with everyone involved convinced that the benefits far outweighed the costs.[2] Still, only a few PTO teams opted to share work responsibilities in this way.

Team leaders offered a number of reasons for their resistance: "It takes time." "It feels risky." "It is easier and less threatening to implement the PTO process with more minimal coverage." And so, despite exponential leaps in the benefits derived by every team that tried this new way of allocating work, most of the teams participating in the experiment resisted large upfront changes in work allocation. Indeed, of the more than nine hundred teams that have now been involved in PTO, fewer than fifteen have set out to use teaming at the start of the project.

For a long time I remained puzzled as to why team leaders could be so resistant to such clear benefits, and I continued to encourage teams embarking on PTO to try teaming. And each time they refused, I found myself disappointed. Eventually, however, I came to appreciate that their resistance was embedded in their sense that to make such substantial change in the midst of all else that needed to be done to deliver results to the client simply felt overwhelming. One senior partner put it this way: "The benefits are clear, and we should do it. But it fundamentally challenges how we do our work. We make decisions about allocating work during the proposal process. We don't make it a priority, especially at that early stage. We should, but we don't."

Instead, teams developed a limited system of coverage that revolved around members acting as *coverage partners* for each other on their nights off. Team leaders perceived establishing coverage partners as much more palatable than *teaming* and were willing to try it. And, as it turned out, coverage partners often started working quite closely together, essentially reaping many of the same benefits that teaming generated. Compared to non-PTO teams, there was more sharing of information, more breadth of understanding of the work, and more engagement in the client's problems rather than only one's own discrete module; there also came to be more of an ability to cover for one another beyond one's night off even across levels of the hierarchy. The benefits were not as large as those from teaming, but it was a much smaller change to make—assigning teammates to cover for each other on their nights off—and therefore much easier to get people to embrace . . . and it still had an impressive impact on the team's dynamics, increasing versatility and flexibility within the team, generating significant personal as well as work-related benefits. In a smaller but still forceful way, the practice of coverage began to chip away at the status quo.

For me, there were two important reminders embedded in such efforts to change the way teams worked. The first is how difficult it is to challenge the status quo—even in the face of hard evidence that change is possible and desirable. When things are going well, people are especially reluctant to tinker with them. That's precisely why so many advocates of change emphasize the need for some sort of dissatisfaction to motivate it, and managers believe it is easier to take over a group or organization in crisis than one that is doing well.[3] Despite very compelling evidence that teaming was more powerful than BCG's traditional way of dividing up work into discrete modules, there was little discontent with the current way and nothing ended up changing in how work was allocated on more than 98 percent of the teams.

The second reminder was the power of small wins. Nearly thirty years ago Karl Weick wrote a groundbreaking article in which he described a set of psychological mechanisms that account for why small wins are preferable to big, daunting change: "When the magnitude of problems is scaled upward in the interest of mobilizing action, the quality of thought and action declines, because processes such as frustration, arousal, and helplessness are activated. Ironically people cannot solve problems unless they think they aren't problems." Weick found that in the face of what are perceived as big problems, people experience a large amount of arousal, which paralyzes them.[4]

The BCG initiative confirmed Weick's observation. While most resisted making a big, ambitious change to restructure how work was allocated, they were quite amenable to a small, doable change. Better yet, that change—covering for each other one night a week—still added up to a substantial alteration of the status quo and eventually began to change the organization's culture fundamentally.

So as you think about your goal, make sure it is both aspirational but also doable, and personally motivating. Most important: your team needs to embrace that goal. After all, PTO is about collective change, and it requires a collective effort to make such change.

The next chapter is all about how to engage your team in the PTO process.

Choosing the Group and Their Goal

Define the Experimental Unit

- Consider work interdependencies and define the smallest group whose core work is done among the members.

Identify a Collective Goal

- Identify the problem (a pressing personal issue) that:
    - Is experienced as a problem by most if not all people
    - If addressed, also stands to have organizational benefits
- Make sure the goal has the following four characteristics:
    - Personally valued
    - Small but doable
    - Collective and shared
    - Concrete and measurable

Keep Focused on the Goal

- The inclination among team members is to make the goal individual—something that they personally care about; even when a collective goal is established, there is a tendency to want to revert to an individual one. Make sure that the team keeps their focus on a collective goal.

- Don't be afraid to refine or change the goal—you are likely to get it wrong before getting it right; that is part of the process.

9

The First Meeting and Beyond

Once the team and goal are in place, it's time for the team to get together to discuss what PTO is and how best to implement it in your context. The central purpose of this chapter is to provide guidelines for this meeting. I have organized the chapter around a set of PowerPoint slides that present the key points that need to be raised in this meeting. I have intentionally tried to capture the key points on PowerPoint slides, to provide a template that can be adapted for use with your own team. Slide 9-1 overviews these key points and serves both as a potential agenda for your first meeting as well as a road map for this chapter.

Cycle of Responsiveness

It is important people involved share a basic understanding of the underlying problem they are seeking to address: namely, the cycle of responsiveness and the potential benefits if it can be broken. As described

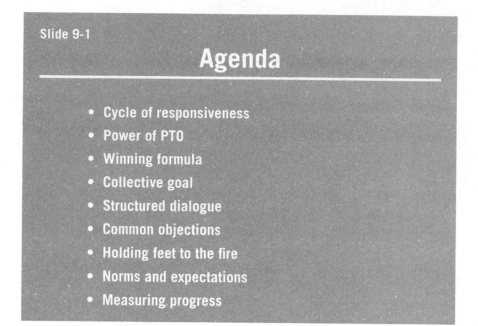

in the introduction, the client, or customer, or the pressure to manage across time zones—or whatever other legitimating factors your team may face in its work—is part of why they're on so much, but it is a much smaller part of the story than most people have come to believe. Instead, the more we expect of ourselves and each other, the more we do, the more requests increase—and the even more we expect of ourselves and each other. Slide 9-2 shows how this cycle—first presented in the introduction—can trap us.

The cycle of responsiveness reveals two important points. On the one hand, there is little you can do to affect the situation individually, other than optimize how you exist given this cycle exists. You can be more efficient and effective. You can take advantage of company policies meant to help you accommodate the demands created by the cycle of responsiveness. But individuals alone, even the CEO, cannot change the cycle because it is deeply embedded in how people interact with one another in the process of getting their work done.

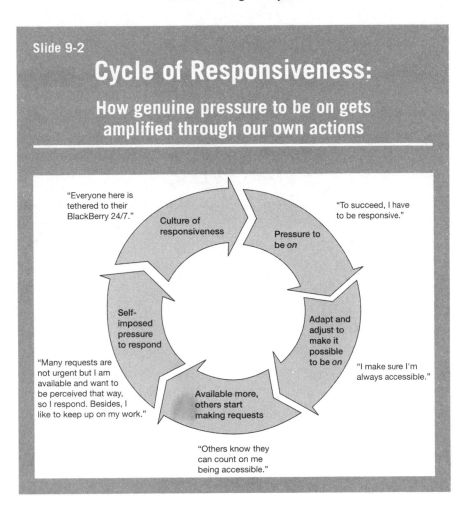

Slide 9-2

Cycle of Responsiveness:

How genuine pressure to be on gets amplified through our own actions

On the other hand, the cycle of responsiveness helps clarify why the change itself does not need to be some large, societal, or even organization-level change. The amplification of expectations is not driven by clients or customers, or even by managing across time zones or some other factor outside the group's control. Rather, a larger part of it is likely to be driven by your team, which means that if you and your teammates work together to change your patterns of interaction, it can have a profound effect on the pressure you each face to be on.

Importantly, if you can break the cycle you will reduce the bad intensity in your work that amplifies the never-ending pressure you feel to

Slide 9-3.

Purpose of PTO

- Break the cycle of responsiveness
- Help team members work together to change their actions and interactions
- Reduce the bad intensity and increase the good intensity
- Create a win-win, benefiting both team's work process and team members' work-lives

be on. As a result, your work process will benefit because it will be done in more efficient and effective ways, and you will benefit because you will be spending your time on more engaging work done in more manageable ways. Breaking the cycle and achieving this win-win, in a slow, step-by-step manner, is the power of PTO (see slide 9-3).

The Winning Formula

PTO's two rules of engagement are essential to its success: (1) striving to achieve a collective goal of predictable time off; and (2) engaging in ongoing discussion of the ups and downs of striving to achieve this goal and of the work process more generally. It is the combination of these two rules that unleashes a powerful process that will inspire you and your teammates to raise increasingly large, difficult issues, and work together to address them. Big changes do not occur all of a sudden. The process builds momentum over time. It starts small. If your team works together toward a small, doable, collective goal and remains open about any struggles that arise, trust and openness, and, in turn, the passion to work together to create change will follow (see slide 9-4).

Slide 9-4

Winning Formula

Collective goal of predictable time off	+	Structured dialogue	=	Better work and better lives*

*Requires supportive leadership at the team level.

The Team's Collective Goal

Team members need to agree that being always on is a problem, and the goal selected is one possible way to address it. However, not everyone at BCG agreed that inability to make a plan was the most troubling manifestation of the always-on problem for them personally or even that a predictable night off was what they needed most to address this unpredictability. What everyone did agree about was that the work was unpredictable, and this had a negative effect on their personal lives.

The goal is a means to a much more significant end—the kind of change that will address the unrelenting pressure to be always on. To be effective, PTO depends on the whole team working together to achieve the collective goal. Team members will have the incentive to "cheat"—not stick to the goal—in order to get their work done as they have always done it; there will also be a tendency for the "cheaters" to point fingers at those who are sticking to the experimental guidelines but going against the status quo of making work their first priority, always.

Again, remember: the goal must be collective in that everyone participates and it must be shared in that everyone shares the responsibility for everyone else being able to achieve their time off. Individuals alone cannot change their work interactions; it's a collective challenge that can be met only by working together, and the goal is meant to motivate exactly that—people working together to effect changes that they alone cannot make. Slide 9-5 captures the essentials.

Slide 9-5

Collective Goal

- Of personal value to all of us
- Means to as well as end
- Collective and shared
- Small and doable
- Concrete and measurable

Structured Dialogue

The other half of PTO's winning formula is ensuring constructive dialogue happens. This is built around three elements. The first is the forum itself—useful, productive dialogue cannot happen if meeting times are sporadic and attendance is not mandatory. The second and third elements comprise two categories of tools that have proven valuable for fostering dialogue in these meetings: (1) tools that create open dialogue regarding the work process generally, drawing out people's emotions and experiences of the work, and (2) tools that create open dialogue based on how the team is working together to achieve the collective goal. See slide 9–6 for an outline of these essentials.

Regular Meetings

It is standard practice for BCG teams to have both a team kickoff meeting and a weekly case team meeting. But, leaders tend to push these meetings down in the list of priorities, rescheduling them, even canceling them, and often allowing less than 100 percent attendance. People are also tempted to blow them off for "more pressing" issues; for example, no matter where we looked, a client meeting always seemed to trump the internal case team meeting. Yet if the purpose of the internal

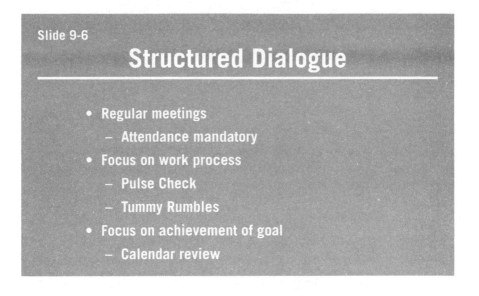

Slide 9-6

Structured Dialogue

- Regular meetings
  - Attendance mandatory
- Focus on work process
  - Pulse Check
  - Tummy Rumbles
- Focus on achievement of goal
  - Calendar review

meeting is to get everyone aligned and to update the senior team members, absence, especially that of senior team members, becomes a big problem.

Also keep in mind that exactly at those most stressful moments when you feel you don't have time to meet is when you need the conversation most. As one consultant astutely described PTO's effectiveness: "I think in that particular setting [stressful cases] it's even more important that you have PTO because that's the sort of setting where people are on pins and needles and are very concerned about getting their particular piece right and not messing up and really over delivering. And if they do have concerns they're less likely to bring them up because they don't want to be the person to rock the boat."

The forum for structured dialogue must therefore be grounded on two basic requirements: (1) meetings must be regularly scheduled—and (2) attendance is required. At BCG, we asked PTO participants to consider team meetings to be as important as any client meeting. And when they put these meetings back into the first-place slot on their priority lists, they discovered over and over the value of talking regularly as a whole group about their work process.

Dialogue About Process

To draw out feelings and experiences, BCG teams used two tools most frequently—the *Pulse Check* and *Tummy Rumbles*. The Pulse Check, as we saw in chapters 1 and 2, asks team members to answer four questions (see slide 9-7):

- How are you feeling?

- How much value are we delivering to the client?

- How satisfied are you with your learning?

- Is the current operating model sustainable for you?

Teams are asked to respond to each question using the cartoon face that best corresponds to how they feel. The Pulse Check is designed to push a group of people who tend to be highly analytical out of their comfort zone and talk about their feelings. From the first question, the

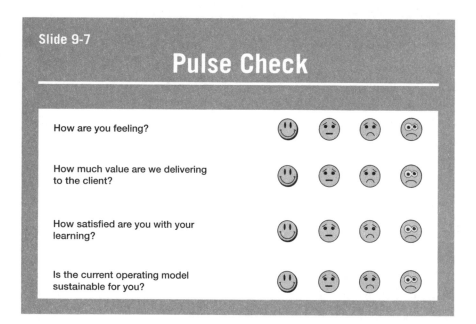

signal is that this is a different kind of meeting: it's not about numbers, not about your work content, not about the client; it's about you and your feelings.

The questions we used at BCG might not be quite right for your group. What you need is a series of questions that get team members to express how they are feeling about the work, how they are doing in terms of delivering that output, and whether their work-lives are satisfying, fulfilling, and sustainable. The key is to tweak these questions to fit the nature of your group and its particular concerns about work and work-life.

The Tummy Rumbles tool further allows team members to express themselves *before* the team meeting (slide 9-8 shows an example).

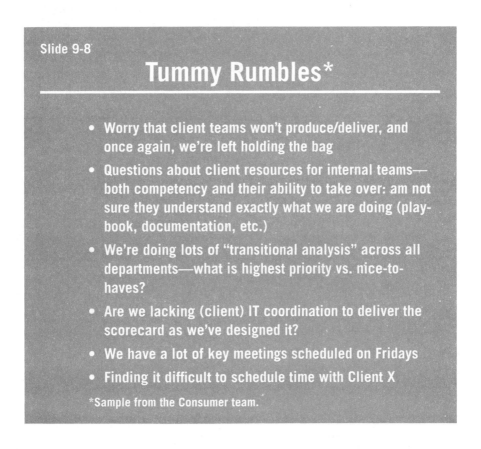

Slide 9-8

Tummy Rumbles*

- Worry that client teams won't produce/deliver, and once again, we're left holding the bag
- Questions about client resources for internal teams—both competency and their ability to take over: am not sure they understand exactly what we are doing (playbook, documentation, etc.)
- We're doing lots of "transitional analysis" across all departments—what is highest priority vs. nice-to-haves?
- Are we lacking (client) IT coordination to deliver the scorecard as we've designed it?
- We have a lot of key meetings scheduled on Fridays
- Finding it difficult to schedule time with Client X

*Sample from the Consumer team.

Dialogue About the Goal

The second category of tools helps teams discuss their progress in reaching the agreed-upon goal. At BCG, teams used the *calendar review* (see slide 9-9) to help team members keep an eye on how successfully they were taking their predictable nights off. At the beginning of each case, teams discussed what were the big milestones for the case and noted them on the calendar. They also discussed any other BCG-related work commitments. At BCG, recruiting could be a major time commitment, typically involving traveling to university campuses to interview potential candidates. These trips were noted on the calendar, as were any vacations or other planned personal events. Then team members chose their nights off. People tended to choose a particular night off each week (e.g., Mondays), and then make alterations up front to accommodate both work and personal engagements. After the calendar was set, people were still encouraged to make changes that might enhance their personal life; for instance, switching a night off to attend an upcoming concert or a Little League game. But nights off were not to be changed for work reasons—doing so was considered a violation of the experiment.

The calendar served as an ongoing reminder of the team's commitments and made it easy to track nights off and whether they were taken and/or changed. Each week, teams discussed what had happened and asked people to raise potential issues looking forward to the following week. When people didn't think they could make upcoming nights off happen, they were asked to speak up. This exercise had two effects: (1) team members began talking about issues that they would never have raised previously (instead, they would have put in the time to deal with them), and (2) they were forced to work together proactively to explore what changes could be made to achieve the goal.

The tool for tracking adherence will be different for different sorts of goals. What is crucial for your experiment's success is to have some visible record of the results from last week and the commitments that need to be upheld next week. Teams need to analyze the past but also have

Calendar Review*

Monday	Tuesday	Wednesday	Thursday	Friday
	1 Lisa, Bob	2 Mark Client A update (8:00 – 8:30)	3 Bill	4
Vacation—Charlie				
7 Charlie	8 Lisa, Bob	9 Mark Prep Client B for SVP Update Client A update (8:00 – 8:30)	10 Bill SVP Update _Training—Bill_	11 Debrief SVP with Client B Debrief SVP with COO _Training—Bill_
Recruiting (SF, evening)—Lisa				
14 Charlie	15 Bob	16 Mark Client A update (8:00 – 8:30)	17 Bill, Lisa _Recruiting (BOS, all day)—Mark_	18 _Vacation—Lisa_ _Training—Mark_
21 Charlie	22 Lisa, Bob	23 Mark Client A update (8:00 – 8:30)	24 Bill	25
28 Charlie	29 Lisa, Bob	30 Mark Client A update (8:00 – 8:30) _Recruiting (CHI, all day)—Bill_	31 Bill SVP Update _Recruiting (LA, all day)—Mark_	Team lead meeting
Prep with B for SVP Update				

*Sample from Consumer team.

some way to surface issues that lie ahead so everyone can be proactive, not just reactive.

Holding Each Other's Feet to the Fire

You need to stay focused on the big picture and the long-term implications of the experiment—particularly when you're up against a tight deadline or a last-minute crisis, when the team will be inclined to abandon the goals for "just that week." One consultant made this point extremely effectively: "There's a saying . . . you should meditate for a half hour every day, and if you're too busy to meditate for that half hour, you should meditate for an hour. That's true of PTO—when we get so busy that we think we can't do it, that's when we need to put even more effort into it. But we need to be forced to do that, because when you're really busy you're tempted to just let it go."

At those moments when the work turns tougher and more stressful, you and your teammates must step up to the challenge and push each other to keep PTO on the front burner (see slide 9-10). The onus is on the team leader, who also needs to encourage team members to push back on each other to maintain everyone's commitment. Team members should be encouraged to question their leaders too, so they don't throw PTO out in the frenzy of the moment.

From the first meeting forward, your team needs to openly discuss this shared responsibility to the PTO process. While getting the work done always is the top priority, the inevitable inclination is to let go far too soon—unless you do everything you can to hold each other to PTO's rules of engagement. Sometimes exceptions are unavoidable—you will need to let go of the rules and move forward, learning from what happened and seeking more and better changes in the future. That course of action, however, should be the rare exception.

Employing a facilitator can be a wonderful asset for getting an outside eye on your progress and keeping everyone true to the process

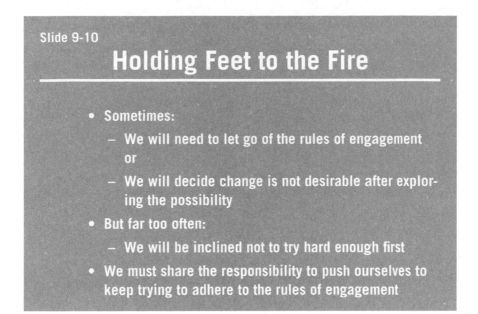

Slide 9-10

Holding Feet to the Fire

- Sometimes:
  - We will need to let go of the rules of engagement or
  - We will decide change is not desirable after exploring the possibility
- But far too often:
  - We will be inclined not to try hard enough first
- We must share the responsibility to push ourselves to keep trying to adhere to the rules of engagement

(I devote chapter 11 to describing the benefits of facilitation in detail). More than likely, however, you and your team will be trying to make the first experiment work on your own. In that case, a coworker, a mentor, even a friend outside the organization would be invaluable to check in on your progress, periodically, and help you try to stay true to the PTO process. And, make sure to leave enough time in your team meetings for members to check up on each other.

Establishing Norms and Expectations

It is valuable to set clear expectations of how team members are to respond when they first feel that conflict between doing what they have always done—practices that the firm has traditionally rewarded—and doing what the experiment requires. Also useful at this point is a more general conversation about the work process and how the group will work together.

Setting Norms

In the first meeting, or in a meeting soon thereafter, the team should discuss the norms that will guide the team's work process, beyond those necessary for the collective goal and structured dialogue. Discussion of where, when, and how the team will work together is extremely productive. (Such as when it is and isn't OK to e-mail, preferred travel schedules and meeting times, working alone or in the team room.) Though these norms are likely to evolve over time, it is useful to have a clear starting point and to find out what people expect of each other and themselves. For many, this will be their first time on a team that makes work practices explicit and agrees on what they should be.

One BCG project leader had this to say about setting norms up front: "It is really helpful to take some time in the kickoff to go around the table and hear from each person about what is important to them. What are their personal boundaries and values? It gets each person engaged, and forces each person to take account of the differences in priority among the group. It also makes people conscious of what others are working for."

Your team's discussion of norms should be quite distinct from your collective goal discussion. Discussing team norms means making explicit how your team is going to act and interact in getting the work done. The collective goal, in contrast, is related to a particular aspect of the work process that your team is going to actively engage *together* to change.

Setting Realistic Expectations

Above all, remember that this is an experiment. Everyone must be willing to take risks, be candid, and be receptive to each other's mistakes. In the end, the PTO process is only as powerful as the team makes it; the more the team works together to challenge assumptions and rethink work processes, the more change that can transpire. The collective goal is not a promise; team members are not entitled to it. The goal is an opportunity for team members to work together to try to make it—and ultimately so much more—the new reality.

Measuring Progress

Make sure to document the results. You want to get some baseline measure before you begin. You also want to collect data periodically. At BCG, we conducted a survey before the first meeting and then weekly and monthly for the duration of the first team. You want to collect data about both how effectively the rules of engagement are being implemented and adhered to as well as the implications of engaging in PTO for individuals' work-lives and the work process.

The data are an important signal to the team regarding how each is responding to the PTO challenge. The results are also important for expanding the experiment beyond your team to begin changing the larger organization. At BCG, the impressive data racked up by the experiment with the Consumer team became a powerful tool for convincing other leaders that they, too, should give PTO a try.

Addressing Objections

The whole purpose of PTO is to get your team to challenge assumptions about how you work. Therefore, it shouldn't come as a surprise if you hear someone say, "This is not possible for me." It's a natural reaction. If the PTO process were so easy to pull off, that would undermine the intent of the collective goal as a forcing function to rethink how work is done. Indeed, if the goal feels easily achievable, there is probably something wrong with it. (See slide 9-11 for some typical objections.)

You might also hear, "The process simply doesn't apply to our situation." When I have presented the BCG story to audiences of managers and other professionals, many shake their heads and dismiss the BCG culture as over the top: "Yes, my life is busy," they concede. "It is unpredictable. But we're not nearly as crazy as those BCGers." I have two responses to this objection. First, it is really easy to point fingers when you read about others and think, "Wow, they are crazy! I am *definitely*

Slide 9-11

Common Objections

- Not possible for me
- Not relevant for me
- I don't want this
- It will result in entitlement
- Too much burden on me

not like that." But take a moment and think about how you really be-have. Many BCGers make the same claim—sure, some BCGers act in these ways, but they personally are "not like that." We do not always want to admit to ourselves, let alone others, the effects of our actions on ourselves and each other.

Second, even if it is true that you and your team don't act under pressures and unpredictability to the degree that BCGers do, it is important to recognize that PTO should not be categorized as something that applies only to extreme cases. Rather, it should be able to catalyze positive change in situations far different from BCG's. The process should be invaluable in any case where the work has more bad intensity than it could. It should apply in any situation where people can benefit personally from working collectively to challenge deeply held assumptions about how the work is done.

I also often hear people say, "I don't want this." From carefully ob-serving people at work, I have found that they are often so deeply caught in the cycle of responsiveness that they have come to accept this person who never stops working as who they are and who they want to be. But what I discovered at BCG is that many who felt strongly that this process was not possible, let alone desirable, changed their minds once they engaged in PTO. You might be very surprised about how much you stand to gain.

Another objection, usually voiced by senior leaders, is that PTO will make team members feel more entitled and raise their threshold for what they expect. The concern is that team members will suddenly think that the goal is the new normal and time off will become a right rather than a privilege earned by investing in the process of making such time off happen. This fear of entitlement was widespread among partners at BCG, but in practice it arose only in the very rare instances when the leader rejected the PTO process from the start.

An equally widespread and very important to address objection is, "This is going to increase the workload of the middle manager." This makes perfect sense as an initial reaction. At BCG, the project leader and/or principal was the integrator and synthesizer of each team member's work. Participating in PTO would require the additional responsibility of ensuring that their team members got their time off, regardless of what was going on at work; then there was the weekly dialogue that can require premeeting work regarding tummy rumbles plus extra time for the weekly meetings for the teams to reflect on their process. Little wonder that PTO could feel like a big burden.

Many BCG principals and project leaders voiced that objection until they understood what was truly involved—and what the benefits were. When PTO is done right, middle managers end up doing *less* work rather than more: they now have their own time off and the team shares the burden for ensuring that everyone gets a night off. Most important, the team comes to share ownership for the work itself and its integration, benefiting the work process in ways that also ease the burden on the middle manager. These effects were so powerful, in fact, that 73 percent of principals and project leaders engaged in PTO— compared with 25 percent of those not engaged—could see themselves at BCG in the long term.

Bottom line: it is natural to resist a process that sets out to fundamentally challenge how your work is done. But we found at BCG that in spite of such initial resistance to PTO among various leaders and team members, once they engaged in the process, its benefits—for individuals and the team's overall work—won them over, and their objections vanished.

Going Forward

PTO is a gradual process that builds over time. Once your experiment takes off, the next big step is to keep fostering progress—providing the support and encouragement necessary for people to continue to surface issues and work together to address them. Do not lose sight of the rules of engagement when the pressure mounts and time feels too short to engage.

Once your team starts to reap the benefits of PTO there is also great potential to expand the process. Read on to learn what is entailed in expanding beyond the team level to create global organization change.

Getting Started: Guidelines for Team Members

This chapter has focused on the team leader's role in launching PTO. However, PTO is a collective process aimed at collective change. It will only work if everyone on the team engages together to make it happen:

- **Be open in the first meeting:** Take risks. They can be small. To turn the possibility of PTO into a reality, you must say what is on your mind. Share your hopes and fears. Let others experience the process—let them see what will happen, the reactions, and the potential power of the process. If you go first, your peers are much more likely to find the confidence to follow.

- **Remember that the collective goal is a means to an end:** Don't fret if the collective goal is not your first choice. Don't get into a struggle with others as to who will benefit most from it. Focus on finding a goal that meets the criteria—not daunting, doable but stretch, small, concrete and measurable, collective and shared, and is of some potential personal value. The goal needs to get at a manifestation of the always-on problem that is fundamental to your work place and does affect everyone, but it need not be the thing that troubles everyone the most nor a solution that is of particular value to everyone. At BCG, unpredictability was a problem for everyone—but not the problem that everyone ranked most irksome. Moreover, some valued a night off a week, but many did not even want it. But they all agreed that the goal (a predictable night off a week) was meant to address a particular problem (unpredictability of the work), which was pervasive. Keep in mind that the real benefit for you—and everyone else on the team—is unleashing the learning process at the core of PTO.

- **Remember that the tools to foster structured dialogue are just that, tools:** What matters is that your team gets together on a regular basis and shares openly what is going on—regarding the experiment and even more importantly regarding your work issues and work-lives in general. What matters is that people attend and people gradually build trust and the willingness to open up. To foster that process, you need to share where you are coming from, ask questions to understand what is going on for others, and be an active listener. Engage in the process.

- **Give others the benefit of the doubt:** Mistakes happen. People may send mixed signals. Don't overreact. Ask questions. Understand their intent. Calmly and clearly explain to others how they are coming across. Give feedback.

- **Holding each other's feet to the fire:** It is one thing to launch the PTO process on your team with the best of intentions. It is another to keep it going when the work demands escalate, crises hit, and work feels overwhelming. Yet it is at exactly those stressful moments that the team has the most to benefit from PTO. You need to remind each other to take the time to stop and reflect; though it might feel impossible to step outside the whirlwind, taking time to think about what really needs to get done and how it will make more time not less because you will be ready to work smarter and more efficiently. Make sure to take some time to assess whether there are ways you could do things differently before you barrel ahead.

- **Be clear about the expectation:** PTO is not about your entitlement to some predictable unit of time off—or whatever the particular goal your team chooses. This is about you engaging with your team in a collective process to rethink your work. If you view the collective goal or the process more generally as something you are now entitled to, you will undermine the intent, and fail to generate the kind of changes everyone is hoping for. The only entitlement that PTO offers is for your team to try to improve the work process, together. PTO has nothing to do with what the organization/your team leader owes you. It is about what you all owe each other—which is working together to improve your work world.

- **Share ownership:** Look for ways to help each other and your superiors do their work better. Remember that PTO is about you all working together to make it happen. Be proactive. Take responsibility. Raise potential solutions, not just issues. Be thoughtful and constructive.

- **Keep the process going:** The process depends on you and your teammates adhering to the collective goal and being open. It is important that you share your thoughts and feelings, your highs and lows, your accomplishments but also your struggles. And you have to share the personal as well as the work. If you don't share the issues that are affecting you, nothing can be done to change them. Moreover, if you just talk about these issues and don't take action, still nothing is likely to change. PTO legitimates you to engage others to work with you to create change. Step up. Speak up. Suggest changes. Try new ways. Work with others to make things different. And keep on doing it.

Part IV

FROM TEAM TO ORGANIZATION

A Firmwide Initiative

As I finished this book, George Martin, Rachel Levine, and their colleagues at BCG had been working on the PTO initiative for close to four years, and while they had achieved impressive results, there was still much more to do. "Up, down, up-down, down, up-up, down-up, up-up-up-up, down-up, up and done." That is how George Martin has described the diffusion of PTO at BCG, and for good reason. Spreading the process beyond the Consumer team's initial success involved effort, patience, and persistence. Understanding what George, Rachel, and the PTO Rollout Team did at BCG provides a number of rich insights into how to take successful results at the team level and expand them throughout an organization.

As you read, keep in mind how this all began. I approached BCG as a Harvard Business School professor with no grand plan beyond observing, and hopefully running a few team-level experiments about turning off in a very high-pressure environment where few researchers had previously been granted access. George, somewhat to my surprise, had graciously allowed me to enter, but when a year later I proposed an experiment, he was less than enthusiastic, one might even say dubious, about the prospects of my experiment, not volunteering any of his own teams to participate. As the managing partner of the office, George kept tabs on my whereabouts and asked for the occasional update on what I was learning, which I viewed mostly as a formality.

Imagine my surprise, then, when George listened to our presentation of the results from the Consumer team experiment and suggested, "What if we make next year the year of predictability in the Boston office of the Boston Consulting Group"—and then went to work making that a reality. His first step entailed creating the PTO Rollout Team—which he led.

As I briefly mentioned in chapter 2, the PTO Rollout Team included both Paul Schwartz and Rachel Levine. Paul had a reputation for his own workaholic tendencies and for driving his teams extremely hard. George believed Paul's stature in the firm as a top revenue producing senior partner—achieved by an attitude toward work that PTO was setting out to change—would lend credibility to the effort among his ambitious colleagues in the Boston Office.[1] Rachel, too, was an influential BCG veteran and a former member of the CEO's executive committee. She became the Rollout Team's "executing partner." (Technically, Rachel was no longer a partner. Just prior to the launch of PTO as a BCG initiative, she had opted to step off the partner track and join the Business Services Team (BST) at BCG while her four children were growing up.) Soon other members of the consulting staff, from multiple levels, were added to support the PTO Rollout Team's activities. And George asked me and my research associate, Jessica Porter, to play the role of advisers to this team.

Building Support

From the beginning, the PTO Rollout Team sought opportunities to build interest and support for PTO with everyone in the Boston office—from senior leaders to administrative staff—as well as anyone else who would listen from other BCG offices. George and Rachel reasoned that if some people became involved and had positive experiences, others would want to participate.

Create Opportunities to Share Results

The PTO Rollout Team's first step was to take advantage of one of George's regular meetings with his fellow Boston partners to present the results from the Consumer team's experiment and let them hear first-hand from the team's partner and project leader. That meeting was followed up with a daylong session with the entire Boston office staff, again with a presentation from the Consumer team.

George and Rachel then took the results to every major constituency in the Boston office—and then the firm—and presented them boldly, proudly, and strategically. They put no pressure on others to embrace the experiment, leaving the Consumer team's results—and team members—to speak for themselves. As George once explained to me, "Our belief was getting a pull from partners was going to be more effective in a BCG culture than trying to push it down partners' throats."

Build Alliances

Every organization has its politics, and early on in the expansion, George and Rachel knew that if they wanted to expand PTO beyond an experiment with one case team, they would have to attract powerful allies to PTO's cause. They identified the partners and principals in the Boston office whom they thought would be supportive, and invited them to join an "advisory committee," thus quickly expanding support for the experiment to nine partners—nearly a third of the partners in the Boston office. They also reached out to colleagues from other offices, thus planting seeds for PTO across the Northeast. The strategic alliances made it easier for them to spread the initiative regionally and ultimately globally, when the time was right.

Their targets of influence were not always the top leaders in a given office. It was not lost on George that PTO's most effective advocate in his own office was his head of consulting staff, Rachel Levine. It was a deft move to get the staffing coordinators on board: They ended up working almost as PTO recruiters, encouraging principals and project leaders to try PTO on their cases and reassuring consultants and associates that joining a PTO team would not jeopardize their careers.

The PTO Rollout Team also looked for allies in unexpected places. They soon recognized that though the PTO process depended on the consulting staff, executive assistants had a lot of control over partners' schedules. The Rollout Team proceeded to build an alliance with the administrative staff, holding focus groups and inviting them to the PTO kickoff meetings; they also asked the head of administrative services to join the PTO Rollout Team. With the schedule keepers on their side, George and Rachel had increased the odds that partners would attend kickoff meetings and PTO check-ins, which signaled to more junior members that their leaders were committed to PTO. It also helped with scaling the experiment, because both office and firm leaders could see there was a broad base of support for PTO, not just among the consulting staff but the firm's administrative staff as well.

Enlist Top Management Support

Very early on in the PTO Rollout Team's push to share their results, Rachel met with BCG's Frankfurt-based CEO Hans-Paul Bürkner to update him on what was happening in Boston. Bürkner asked her to make a presentation to his executive committee (EC), comprising top leaders from BCG offices around the world who work with him as the firm's governing body, setting BCG's agenda deciding which global and regional initiatives to take, and recommending certain issues that the firm's partners needed to address. To prepare for that command performance, Rachel, a former member of the EC herself, made sure she spoke separately with most of its members to enlist their support. Rachel and George's next stop was the firm's semiannual World Wide Officer Meeting (WWOM)—and they were given such a prized slot on the agenda that they decided to hire an acting coach to help them prepare their presentation before the firm's global partnership. (Such careful preparation is not unusual, considering the pressure of the chance to impress so many of the firm's top people with one presentation.) They—

and PTO—were a big hit. George and Rachel continued to update the EC every six to nine months as the experiment spread throughout the firm. (They also made a second appearance at the WWOM three years later to update the firm on PTO's progress.)

Create Peer Pressure

As some teams started embracing PTO, others started to feel pressure to do so as well (remember Ron, the highly regarded partner profiled in chapter 6 who resisted participating, but felt pressure to do so, first from his team members and later from other partners with whom he worked). And when they tried it, most decided that PTO was worth doing again. That was exactly what George and Rachel had hoped.

This pressure built at the office level as well. The more PTO caught on in a given region, the more pressure other offices felt to participate. Every month, the Americas management team would meet and periodically the regional chair would ask Rachel to give an update on PTO, including the percentage of each office that was doing PTO. While the regional chair didn't exert any pressure on offices to take up PTO, it became awkward not to engage. And this same pressure that spread PTO across offices within the Americas started building steam in Europe and Asia as well.

Create and Sustain Champions

As people tried PTO, many had positive experiences and in turn became champions themselves. One of the most powerful types of champions was the former skeptic. These skeptics fell into two categories: (1) those who could not imagine themselves or their teams taking nights off ("How can people take units of predictable time off, given the nature of our client-service business?") and (2) those who could not imagine any value of PTO given their personal effectiveness as a manager ("How can PTO be of any value, given how well I already manage?"). Converting either type of skeptic turned out to be of great value—and a surprisingly frequent occurrence.

In chapter 7, we met Tom, the partner who had described himself as having "a work-life balance problem but didn't know how to fix it."

Tom later recalled his initial skepticism toward PTO: "I was concerned we would either set false expectations around work-life balance and disappoint our staff, or we would actually meet those lifestyle expectations and disappoint on the business side, disappoint the client." On his first PTO team (Healthcare Lean I), Tom called into the case team meeting from vacation and opted to take Friday night as his night off. But we later saw, in the Healthcare Lean II case, how much Tom changed—to the point where he was scolding team members for doing too much rather than encouraging this behavior. Three years later, he reports that he actively pursues PTO, not just practicing it but embracing it: "I have an option not to do it, but I do PTO on almost every case because I want to." Tom sees himself as deeply, and genuinely, committed to the process:

> I'm a very skeptical guy when it comes to the soft side of running businesses in general, so I'm not just saying this. I find actually that forcing the discussion, stepping back and forcing yourself to talk about, "Are we getting the best out of the team?" ultimately brings you things that you wouldn't be able to achieve otherwise. It's an open communication that ultimately leads to higher motivation and engagement from the team. Even if you were not to change the work plan, even if they were doing the exact same set of activities, people feel better about doing them. But [they don't end up doing the same activities because], frankly, it forces you to address the issues that you've seen. It's your duty to actually address it, to take the feedback and make changes.

After participating in PTO, Tom went on to win—the next two years in a row—the highly prestigious Northeast award given to between 10 to 12 percent of the partners globally for high scores on both revenue generation and upward feedback.

In contrast to the workaholic manager who initially saw no possibility of turning off but evolves as part of engaging in the process, there were also those managers who felt that their teams already could voice issues and address them, and that they were already providing the time off that their people needed. Ron, mentioned above and in chapter 6, was a case in point. He had already won the prestigious Northeast award twice—before PTO—and waited nearly a year before trying PTO because he was skeptical that good managers such as himself would find any value in it. Yet he became a convert soon after trying it. His own transformation further committed Ron to helping convert other skeptics as well. He explained, "I became an informal and formal supporter of the concepts behind PTO . . . There were some people who were probably just like me who said, 'Do we really need to do this if things are going well?' and I was constantly having the conversation about how we need to run our cases well, respect our teams, be open so we can improve the product *and* work-life balance . . . that's what PTO is all about."

Champions helped George and Rachel move the initiative forward. They helped get more teams to experience PTO. They also helped fuel the process in another, more indirect way. As more teams were involved, more positive results were recorded, and more enthusiasm mounted among George, Rachel, and the growing group of champions. It was a positive reinforcing cycle that at its core rested on PTO teams being successful.

Move Forward Cautiously, but with Conviction

The PTO Rollout Team had no grand vision. They had no detailed plan for how to proceed. They simply stuck to the belief that a "viral rollout" was the best strategy. PTO had something to offer and they wanted to help others get it right. That often meant pushing through resistance and not getting sidetracked or discouraged along the way.

Make Sure the Right Conditions Are in Place

"This might seem simple, but it is deceptively complex," was the way that George often characterized the process. He worried that partners from other offices would merely take the PowerPoint slides that were used to describe PTO and try to do it on their own, without fully understanding the complexity. Both he and Rachel were well aware that if offices modified the rules of engagement or rolled PTO out without full leadership support, it would only increase the risk of failure.

As it was, the firm's top leadership team was eager to move faster than George and Rachel. Immediately upon hearing the Consumer team results, CEO Bürkner had not only suggested the presentation to the EC but also had suggested launching official PTO pilots in the United States, Europe, and Asia. Rachel, however, had persuaded him of the importance of getting it "rock-solid" in Boston, first. Time and again, Bürkner and his executive committee pushed George and Rachel to move more quickly. But they stuck to their conviction that three conditions had to be met for a new office to get involved with PTO: (1) office leadership needed to understand what PTO is in all its deceptive complexity; (2) office leadership needed to put resources behind the effort, and (3) there needed to be a genuine pull from the office leadership. "For three years," said Rachel, proud of how conservative they had been in the face of the CEO's enthusiasm, "I've gone to the EC every six to nine months, and every time I've managed to put them off."

As the initiative headed into the fourth year, George and Rachel agreed that they had achieved enough success virally that they were finally ready to move more quickly. As George explained, "We are now at the tipping point and we can be a bit more assertive and encourage offices to do it. And at some point if some people don't do it just in a voluntary way, we'll drive it more aggressively." The CEO and the EC seized the opportunity, declaring that PTO would become a global initiative. Rachel explained her change of mind: "The power is that now we are rock-solid and when people question what it is that they are being asked to implement, they will be pleasantly surprised when they look beneath the hood and learn more." Moreover, she shared the senior leadership's concern that they were now at a risk of uneven penetration with global training and recruiting efforts highlighting PTO, so that people who were not part of the effort might be resentful if they did not have access.

Persevere—and Push Through Resistance

When we initially launched the first experiment at BCG, the only thing that was certain was the widespread pessimism about its chances for success among the Boston office consulting staff. Even BCGers desperate for change, including talented consultants who were already planning their exit from the firm to try to salvage some kind of balance in their lives, didn't think we had a chance. The Consumer team results did little to overcome such skepticism. As one partner put it, "This will always be a really intense job. I would love it if your research could markedly improve the lives of the consultants, but I don't think it will be able to because that is just the nature of the work we do."

Such pessimism was justified. BCG had had many well-intentioned change initiatives that had made little difference. Just the previous year, a quarterly conference had been devoted entirely to career development, to small effect. The firm had deck upon deck of slick slide presentations about "best practices" and "how to work more efficiently." Yet, in the end, little seemed to change.

But George and Rachel pushed on. They met resistance in every form imaginable along the way—from partners who didn't think unpredictable schedules were a problem worth addressing and consultants who didn't want a night off to a much more formidable and unexpected obstacle—a historic global recession that stalled the rollout in offices on the verge of committing to it. George and Rachel embodied the flexibility of PTO: when one partner resisted, they found another willing to sign on. When the economic downturn hit, they found an argument for continuing the rollout not in spite of the economy but *because* of it: "This is the time it is most important to protect our culture," Rachel implored the partners in Boston. "Now more than ever we need people to be working smart and efficiently."

Avoid Dilution

George and Rachel had to navigate the PTO rollout very carefully. It seemed that at every turn people wanted to make alterations in exchange for buy-in. George and Rachel stuck to their go-slow strategy of letting PTO's success do the talking, sometimes having to beseech PTO enthusiasts *not* to roll out a new team before they were ready.

For instance, when they first began talking to BCG's New York partners about what they were doing in Boston, the New Yorkers put their own spin on it. They loved the idea of an efficiency initiative to help teams improve how they worked together; they were less crazy about promoting an experiment that benefited individuals' personal lives. The easy route would have been for George and Rachel to agree to dilute the PTO initiative in exchange for the New Yorkers' buy in. Instead, they argued that if New York discarded personal issues, the office would also be throwing out the gains in productivity and effectiveness that PTO delivered; then George and Rachel waited patiently until they found one New York partner willing to execute the experiment as it was supposed to be done. His peers would see the benefits, and sign on.

Learn as You Go

The PTO Rollout Team was never beyond learning. They knew that they had to deliver results but also continue to improve the process as they went forward. This included collecting data so they would be able to track progress but also recover from various setbacks—and learn from them.

Keep Track of Progress with Metrics

Before the first BCG team began the experiment, we tried to capture a baseline measurement for where the team stood regarding a range of work and work-life issues. These included questions about collaboration, innovation, effectiveness, efficiency, client value, ability to turn off, work-life satisfaction, job satisfaction, and career sustainability. Then each month, we captured data that allowed us to gauge change over time. Initially, we surveyed only members of PTO teams, but as the initiative expanded officewide, we surveyed those on nonparticipating teams for comparison purposes.

It also turned out to be valuable to get information regarding how teams varied in their engagement in the process. Asking questions that measured the level of leadership support, the level of commitment to setting and achieving a goal, and the frequency and level of openness of structured dialogue was extremely helpful for evaluating, explaining, and promoting why some teams did better than others. George and Rachel used those results to convince future teams to "double down" on areas where they had flexed too much . . . such as teams who tried to implement the structured dialogue without committing to the collective goal.

As the initiative expanded to other BCG offices, they, too, often ran some sort of baseline and/or initial surveys to track their own results. As the expansion continued, the PTO Rollout Team established a global survey to be administered twice a year. In addition to keeping track of the experiment's progress, these metrics became a valuable tool for maintaining the enthusiasm for PTO in offices accustomed to the experiment and creating momentum in offices new to PTO. And as we noted above, they fueled the behavior of champions who in turn were at the core of the grassroots diffusion of PTO. It was also reinforcing because as more teams participated and had positive responses, the results looked all the more compelling. In the end, establishing a set of metrics provided evidence that change was possible, inspired people to participate, motivated them to continue, and helped them understand how to refine their efforts most effectively.

Learn from Mistakes

As the PTO initiative entered its second year, BCG was hired for a large postmerger integration project (PMI) centered in the Northeastern United States. This was a huge win for the firm. At a time when the economy was still in reverse gear, unemployment skyrocketing, and the competition agonizing about layoffs, BCG went from having many unstaffed consultants to a staff shortage in some Northeast offices, almost overnight. The firm had done major PMIs before, but this one would require the largest team in BCG's almost fifty-year history: well over one hundred consultants from the United States and around the globe, assembled in close to fifty subteams.

PMIs are notorious for their long hours, intensity, and propensity to burn out staff. But in hard economic times, people were willing to put up with almost anything to keep their jobs. Still, the lead officer on the PMI decided to implement PTO across the entire PMI team, hoping to reduce stress and optimize productivity. His decision also provided PTO with global exposure.

Given the intense pressure of any PMI, the sheer magnitude of this case, the limited resources of the PTO Rollout Team, and the persistent recession, there was a great deal of variability in how PTO was implemented across the subteams—and it had significant costs. What had begun as an extraordinary opportunity—to have well over one hundred consultants doing PTO around the globe—had turned into what PTO's biggest promoter, Rachel Levine generously described as "a little bit of a disaster." Offices where knowledge of PTO was limited to not much more than rumor reinvented the process in their own ways, which created a new set of challenges. As Rachel pointed out, "We allowed PTO to flex too much, particularly on the predictable unit of time off."

Many of the participants ended up associating the process not with a team experience featuring more openness in meetings and predictability in their workweek but with the frustration and lack of control over their schedules that comes from being on a particularly intense PMI case. It left them with a bad taste and skeptical about PTO's potential to make a difference at BCG. As one of the more dubious consultants characterized PTO, "It will gain notoriety, spread to the rest of BCG, be used as a recruiting tool, and eventually die a quiet death."

George and Rachel, however, turned this setback into an opportunity to reinforce PTO's rules of engagement—the collective goal of predictable time off and structured dialogue. They presented comparative data from the PMI teams that effectively demonstrated that teams without a collective goal were not seeing the same benefits as those with it. They used the data to encourage partners on the PMI to adopt a goal if they hadn't. They also used it to show to others that both the collective goal of predictable time off *and* the weekly check-ins to discuss the process were essential.

Advocate for Changes in Formal Structures to Support PTO's Evolving Practices

As the experiment gained traction, the PTO Rollout Team began to lobby for changes in BCG's formal reward structures. Some of the changes were fast coming but many have taken years to get approved. Changing the formal reward structures is complicated at BCG because the reward system itself is global—what is rewarded in Boston has to be the same in Dallas, Helsinki, and Tokyo. One of the firm's first formal changes regarding PTO appeared on the forms used to capture upward feedback for the partners—an important factor in deciding partner compensation. Prior to PTO, there was only one question on the form related to a sustainable workload and zero encouragement for partners to keep the workload sustainable for themselves. In fact, before PTO, the form featured one question that could be interpreted to suggest that partners should place their personal lives at the bottom of their own priority list: "Puts the interest of the client/team/practice ahead of self-interest." With the advent of PTO, this was revised to read, "Puts client interest ahead of BCG interest." Two additional measures were also added: "Within reason, enables team members to make and keep key personal commitments and plans" and "Is an effective role model for a sustainable career at BCG."

The influence of PTO on the upward feedback forms for partners happened relatively quickly because the firm was already in the process of updating them. It took more time to implement changes in the feedback forms for principals. About two years after starting PTO in Boston, the following questions were added to their global upward feedback forms:

- Effectively teams with others

- Maintains an acceptable pace of work, given client's needs and timeline

- Is an effective role model for a long-term sustainable career at BCG

- Drives open dialogue among team members regarding case and personal priorities

- Establishes norms that balance client, project, and personal needs; checks in on norms/personal needs regularly

The following measures were also added to the review forms that partners used to review their principals:

- Drives open dialogue among team members regarding priorities

- Effectively teams with others

- Is an effective role model for a long-term sustainable career at BCG

In an effort to further embed PTO practices into the culture at BCG, the PTO Rollout Team also worked with colleagues in charge of training and development to get PTO sessions incorporated into BCG's official training programs.

Communicate, Communicate, Communicate

An important part of expanding the experiments was simply talking to and then staying in touch with all the key constituencies—allies, stakeholders, experiment teams, and the rest of the staff. During PTO's first year in the Boston office, George Martin made a point of updating the entire staff at his monthly meetings regarding the results of the monthly PTO surveys of the office. The results from teams participating in PTO, compared with those not involved, were positive along a wide range of dimensions, from teamwork process and value delivery to job satisfaction and work-life balance. Sharing these monthly updates increased overall enthusiasm for the experiment.

Such constant communication also helped to keep focus on the rollout. Even with a small percentage of the office initially participating in PTO, the rest of the office knew what was going on and remained interested in how it turned out. From early on, there was a buzz in the office, a persistent curiosity about how things were going. Everyone recognized the personal upside if their colleagues could make the experiment work and bring some predictability into the way they all operated. Was change really possible? This air of suspense was important for sustaining interest across the office hierarchy—among leaders as well as the junior staff.

It certainly did not hurt PTO's growing reputation that CEO Hans-Paul Bürkner sent periodic e-mails endorsing the initiative. At the end of the first year, he introduced PTO to all of BCG's offices worldwide, including in his e-mail this comment:

> PTO is not a panacea for all the work-life balance issues we face. This is a tough and demanding job. It does, however, provide a good set of principles and ideas for improving the case team experience. PTO has proven to enhance not only work-life balance but also client value delivery, consultant development, and overall case experience.
>
> Like all major change efforts, any rollout must be done in a well-planned way. And while these ideas are conceptually simple, there are real complexities in implementation. The U.S. is currently rolling it out, we are piloting it in Europe, starting in London, and then will identify one Asian office. We have also introduced PTO on a global scale with the [company name omitted for confidentiality] PMI where we adopted it in most teams around the world.

Bürkner also expressed his support for PTO in an official company video:

I think the key for us is to be passionate about PTO, but also to be very persistent. As we know, the devil is very often in the details, there may be cultural constraints in one or the other offices, there may also be people being critical, or even rejecting the idea because it was not invented by them. So I think we need to do a lot of convincing, and we need to ensure that a lot of teams are trying it, hopefully having good experiences, learning from it, revising the process to some extent, where it needs improvement, but they keep on pushing very, very systematically and persistently, until we have the large majority of the BCG people being not only convinced but being passionate about it.

BCG began including a description of PTO in its recruiting presentations on university campuses—clearly positioning PTO (and thus the firm's attention to improving work-life) as a potential edge on their competition. A key talking point in the firm's recruiting materials was: "PTO is an innovation to fundamentally improve the case team process so we can deliver both superior client value and greater employee sustainability." BCG was also careful to note that PTO is "for all employees, not just for those with specific personal needs."

Manage Expectations

As enthusiastic as BCG senior leaders have become about the process, they also find it important to be clear about expectations: a frequent refrain is "PTO does not make our tough but rewarding job 'easy,' but it does make it better." The advantage of repeating this phrase over and over is that it keeps people realistic about the potential for positive change while underpromising on results.

PTO at BCG continues to develop and grow—picking up steam as it moves forward. Most recently, the firm's leaders made PTO part of the firm's worldwide people management strategy. Gradually, the culture of the firm and its core work practices are changing. But, as with any good change initiative, it's often two steps forward, one step back. And, as George Martin says, "If you are not always worried . . . you don't know about change."

Diffusing Throughout Your Organization

As you think about translating BCG's efforts into your own, the core message to keep in mind is that diffusion will be a slow, deliberate process that takes passion and commitment. Expanding the process in your organization will require champions who are ready to carry out your vision. If you have achieved positive results on your first team and you want to take PTO further within your organization, as George Martin and Rachel Levine did at BCG, keep the following in mind:

- **Build support:**
  - Create opportunities to share results.
  - Build alliances.
  - Enlist top management support.
  - Create peer pressure.
  - Create and sustain champions.
- **Move forward cautiously but with conviction:**
  - Ensure conditions for success:
    - Leadership understanding
    - Resources
    - Genuine pull
  - Persevere—and push through resistance.
  - Avoid dilution.
- **Be open to learning as you go:**
  - Keep track of progress with metrics.
  - Learn from mistakes.

- **Advocate for changes in formal structures to support PTO's evolving practices:**
  - Revise performance metrics and review forms.
  - Create or expand trainings to include PTO.
- **Communicate, communicate, communicate:**
  - Both formally and informally, at every level, make sure to get the message out there—and keep it alive over time with additional forms of communication.
- **Manage expectations:**
  - Emphasize potential for positive change while underpromising on results.

Introducing Facilitators

There is one last critical ingredient in BCG's success in diffusing PTO throughout the firm, and that is the role played by the facilitator. While running an initial experiment without a designated facilitator is quite plausible, we found that, as the number of teams increased, the presence of facilitators proved invaluable for keeping the process moving smoothly, sustaining interest, and expanding the effort. As one BCG partner put it: "PTO is a best practice, but let's be honest—we just don't do it without a facilitator."

Facilitators collected and analyzed data to share the progress and continue to refine the conceptual thinking around PTO. They looked for ways to embed the PTO process into the firm's existing systems, such as evaluations, upward feedback forms, and training sessions. They helped new offices get started. But most important of all, facilitators were there to help each PTO team establish the rules of engagement and stay true to the process, especially when stressful times hit and increasingly less-informed leaders became involved.

The Genesis of the PTO Facilitator at BCG

Discovering the power of PTO and what made it work was full of surprises from the start, and one of the biggest was how much facilitators contributed to its success.[1] Initially, we acted as facilitators as much to ensure engagement in our experiment and to collect data as to lend a guiding hand. During the Consumer team experiment, for example, we participated in the weekly case team meetings, ensuring that the calendar review, Pulse Check, and Tummy Rumble discussions occurred. We also met one-on-one with team members to learn about their PTO experience.[2]

As the research transitioned from our initial HBS-led experiment to a BCG-led initiative overseen by George Martin, Rachel Levine, and the PTO Rollout Team, it was immediately clear that we wouldn't have the time to continue collecting the same level of detailed data or guiding the process in the same way. The alternative was for BCG to create a team of facilitators selected from their own staff—but trained by us—to oversee the next wave of experiments. That decision alone was a big deal for the Boston office: taking people out of revenue-producing client-service work for three- to six-month rotations as facilitators—and at a time when the firm's workload was at full capacity—was costly. But we all viewed the need for facilitation as an interim step to help BCG ramp up experiments with several more teams, and the Boston leadership decided facilitation was worth the short-term investment.

Over time, stories of how facilitators helped transform resistant leaders have multiplied, as has evidence that teams with little or no facilitation often do not achieve the full potential of PTO, even when they are led by PTO advocates. We soon realized that facilitation was an important part of the ongoing process. Facilitators served as an ever-present reminder of the purpose of PTO—and the need to keep challenging the status quo—in a culture where there were constant pulls to keep on doing things as they had always been done. George Martin summed up the Boston office's experience with facilitators in a video about the PTO process directed at the rest of the firm: "We are actually finding that having the discipline of having facilitators track, measure, and support teams is incredibly valuable to case teams, so you need to be ready to invest those resources. And you need to be prepared to keep going at it. [PTO] is really easy to be a fad for three months, but if you want it to be long term, facilitation has to be a part of how you operate."

The Power of the Facilitator

Recall Jay, the resistant project leader in chapter 7 who successfully undermined the PTO effort on the Healthcare HR team, despite George's support. The leadership of another of the original ten PTO teams—what I will call the *Tech Efficiency* team—shared much in common with the Healthcare HR team. Both teams had support for PTO at the top; both had a project leader who felt that PTO had been imposed on him. "I took a resigned and cynical tone about the introduction of PTO on this case," confessed Tech Efficiency's leader, Ed, echoing Jay's (the Healthcare HR leader from chapter 7) initial resentment about being forced to participate in the experiment. "PTO is about making life more manageable and putting work-life balance front and center. This was just not a case where it would be easy to deliver that." And Ed made no effort to hide his resistance to the rest of his team. According to the associate, "Ed made it clear from the start that this was not going to be a PTO case, at least for him." As proof, she added: "He was the first to sacrifice his night off."

Despite both teams starting with resistant project leaders, the outcomes were quite different. For the Healthcare HR team, there was a sense that PTO had not achieved nearly as much as it could have. Members of the Tech Efficiency team, in contrast, credited PTO for making an out-of-control case bearable. "Without it, I might have quit already," confessed one team member.

So why the difference? A key factor was the presence of an engaged facilitator. The first few weeks of the Tech Efficiency case were a sprint.

Ed, the project leader, had known it would be from the start. The partner had warned him that the make-or-break point of this seven-week case would occur within the first two weeks. Yet, halfway through the project, Ed realized things had still not improved: "I had thought that interesting work and high-quality output would be enough to satisfy the team," he explained. "But I sensed the team was beginning to revolt under the workload."

That's when he realized that the experiment, which he had been resisting, might be of some value. He turned to the facilitator who had been assigned to his team to get more insight into his team members' thinking. What was reported back to him was not exactly what any project leader on a tough case wanted to hear: the team didn't feel appreciated; they had a sense the case was already failing; that they were failing; and that they thought he was a "jerk," "condescending," and "difficult to work with."

Ed took that criticism hard. "It totally surprised me and it ruined my day," he recalled. But instead of turning defensive or vindictive, he tried to learn from it. "I knew I needed to take action."

He turned to the partner in charge for help, and together they spoke to the facilitator, spending half an hour talking about the team's perspective, acknowledging that they had been pushing the team hard. Ed and the partner then talked to the team, explaining that they were going to continue pushing toward delivering high-quality output for the client. "For that, we are unapologetic," Ed told the team. He then set out the leadership's new guidelines for going forward. "We will tell you if things are not right. Otherwise, have faith that we like you as people, we like this team, we enjoy working with you, and we want you to feel comfortable talking to us. If there is something I am doing that is making it harder for you to work, I want to know; that is not my intent and I don't know I am doing it unless you tell me." A consultant on the team described Ed's behavior as "incredibly open and responsive to the feedback."

As a result of Ed's quick and forceful response to the feedback, the Tech Efficiency team looked back on the PTO process in terms of two intervals—preintervention of the facilitator and post. "It humanized everyone on the team," explained one consultant. "Before the intervention, the case was not sustainable, even for a couple more days." According to the team's one associate, "The case itself was an absolute disaster at first. I was on the verge of tears most of the time, until the intervention. That was priceless . . . After the intervention, the conversation was more honest. The dynamic changed. I was able to let people know when I was approaching my wits' end."

Ed later reflected on his change of attitude: "I came to recognize the importance of discovering what was going on—whether through the facilitator or by asking the team directly, which I intend to do in the future." He further noted that taking a half an hour a week to discuss the work experience would not have happened ordinarily on such a tough case, with so little time to do anything but work toward the imminent deadline. But he ended up finding the Pulse Checks "very useful." Not only did he get a clearer sense of how people were feeling about the case, but what he heard from team members also tended to be a lot more nuanced. "Someone could now say 'I feel good about the work, the value delivery to the client, but I don't feel good about the hours,'" he explained. "This is a very different message from, 'This case sucks.'" He had come to realize PTO encouraged more productive complaining. "As a project leader, there is not much you can do if you don't understand the problem," he pointed out. "But PTO forces people to figure out what is frustrating them [and] give it some more granularity, which makes it more understandable and actionable."

In the end, this project leader who had been so openly resistant to PTO concluded that the experiment had "an overall positive effect. It reinforces communication and gives consultants a voice." He even recommended using PTO to another project leader on a very intense case "because the case is going to be intense regardless, but PTO still helps facilitate communication, which is very, very valuable."

Facilitation, however, is only as useful as the facilitator's capability to deliver feedback—and the leader's willingness to receive it. The best leaders could handle constructive feedback, and then turn it to their advantage. Ed was able to put his ego aside and take action, repairing his relations with his colleagues.

There was a very different relationship between the project leader and the facilitator on the Healthcare HR team, mainly due to the fact that on many of the early PTO teams there was a great deal of experimentation around what the role of the facilitator should be. The Healthcare HR team was experimenting with what the PTO Rollout Team had labeled "lite-facilitation." In those cases, the experiment began with a shorter-than-usual kickoff meeting of fifteen or so minutes (rather than the more typical one- to two-hour kickoff) discussing what PTO was and how it would play out during the case. After that, the Healthcare HR facilitator was not always on hand but was available to the team on call. Unlike facilitators for many other teams, the Healthcare HR team facilitator did not attend the PTO check-ins or meet weekly with each team member one-on-one. As a result, by the time it was clear that the team had some serious problems, the facilitator was unable to intervene effectively because he had had so little involvement with the team (or any advance warning of what was happening).

It is fair to wonder whether any amount of facilitation on the Healthcare HR case could have improved the experiment's odds in the face of the all-out resistance to PTO by Jay, the project leader. Probably not: as Jay proved, a project leader can undermine the experiment in too many ways for it to succeed. But the results from so many experiments convinced all of us that more and better facilitation was preferable to less.

The Facilitator's Many Roles

Over fifty years ago, in his seminal book *The Presentation of Self in Everyday Life,* Erving Goffman provided a brilliant sociological depiction of Shakespeare's famous line "All the world's a stage."[3] Goffman argued that in normal social interaction people attempt to shape the impressions they give according to some shared set of guidelines about how one is supposed to act.[4]

Facilitators encouraged individuals to challenge those guidelines and try out new roles. At the same time, facilitators acted as a new type of audience, subscribing to a new system of practices, conventions and procedural rules, and applauding a new set of actions. The facilitator also played the role of acting coach, helping individuals to perform their roles better according to the new script.

Facilitators were involved in setting up the team for an effective kickoff meeting, as well as attending it. They then met weekly with the team members individually, usually for about fifteen minutes, but sometimes as long as one hour, depending on the person's desire to speak with the facilitator that week. These one-on-one weekly conversations turned out to be an easy way to gather information helpful for pushing the team to challenge their assumptions and strive collectively to find new ways of working. They also aided facilitators to be more effective in their second role—attending the team's weekly meeting to discuss the experiment's progress. We found that teams benefited most from the weekly meetings when facilitators attended but played a back-seat role—with the team leadership presiding over the discussion. The facilitator's mere presence ensured that the conversation occurred, and gave it legitimacy. The facilitator might also bring up a topic that the team needed to address but had not raised.

The facilitator was also instrumental in helping the team leadership as well as team members understand PTO, explaining up front to the partners and principal and/or project leader the PTO process and tools (the weekly calendar, Pulse Check, and Tummy Rumbles), and stressing the importance of each leader's commitment to the process. An effective facilitator was also a coach, encouraging and helping everyone from the most junior to the most senior team members, individually and collectively, digest what happened in their day-to-day work-lives and explore whether change was possible—and then push people toward discovering new, innovative ways of making that change.

Helping Raise Issues Effectively

Facilitation was a particularly valuable tool for helping team members figure out how to raise issues with their colleagues, frankly and fairly. A consultant described how the facilitator helped him figure out how to bring up a scheduling conflict. From the beginning of the case, the calendar showed the team spending the last week at home. This consultant had in-laws coming from Mexico that week and had booked tickets for a Red Sox game and rock concert, along with other plans. As the case was winding down, the project leader announced the possibility that the team might have to spend that last week at the client site. The consultant raised his scheduling problem with the facilitator "as exactly what PTO was trying to avoid," and sought advice on how best to voice his frustration over this last minute change of plans. "The facilitator was very helpful in helping figure out how to deal with it," recalled the consultant. "In the end it was a perfect example of open communication. Per the facilitator's suggestion, I opened the conversation with, 'In the spirit of PTO open communication, I wanted to let you know' . . . and the project leader agreed that regardless of what the team did, I could stay home that week."

Many team members noted that facilitators guided them in handling their frustrations in a "solution-oriented way" rather than simply expressing their issues. As one person put it, "Instead of saying something like, 'This is not acceptable,' I learned to approach it by saying something like 'This is what I think could be improved and this is how we could get there.'" The facilitator had helped this consultant understand that the team leadership supported PTO and expected team members to raise the issues that concerned them—for the benefit of the entire team. The facilitator had also helped the consultant understand that the team leaders expected the consultant to take ownership of the problem and work with the leadership to address it.

These examples share a common theme: the facilitator did not raise the issue on the member's behalf but rather encouraged and helped team members to discuss their concerns among themselves and share responsibility for resolving the issues as best they could.

Providing Back-Channel Feedback

When appropriate, and without violating the highly valued promise of confidentiality, facilitators might also choose to raise issues or help individuals raise issues among themselves in the weekly meeting or in a smaller, more informal setting. "There were issues I was uncomfortable raising," explained one young associate, "and the facilitator helped to get quick, efficient resolution from partners, principals, and project leaders on outstanding issues."

Team leadership also appreciated the facilitator's back-channel role regarding team members' concerns about both the case content and work-life issues. As one project leader in a particularly difficult case noted, "From a project leader, managing perspective, this was always going to be a difficult case, PTO or not. But PTO facilitation made it a little easier for me. It provided me a sense of where the team was at so I could try to keep up enthusiasm and make it a better experience for everyone."

Such messages were sometimes difficult to hear; but, as we saw with the Tech Efficiency project leader, Ed, managers generally appreciated knowing how the team felt so they could take measures to improve the situation, if possible. "I'm not going to lie," confessed one partner. "I got some hard messages from the team, which probably wouldn't have come up without a facilitator. But we were able to think proactively about addressing these concerns and morale is much better now."

Providing Space for Reflection

The weekly one-on-one meetings with the facilitator also helped team members think through how the case was going and how the team was functioning. So often we get caught up in the day-to-day demands of our work that we don't take the time to stop and reflect. Indeed, we convince ourselves that we don't have time to stop and reflect. Yet this act of reflection can be very powerful, saving us time in the long run as we recognize we are working in ways that are undermining our larger intent. Meeting each week with the facilitators forced time for reflection into the busy schedule. And people benefited.

As one consultant explained, "Usually you are just thinking about the next three things you have to do. The facilitator check-ins caused me to reflect, 'I'm feeling stressed—what exactly is going on? Should it be this way?'" He concluded, "Without the check-in, I probably would have missed out on the opportunity for things to surface."

And a facilitator observed, about his interactions with a partner, "I would just start the meeting by saying, 'How is everything going?' and he would sit back and start thinking about the case. He'd say, 'I think X is going well, Y isn't going well,' and then he'd reflect on how a member of the team was struggling, another member was doing really well, and the team was running really hard because there was a lot of uncertainty from the client. By the time he was done he would have come up with a set of action items, and he'd take a breath and say, 'this has been really useful, thanks.'"

Providing a Sympathetic Ear

Facilitators also provided immense value being good listeners, and quickly became a regular sounding board and resource, especially for junior members of the team. "The facilitator was like my life coach," explained one associate. "I just found it really helpful to be able to vent. It was an emotional release and sanity check."

While junior team members were quicker to point to the emotional value of facilitation, BCGers up and down the hierarchy appreciated having an easily accessible person to listen to them as they tried to process aloud what was happening on the case—regarding the work process in general as well as meeting their predictable time off goal. A principal explained, "It was almost like a shrink session where once you talked about something and vented it was out. Getting it off your chest and having somebody listen was 70% of the value, and the facilitator was thoughtful and helpful."

Holding the Team's Feet to the Fire

The facilitator also could be very helpful to encourage the team to stop and reflect when they reverted to bad habits, especially when the pressure mounted. "I look for opportunities to set up win-win situations, so everyone on the team does better," explained one facilitator. "For instance, a partner might see a situation as, 'We have a readout in two weeks and they need to get there regardless of what it takes, even if that means everyone will run hot for two weeks.' I try to reframe this for the partner, as, 'Yes, we have a readout in two weeks, but after that there are still four more months on this project. If we burn them now, they'll spend the rest of the project nursing this burn; and, in the end, the whole project will suffer.'"

An effective facilitator pushes the team to take the time to stop and reflect, despite all the pressure—pushing them to devise new practices that will actually better enable them to meet their deadlines. Put differently, the facilitator is asking the team to do what seems impossible, given all the time pressure. How many times in the throes of a seeming crisis at work did you barrel ahead, believing you had no choice but to get the work done at all costs—only to realize in retrospect there were better ways you could have worked, had you carved out the time to consider what you were so caught up doing?

The facilitator is there to ask the questions team members do not tend to raise, particularly on deadline: Why are you not trying harder to take your night off? Do you really have to work in this way? What more can other team members do to make this goal happen? Is there really no alternative? Sometimes the honest answer is "it has to be this way." But often, by pushing the team to reflect, the facilitator can help team members recognize that there are alternatives. And the PTO initiative proved over and over again, it is exactly at these moments when change seems so unlikely that the team reaps the biggest benefits from considering the possibility of change.

Being an Effective PTO Facilitator

Of course, every case and every team are different. But over the three years and fifty-five facilitators who have been involved to date, several practices of effective facilitation emerged that hold true across the PTO process.

Ensuring Confidentiality

Confidentiality is at the heart of all that the facilitator does. Facilitators are an outside and safe ear to talk to about issues that might be difficult to raise with teammates. Thus, the facilitator often becomes aware of issues that some or all of the other team members may not be aware of. The facilitator can raise issues in aggregate for the team, being careful never to reveal an individual's perspective or experience. They can push people to raise issues with others, or even agree to help raise them. But facilitators must also accept the constraints of confidentiality when an individual is not yet ready to raise an issue. For instance, a consultant on one PTO case was having medical issues that impacted his performance, but he was not comfortable sharing that information with team leadership. While the facilitator encouraged the consultant to be honest with his project leader and advised him about other sources of support from the firm, she had to respect the consultant's privacy and wait until he was ready to discuss the issue with his team.

As frustrating as such silence might be, the alternative is just too dangerous. Any breach of confidentiality will cause trust to be lost on several levels. The individual will feel exposed and betrayed, and will no longer trust the facilitator or the PTO process. The rest of the team will likely find out, which will also undermine their trust in the facilitator, making it impossible for the facilitator to be effective in helping the team build trust with each other.

Worse still, such a breach can cause shock waves to the initiative, as members of the team go on to future teams and talk to peers about what happened. This undermines the credibility of facilitators and of PTO overall. One facilitator described having to regain the trust of team members who'd felt betrayed in the past. "At a PTO kickoff, a consultant announced that she would not be participating in the one-on-ones with me, nor would she advise anyone else to, since she'd been burned by a facilitator on her prior team. I had to prove myself over and over to her, and the whole team."

Balancing Flexibility and Rigidity

Facilitators need to help each team adapt the PTO regimen to the reality of their specific case—and then push every team member to stick to the PTO process, even when they might not think it is to their immediate advantage. It's a delicate balance: too much flexibility allows the team to stray from the core principles of PTO; but pressing PTO too rigidly is likely to undermine the team's trust in the process, leading members to the conclusion that conducting the experiment is not realistic, given day-to-day demands of the work. As important as it was at BCG to make sure that PTO team members took their predictable nights off, sometimes in the heat of a case time off was impossible. Some cases were so demanding that a few hours off on the weekend was a stretch goal for that team. The facilitators had to help the team set realistic rules of engagement and know when and how to push hard but also ease up.

Staying Out of the Spotlight

Although it is part of the facilitator's task to orchestrate interactions between team members, facilitators are most effective operating behind the scenes. The best facilitators were able to get team members to engage with each other without leaving any fingerprints. As the BCG Boston office head staffer Rachel Levine so nicely phrased it, facilitators need to "take pride, not credit." The team—not the facilitator—must own the process.

One BCG facilitator explained how he communicated this to the team: "I say, 'This is your process, you should be talking to each other, not me. I will be there to make sure it happens, to help keep you on track. But the best outcome is when you make this a part of the culture of the team, make this a part of how you talk to each other all of the time, not just during the kickoff and PTO check-ins.'"

Managing Expectations

Facilitators play an important role helping the team manage expectations around the collective goal and around how to make reasonable personal requests (so partners don't automatically dismiss them as too demanding or entitled). PTO could make a marked difference in a case team's experience, yet it would never make consulting a 9–5 job. The facilitator needed to communicate this to the team in such a way that team members didn't expect more from PTO than PTO could possibly deliver. At the same time, the facilitator needed to convince the team to engage in PTO fully—to embrace both the collective goal and the open dialogue and to push themselves to work together as a team to attempt to make changes they didn't necessarily believe possible at the outset.

Speaking Up

Like team members, facilitators also needed to have the confidence to speak candidly to everyone involved in the experiment—including the most senior participants—sharing what they were learning, challenging the status quo, pushing back on assumptions, raising questions, getting others to rethink plans and actions, and, above all, pointing out opportunities to do things differently. This was no easy feat, especially in the face of leaders who considered the facilitator, not to mention PTO, a distraction from the "real work" of delivering to their client.

In stressful periods during a case, even the most supportive partner or principal can view PTO as overhead, and it took skill for the facilitator to press for the overall value of sticking to the experiment. Skeptical or even downright resistant leaders would always be the most challenging test, but the BCG experiment proved that facilitators were most effective when they stifled their own defensiveness and nurtured mutual respect between themselves and the leaders, so that the whole team could take note and engage in the process.

Who Are the Facilitators?

While the role of the facilitator—and who fills it—continues to evolve at BCG, most facilitators are members of the consulting staff who rotate onto the PTO Rollout Team for three to six months and then return to client work. Facilitators are not working members of the teams they facilitate and do not have content expertise; their primary responsibility is to support seven to ten teams, focusing on team dynamics and being a thought partner guiding the discussion about the process (not the content of the work).

By the time the initiative had completed its third year, thirty-six people had already served as facilitators and nineteen more were actively playing that role. Fourteen of the nineteen facilitators were members of the consulting staff and had been pulled out of client-facing work (ten of them full-time, four of them in different part-time arrangements). The remaining five facilitators were from the firm's Business Service Team (BST)—the administrative staff who support the internal functions of the firm, such as staffing, HR, recruiting, IT, finance, and administrative support. The PTO Rollout Team was increasingly experimenting with both types of members, those who rotated in for a few months from client-facing work and those who were part of a stable core who remained a part of the team indefinitely.

Where your facilitators will come from if you decide to take PTO beyond the team level remains an open question. Being a facilitator can be a tremendous opportunity for learning and development for colleagues in your organization, especially those who are on a managerial track. I describe in the next section how BCGers benefited from being facilitators. If your company has its own internal consulting group, they too may provide a possible source of facilitators. The possibility also exists to bring in outsiders to help diffuse this process. Whatever you choose, the role of the facilitator will be much the same: to help inform each team about the process, to meet one-on-one with team members on a regular basis, and to participate in the regular team discussions about the goal and the work process more generally.

Benefits of Facilitation—for the Facilitators

Facilitating PTO teams ended up becoming a career plus for BCG facilitators, exposing them to a range of leadership styles and seeing close up what made certain leaders more or less effective with their teams and clients. As Rachel Levine liked to say in the training session for facilitators, "In the end, you should have two lists—one of all of the great things you've seen and that you want to try on your own teams and the other is your 'Just shoot me' list. That's the list of things that you tell your friends, 'Just shoot me, if I ever do this myself.'" Levine compared facilitating PTO to the "case method" in business school—a quick education in management styles for a consultant or project leader. She also has described facilitating "as a boot camp to learn how to manage a project well."

Partners who worked with team leaders who had been facilitators often noticed a marked improvement in their project and team management skills. "It's a great opportunity for the facilitator to see lots of different case experiences," explained one partner. "And actually see the good, the bad, and the ugly of the case experiences."

The facilitators agreed. One described the role as "taking a crash course on being a principal/project leader—I saw many different styles. As a new project leader, that's fantastic exposure and helps me develop my own management skills and style." Another former facilitator was even more enthusiastic: "I'm convinced being a facilitator made me a much better principal, and that PTO is responsible for the great reviews I've been getting."

As the evidence accumulated, partners continued offering the opportunity to facilitate PTO teams to high performers, typically second-year consultants or first-year project leaders—a clear signal to the rest of the office and firm that this initiative was being taken seriously and facilitation had become a significant plus for people's career prospects at BCG.

Going Forward with Facilitation

As you consider the possibility of expanding the experiments and engaging facilitators to help aid that process, keep in mind that facilitators' core purpose is to help teams understand the PTO process and stay true to it. Facilitators are always beneficial as it is easy to revert back to old behaviors, but facilitators are particularly useful when people involved are less informed about PTO and less committed to it.

Over time at BCG, I have gained an increasingly rich understanding of what is PTO, why it works and how facilitators contribute to this process. In the next, and final chapter, I sum up what I have learned about PTO, and what is involved in ensuring its success.

Practices of Effective Facilitation

- Ensure confidentiality:

  - Protect confidential information in all circumstances.

  - Share only aggregated or blinded information.

  - *Remember:* Any betrayal of confidence sets back both the team and the larger effort.

- Balance flexibility and rigidity:

  - Take the context into account to create rules that are achievable.

  - Keep both the demands of the work and the expectations of PTO in mind.

  - *Remember:* Encourage teams, within reason, to embrace *both* rules of engagement.

- Take pride, not credit:

  - Allow leadership to take credit where possible to build credibility with the team.

  - Help teams build skills and confidence to own the process.

  - When interjecting is necessary, take care not to dominate the discussion.

- – *Remember:* The objective is to get the team to engage in the process, not to run the process for them.
- Manage expectations:
  - – Frame value of PTO in realistic terms—PTO will not solve every issue.
  - – Encourage teams to strive—benefits are proportional to the degree they embrace.
  - – *Remember:* People need an aspirational goal to push them to great heights but a realistic goal to prevent disillusionment.
- Be persistent (about the importance of PTO):
  - – Help teams push themselves, even when things are stressful.
  - – Push the team not to let PTO go when things get busy.
  - – *Remember:* PTO is most needed exactly when people find it is hardest to make time for it.

Reimagining Work

Before we started to experiment, we heard the constant refrain up and down the BCG hierarchy:

- "We have to always be on."

- "It is a 24/7 job."

- "I cannot possibly turn off, this is who I am."

- "Our clients pay top dollar for the highest-quality service."

- "Our clients have many choices. They will go somewhere else if we don't deliver."

The central question motivating the research was: Could these norms and expectations be changed—collectively, without undermining the work? The best that *individuals* can do is find ways to exist within their world, where these norms and expectations persist. But could they change these norms and expectations—as a group?

I had intentionally chosen an extreme case, an elite management consulting firm, where being on was believed to be at the heart of the

firm's success with its clients. If turning off was possible at BCG, I reasoned, it should be possible most anywhere.

The results from the survey that we had done of over sixteen hundred managers and professionals worldwide had taught us that the
more unpredictable the demands of the work, the more people are *on*.
The same data also suggested that the more people are *on,* the more
they accept this way of working and perpetuate the unpredictability,
rather than considering the possibility that alternatives might exist. Our
initial research at BCG showed us that BCGers were caught in a similar
cycle of responsiveness, where their own actions were perpetuating and
amplifying the bad intensity—the wheel spinning; the lack of communication; the last minute, late-night changes; the weekend "emergencies";
the never-ending pressure to be on.

Our question therefore became whether this cycle could be broken.
And what we discovered at BCG is: *such change is possible.* So much of the
unpredictability that had seemed deeply ingrained in their work turned
out not to be inherent to management consulting at all. When teams
embraced PTO, and started voicing both personal and work issues and
working together to address them, they found they could reprioritize
work, reconsider what needed to be done, push back on deadlines, reduce last-minute requests, and gradually eliminate much of the low-
value-added work. As a result, the work process benefited and the work
team members did felt more engaging while also being more manageable, more predictable.

Even deeper changes occurred when PTO became an organization-
level effort—what it meant to do good work and be a good worker began to shift fundamentally.

Doing Good Work

The experiment started out in a culture where always being *on* was a
"badge of honor" and to admit a desire to turn off was to admit weakness, an inability to cope with the demands of the work. As one consul-

tant put it: "The BCG culture infuses a lot of guilt in people if they are not working, since all of the success stories you see are the people who work constantly . . . It is pretty upfront at BCG that the rewards go to people who are seen to be slogging. Of those people who are seen as valuing work-life balance, there are very few who do spectacularly well at this firm . . . On a traditional BCG case [non-PTO], you have to demonstrate how hard you will work no matter what." In a client-service organization, where the expectation is that professionals are at the client's beck and call, it is not surprising that people would be rewarded for working in this way.

PTO, however, shifted expectations about what it meant to do *good work*.[1] As one project leader put it, "The assumption is always to work harder and longer, but PTO gives us a tool to work differently." "What has improved dramatically is that I feel I can be *off* if there is something I want to do that would make it difficult to remain *on*," explained a different project leader. Another noted, "Doing good work is no longer about how much work one does—it is about doing the right work . . . Our team has adopted the motto: 'Right work, work right.'"

As people changed how they worked in response to PTO, they became more efficient and effective. In chapter 2, we compared teams that embraced PTO with those that dismissed it, and noted that 75 percent of those on teams that embrace PTO report doing everything they can to be efficient, compared with 42 percent of teams that dismiss PTO. Similarly, 80 percent of those on teams that embrace PTO report doing everything they can to be effective, compared with 51 percent of teams that dismiss it. In turn, as it became evident that the work could still get done as well, and often better, people's willingness to take risks with regard to the issues they raised and attempted to address—both work and personal—further increased. More changes in work resulted, leading to an evolution in what was "acceptable" to say and do. Some of this inspired changes in the firm's formal reward structure—altering it to better align with the new ways teams were doing their work.

As I pointed out in chapter 10, changing the criteria for rewarding good work was complicated at BCG because the reward system itself was global and therefore changes had to be global. In some places, the changes in work practices made it increasingly apparent that new ways of working were preferable, and changes in the reward system followed; in other offices, however, the changes in the reward system predated changes in the work practices, because they were later adopters of PTO. In the latter, the changes in the reward system were more difficult to sell, but they played a helpful role in motivating the ensuing changes in work practices.

Workaholics or *Successaholics?*

We discovered that as the definition of *good work* began to shift so too did the meaning of being a *good worker*. It was not unusual at BCG to ascribe the tendency of always being *on* to a personal trait—labeling people *workaholics*. However, many people who had previously been considered workaholics—by themselves and others—forced to try a night off quite unexpectedly enjoyed it. These people turned out not to be workaholics but what I began calling *successaholics*. They were obsessed with their work because of the satisfaction they got from the kudos for achievement, not from long hours as an end in themselves. When similar benefits were attached to a different way of working (i.e., turning off), they changed their routines, reluctantly at first, but ultimately to their great satisfaction.

Sue, for example, attached little value to the notion of time off. A second-year consultant who had spent the past year in China working eighty-five hours a week, "considered working 75 hours a week to be like being on vacation," in the words of her manager. She was very proud of her work ethic. "When I first heard about PTO," Sue recalled, "I laughed. I was very skeptical. I have no problem doing three red-eyes in a week and working crazy hours." She admitted that, "I saw no value in the night off." However, she also conceded that after her first night off, she began to change her tune. "I found it very relaxing," she confessed. "It made me feel my life was more manageable." And within a few weeks, the same Sue who had resisted a night off was feeling the power of PTO: "The fact that I could just say 'I want a night off' and not have to give a reason, not even say I was tired, was amazing."

Many other BCGers who entered the experiment with an equal lack of commitment or outright resistance also ended up as impressed with PTO's power as Sue. For many, it was the first time in their careers that they were experiencing what it was like to truly turn off—and, despite some anxiety, they tried it, and almost always and much to their surprise liked what they experienced. Moreover, in the process they came to appreciate that working all the time might not actually be best for their work or themselves. As a consultant reflected: "One thing PTO has done is forced me to recognize it, my own intensity. PTO showed me that it is not the only way, and probably not the best way."

Consider Tad. He was the kind of person who was frequently in the *red zone* (working sixty-five or more hours a week), regardless of the case he was on. Tad was extremely committed to his job and loved the intellectual thrill of consulting work. As he was about to begin his first PTO case, we asked Tad what he thought would be the most challenging part of the experience. His reply: "It's going to be really hard to let go of my passion to push the logic and solve the problem. It's hard to let go of that; even on weekends I can't let go. It's in my nature to push the work, push the case, to get as deep as I can, and take it as far as it can go. I have a passion for getting the job done, and that's hard to let go of because I'm always thinking about the work."

Tad was also very conscious of what he thought it took to be a strong performer: "There's a lot of pressure from BCG being up or out, and I'm concerned that [participating in the time off experiment] may not be the best move . . . If the CDC [Career Development Committee] looks at someone who has been staffed on a project that's cranking—getting on an airplane and traveling and working long hard hours—versus someone who is working locally and taking time off, they are going to promote the person who is cranking. It's hard to imagine it won't have an effect."

Tad felt pressure to be connected, always. After an important client presentation, Tad told us "I actually turned off my BlackBerry when I was sitting in the presentation and it felt strange. I was worried that people were trying to get a hold of me, which they were, and they just had to wait for me (which they did.) I had my BlackBerry off for four hours, and that was hard." And if it was hard to be off for a work reason, it was even harder for Tad to be off for a personal reason. About his nights off, Tad noted, "I would rather check my e-mails on my time off and know what is going on, than get caught off-guard by an 'Oh my God, Tad, this is blowing up' phone call. My personal preference is just to see the e-mails as they come in." It took Tad time to get over this, and for many weeks he checked e-mail when he was supposed to be off.

With each week of the experiment, however, Tad became more committed to spending his time off with his family, rearranging his schedule to go to his young daughter's doctor's appointments and music classes. By his second PTO case, he was finally able to completely turn off, and exclaimed after the first weekend on the project, "It was the first Saturday in three years I did not check my BlackBerry!" Disconnecting from work had once been almost inconceivable and undesirable, but as a result of PTO's forced time off, Tad learned that disconnecting was not just feasible but quite rewarding. He became so taken with the positive benefits for himself and his teams that he has gone on to make every case he manages a PTO case. Indeed, Tad has become one of PTO's biggest champions.

Watching Tad, Sue, and so many others like them go through the PTO process has taught us that consultants, in general, thrive on the praise for a job well done rather than the nonstop work, per se.[2] As these successaholics experienced time off, in a context that now valued it, they reevaluated how they wanted to work. Consider Sue's reaction: "For me, the single biggest effect of PTO was coming to terms with the fact that I *deserved* time off. I deserve this. I should not feel ashamed of asking people for time off. That should be fine." Her reaction was a far cry from the Sue who "laughed" when she first heard of PTO and "saw no value in the night off."

Radical, Emergent Change

PTO changed how people worked together and what was rewarded. It altered what mattered to people. In the end, it affected people's expectations of themselves and each other, regarding how much they were *on* and when they could turn *off*.

David Nadler and Michael Tushman, in their now-classic book *Competing by Design*, introduced the *congruence model*—that is, the culture (norms and expectations), the task (what the work requires), the structures (what is rewarded, what is communicated in training), and the people (who is hired and their sense of identity) must be consistent.[3] Moreover, Nadler and Tushman argue that for effective cultural change to occur, it must be accompanied by change in each of the other three components so that they fit together in a new system—or are *congruent*. They further suggest such change happens in short discontinuous bursts of major activity. And, "It is executive leadership which initiates, shapes and directs strategic re-orientations."[4]

What we have done at BCG is break the cycle of responsiveness and create a new system where all the components are now congruent around a new culture focused on getting the work done in ways that minimize the bad intensity and maximize individuals' control.[5] What we further discovered is that the PTO process enabled such change to occur in a much more viral way that still fundamentally shifted the alignment but in small, doable steps that were *not* initially driven from the top.[6] Indeed, senior leaders did not have some grand vision for PTO, nor were they even involved in instigating the PTO process. Only later in the initiative, after the first experiment and then gradually over the next few years, did they become increasingly supportive—legitimating the effort and marshaling resources for it.

The process of change catalyzed by PTO is best characterized as an *emergent process,* based on small wins that amount to radical change.[7]

Toward a More Humane Workplace

What started as an exploration as to whether the cycle of responsiveness could be broken has ultimately transpired into so much more—a process to change the culture of the organization and create a more humane workplace. Many organizations are experimenting with various ways to give their employees the kind of flexibility in their work schedules that would help them better accommodate some of the pressures of work on personal and family lives and help them thrive in the workplace: part-time work, job sharing, flexible schedules, compressed workweeks, sabbaticals, maternity leaves, etc. The problem is that taking advantage of these alternative ways of working often conflicts with the cultural values of what constitutes "doing good work" and "being a good worker." The unfortunate—and unintentional— result is that employees find themselves penalized for participating in the very programs that their own companies are advocating to help them.

That's exactly what had happened at BCG in the case of part-time work. For several decades, BCG has offered its consulting staff a part-time option—working 80 percent of the time for 80 percent of the pay or 60 percent of the time for 60 percent of the pay. But those who tried to take advantage of this policy tended to find that the firm's culture trumped the firm's best intentions. Part-timers who tried to be flexible about when they took their time off—choosing to be absent only when it suited the demands of the team's work—ended up working just about full-time for a part-time salary. Part-timers who tried to protect their shorter week by taking off preset days were often blamed for being rigid and not making the work their first priority; because they were not always available, they fell short of others' expectations (and often their own) as to what it meant to do good work and be a good worker. In both cases, part-timers almost always failed to find a way to work part-time and be valued for doing so.

With PTO, it was different. When PTO teams experimented with different ways of working, they were not behaving in ways that were at odds with the predominant view of doing good work or being a good worker.[8] And they could begin to reap benefits—rather than suffer negative consequences—from attempting to work differently.

Many initiatives focus on helping individuals accommodate the workplace while others focus on making the work process more efficient and effective. But the former tends to leave individuals working in ways that are at odds with the prevalent culture, and the latter tends to leave individuals without any benefit—the temporal gains are reinvested in the work process itself. PTO reconciles the inevitable conflict between managing people in a 24/7 environment and maintaining the organization's competitive edge in the global marketplace by no longer relegating personal issues to eternal second place. Rather personal lives are placed on center stage where they can inspire rethinking the work process itself in ways that are a win for individuals' work-lives and a win for the organization. Fundamentally, rather than help people accommodate the always-on pressure, PTO strives to help people challenge its very existence, finding new ways to do the work that better meet their own needs and desires while simultaneously not hindering—and often improving—the work process. Individuals can work differently without penalty from their superiors and without that internal nagging feeling that they are letting others and themselves down, and the work process can be more efficient and effective. As one BCG partner summed it up, "The value of PTO is in fighting that assumption that work-life balance and effective case teams are mutually exclusive. Because they're not."

Embrace the Challenge

When George Martin first heard our results from the Consumer team and announced that he wanted to expand the experiment to more teams, I hesitated. We had not had time to analyze our results, let alone create a plan for moving forward. But I quickly came to recognize that the time was now. He was offering us a remarkable opportunity to put our research to the true test.

Four years after conducting the first PTO experiment and nearly a thousand teams later, I feel that I finally understand why PTO amounted to so much more than predictable time off for a group of hardworking consultants. PTO's rules of engagement unleash an ongoing process of learning and innovation that continually improves how individuals work in ways that benefit both their work-lives and their work. And it does so because the collective goal of personal time off and the structured dialogue—working in tandem—catalyze open dialogue, passion, and collective experimentation. That's the magic of PTO.

BCG's efforts to create change in its culture continue to be a work in progress, often hindered by the confusion that we caused as we muddled through, discovering what made PTO work as we went along. As I wrote this book, I often found myself looking forward to the day when BCGers could read how I had come to make sense of PTO and what would best propel it forward. I am hopeful that the book will help them gain a richer understanding of why they are doing what they are doing, and thus help them to do it even better. I am also hopeful that everyone else who reads this book will be able to start the process at the point where BCG is now and take it to the next level.

I have only just begun to implement PTO in other industries. However, after watching this process work its magic on BCG teams around the globe—and begin to change the culture of a firm where change was believed impossible—I am convinced that PTO is powerful enough to change most any team and, ultimately, organization. The next step is up to you—to take what we have learned at BCG and make PTO your own, adapting the core principles to best fit your world.

I hope you will embrace the challenge and start your own experiment, engaging with your team members around how you act and interact, aspiring to eliminate the bad intensity your team experiences, and seeking to improve both your team's work process and the work-life of everyone involved.

Good luck on your journey. Please keep me informed about your progress, so we can continue to learn together about how to make the workplace more productive, fulfilling, and humane.

APPENDIX

About the Research

For my academic colleagues and anyone else interested in what we actually did and what data we collected, this appendix shares our journey.

The research for this project spanned six years and went through four phases. My research associate, Jessica Porter, and I studied the Boston Consulting Group, first as ethnographers seeking to understand what people do all day and why (phase 1) and then as action researchers—running field experiments and seeking to create change (phase 2). When the experiments proved successful and BCG continued to run them on their own, we closely observed the first ten teams involved in this initiative (phase 3). And as their initiative has continued to expand, we have had the privilege to continue to study it (phase 4).[1]

I have also studied managers and professionals beyond BCG to understand the generalizability of the phenomenon observed (namely, the pressure to always be on) and its implications. I engaged in interviews as well as conducted several large surveys of managers and professionals from around the globe.

Phase 1—BCG Interviews and Observation

The research at BCG began in June 2005. A friend introduced me to George Martin, the managing partner of the Boston office. At the time, BCG Boston was struggling with particularly low employee satisfaction scores. George was intrigued by my offer to explore the firm's work culture, figuring he might come to better understand what was going on. I mentioned a desire to run experiments but asked for no commitment—until I spent some time at BCG, I didn't even know exactly what the focus of the experiment would be.

Initial Interviews

We interviewed members of the consulting staff in BCG's New York, Chicago, and Atlanta offices, as well as in the Boston office—thirty-eight people in total—for sixty to ninety minutes each. We asked about their background, their work experience before BCG, their travel patterns, and their sense of their career trajectory. We asked about how they spent their time. We asked them to recount the prior day in as much detail as they could recall from when they woke up until they went to bed.[2]

Two questions turned out to be particularly informative. We asked if they could make plans for a Wednesday night, and found that at every level they were not able to do so. A typical response was that any plans they made during the week came with the caveat, "I'll be there if I can." We also asked consultants if they would be interested in working 80 percent of the time for 80 percent of the pay, if they could do so with no stigma attached; the vast majority—younger and older, married and single, with young children and not, men and women—said they would be eager to make that trade.

Initial Observation

In addition to interviews, we also engaged in various kinds of observations. Before conducting our first experiment, we observed a series of BCG Boston office events, including several all-staff meetings, a one-day off-site retreat, and a meeting between partners, principals, and project leaders to discuss work-life balance. We also observed informal events such as Friday-afternoon drinks to celebrate promotions and an end-of-year holiday celebration. And we attended the firm's annual women's conference for the consulting staff in the Americas.

We also observed consultants at every level at work. To get a sense of a day in their lives, we shadowed people from when they arrived at work until they left—including traveling with them, riding in taxis, and going to their hotels. We spent a total of fifteen days shadowing a partner (5 days), a principal (9 days), and a project leader (1 day). We also spent 110 hours observing three strategy cases, observing team members at work individually, in dyads, and in larger team meetings.

As we observed their work-lives, we became increasingly aware of the importance of the proposal writing process in setting up the demands that teams face in any given case. We decided it would be ideal to see a case from its earliest days through its completion. We spent forty-two hours studying a team as they prepared a large cost-reduction proposal, only to see BCG lose the job. We spent another twenty-eight hours studying the creation of a second proposal on manufacturing operations improvement, the team again very excited about the opportunity; yet once again BCG did not win the work. After observing two teams go through an intense proposal-writing process, we decided we now better understood the core elements of the proposal writing process and, instead of trying to find a third team at the very beginning of the process, we chose to observe a project that the Boston office had just sold—a strategy case scheduled to last twelve weeks; we studied it from the official kickoff to the end of the project.

We were able to travel with this team to the client site and observe both the team at work as well as their interactions with the client—including client meetings. We observed this team in all sorts of meeting situations: scheduled meetings, impromptu gatherings, conferring at the airport, at the hotel, in the car to the client, at lunch, at dinner. Over the course of the twelve weeks, we spent thirty-four days on the road with the team, along with five full days and four half days observing them in the Boston office. For 20 percent of those days, we picked a particular person to shadow all day (they joked that we followed them everywhere except to the bathroom). On the other days, we sat in the team room and joined meetings and conversations. In addition, we collected all their internal e-mail exchanges and asked each team member to answer two questions every morning for eight weeks: (1) How many hours did you work yesterday? and (2) How many hours do you expect to work today? We discovered that 76 percent of the time this team misestimated their work hours, 37 percent of the days working 2 or more hours more than they had expected to at the start of the day.

We were beginning to form a rich picture of what it was like to work at BCG, but we were also well aware that we had ended up studying predominately people working on strategy case teams. To gain a more balanced perspective, we sought out an implementation case. (BCG's work is roughly half strategy and half implementation.)

The opportunity presented itself for us to observe a project involving a Boston client—an eight-week "delayering" case (helping the client reduce layers of management by restructuring and combining positions and departments). Again, we had access to the team at the client site as well as sitting in on client meetings. After four weeks the client abruptly decided to end the project, so our observation spanned only the first four weeks. During that time, we observed the team at the client site for a total of ten full and two half days; we also accompanied them to a case team dinner at one of Boston's fanciest restaurants. We interviewed the entire team, both before we started the observation and after the project ended.

Interviews with Top Performers Who Chose to Leave

BCG is an "up or out" firm, and some attrition is desirable. But the firm does not want to lose its top performers. Seeking to understand what motivated its top performers to leave, we had BCG identify the top performers who had voluntarily left the firm in the last few years. Of the twenty-seven people we randomly selected eleven to interview. We met them at their new offices, in their homes, and at coffee shops, interviewing them each for one to two hours. We asked about their experience at BCG, why they had left, and how their new jobs were similar to and different from their experience working at BCG.

Their answers were quite insightful: nine of the eleven interviewed cited work-life issues as a major motivation for leaving. Of the nine, five said work-life issues had triggered their thoughts about leaving the firm, but they would have eventually left anyway; the remaining four said work-life issues were not only the trigger for their leaving but had these issues not existed they would have stayed at the firm for the long term. Most surprising, all those interviewed reported that their new jobs were intense, and the majority still had to travel. The difference was the greater degree of control they perceived over their new schedules—both in terms of hours and travel.

We also interviewed top performers who were still at BCG—four chosen randomly from a list of eight people BCG gave us. Strikingly, all four reported that they were planning to leave within the next two years, because of work-life issues.

Phase 2—The HBS-Facilitated Experiments

It became clear to us that although the work was very demanding, that was not the core problem for the top performers: it was the unpredictability of the demands. People were leaving because they couldn't plan their lives. Even the alternative of 80 percent or 60 percent, "part-time" work, was failing because people couldn't get their time off *predictably*. Moreover, we came to realize that much of this unpredictability was created internal to the organization: it was not the client driving the unpredictability but the BCGers—often unintentionally and unknowingly—themselves.

And so we proposed an experiment. Each member of a team would attempt to work 80 percent—with a scheduled day off each week. BCGers at every level of the hierarchy had expressed interest in working 80 percent of the time for 80 percent of the pay, if they could do so with no stigma attached. Our question was whether it was possible for people to work 80 percent—taking a predictable day off each week—without undermining the work.

Experiment 1: A Predictable Day Off a Week

While leaders of the Boston office were not optimistic that the experiment would succeed, there was enough interest that George Martin sanctioned funds to increase a team of four people to five so that everyone could cut back to work 80 percent (but still be paid 100 percent). We had searched high and low to find this team, and finally Rachel Levine, a partner at the time and our internal liaison at BCG, felt compelled to let us experiment with one of her cases because—as she tells it—she felt responsible for us and we had failed to find another team. In the end, the client had the same number of FTEs (full-time equivalents) from BCG—five consultants working at 80 percent rather than four working at 100 percent. The BCG principal on this project did not reduce his hours because he was allocated to spend only 50 percent of his time on this project.

We conducted this experiment on a local case with a new client with whom BCG had great interest in building a long-term relationship—attracting local work was a high-priority initiative of the Boston office because, as it meant no travel to the client site for the consulting team, it was particularly appealing work. At the time we began the experiment the case had been ongoing for eight months; it was viewed on the high end in terms of how demanding it was, both because of the nature of the work as well as the team's desire to do a particularly good job. Rachel Levine, the executing partner on the case, confessed to much anxiety about breaking the news to her key client contact that her team was going to run an experiment to see if everyone could work 80 percent. She explained to the client: "BCG teams work incredibly hard and we are doing this to help us learn if there are better ways to manage our work so that our consultants have better balance and we can still deliver as good or better product to you, our client." She also promised that the experiment would be halted immediately if there was the slightest concern about the quality of BCG's work and gave the client her cell phone number with instructions to call anytime.

Whereas on a typical team each person would be responsible for 100 percent of his or her own module, this was not feasible for this team for two reasons. First, not all modules could simply be done in 80 percent of the time. And second, as part of the experiment, there was an intentional division of work that built in overlaps to ensure team members' willingness and ability to cover for each other on each other's day off. For instance, one consultant was tasked with the transition of the sales operation and another with the transition of HR. The transition of the sales operation was believed to be a 100 percent job. One consultant was assigned 70 percent of this job while the second consultant was assigned 30 percent. The HR transition was considered 60 percent in total and was split 10 percent to the first consultant (who simultaneously was assigned 70 percent of the sales operation transition) and 50 percent to the second (who was assigned 30 percent of the sales operation transition). While this may seem confusing, the intent was simple—to ensure that people each had primary responsibility for some work and secondary responsibility for other people's work. This was a new concept at BCG. The team came to talk about it as the "captain" and the "second in command."

We interviewed each of the five team members as well as the principal and the executing partner for sixty to ninety minutes each both before and after the experiment. We also interviewed each of the five consultants working 80 percent weekly, for twenty minutes to one hour, after their scheduled day off—whether they took it or not.

We were present for fifty-three of the fifty-six days that the team was at the client site (four days a week for fourteen weeks). We had the team fill out daily and weekly surveys and had access to the monthly survey data that BCG collected for all its teams, which enabled us to compare the experiment team to all other Boston office teams during the same period along four dimensions: delivering client impact, executing efficiently/effectively, progress on development goals, and acceptable work-life balance.

FIGURE A-1

Monthly trends

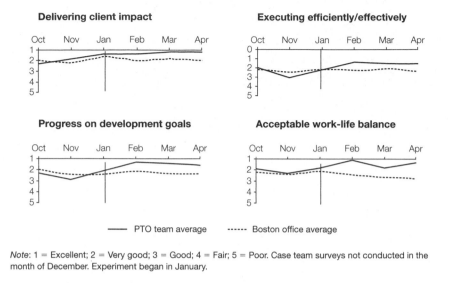

Note: 1 = Excellent; 2 = Very good; 3 = Good; 4 = Fair; 5 = Poor. Case team surveys not conducted in the month of December. Experiment began in January.

During the fourteen weeks of experimenting, it turned out that this team outscored the Boston average for all teams on all four dimensions (see figure A-1). It also turned out that 68 percent of the days off were taken as scheduled. Only 10 percent of days off were canceled outright; another 22 percent were rescheduled to accommodate the work. The partner reported that she was surprised by how well the team had done. She had guessed they would have to cancel or reschedule 60 or 70 percent of their days off. And though we were disappointed by the less than 100 percent success, from BCG's perspective the experiment had been a big success.

To make this possible, team members established rituals to hand-off work before their day off as well as hand-back work when someone returned. The team also began to share information across the whole team more frequently and openly than they had before. For instance, they developed a blog that collected nightly updates on their work that all the team members posted; originally conceived as a way to update coverage partners, the blog posts turned out to be valuable to other members of the team as well. Sharing the details of work in this way led to deeper understanding about what the others were doing, which in turn increased understanding and investment in the project as a whole among the entire group, including the project leader, principal, and partner.

We also interviewed the five key client contacts, all of whom reported that the team's output continued to be as good or better after the experiment began. Given that the team had worked for the client for eight months prior to the experiment, the client had a good point of comparison of before versus during the experiment.

Experiment 2: A Predictable Night Off a Week[3]

Having found such positive results with the day off a week experiment, there was great interest to explore whether it was possible to have a predictable time off goal that was doable for the full-time workforce, which would open up the possibility of a much broader application of the experiment. It took six months to find a team. The experiment was ultimately conducted with the *Consumer* team, which we describe in detail in chapter 1. We spent twenty-nine weeks observing this team, traveling with them on three occasions and spending a total of seven days observing them outside the Boston office and an additional ten days observing them in the Boston office (usually on Fridays). When we were not there in person, we listened in by phone to their weekly check-in meetings—eighteen times. It was typical of other participants as well to join by phone since most of the time one or more of them was not co-located at the time of the meeting. We interviewed each team member for sixty to ninety minutes before and after the experiment, and did brief interviews (fifteen to sixty minutes) with each team member every two weeks, either in person or by phone. In addition, we conducted weekly debrief surveys following their scheduled nights off to track whether they took, canceled, or rescheduled the night off; how much support they felt from their teammates; and whether any of their work shifted to other times as a result of the night off.

Taking a predictable night off a week turned out to be both feasible and highly advantageous. The results for the work process as well as work-life were positive and are documented in chapters 1 and 2.

Phase 3—The First Ten BCG-Facilitated Teams[4]

After the success of these experiments—particularly the predictable-night-off one—the Boston office embarked on an initiative to expand the night-off experiment to more teams. We stayed involved to help oversee the process and capture the learnings. Up to this point, our focus had been on whether change was possible; we now shifted to studying what making such change would entail.

We were involved in several months of meetings that George Martin and Rachel Levine held to create a plan for moving forward. We helped design the all-day, all-office staff meeting at which they shared the results from the Consumer team and launched this new phase of PTO experiments.

After this all-day meeting, teams were invited to volunteer to take part in the next phase. Table A-1 shows the characteristics of the first ten teams that signed up. They represented a nice mix of travel and local, strategy and implementation, and all-Boston and cross-staffed teams. They came from five clients, enabling us to observe both different client relationships across different industries but also multiple teams from the same client over time, addressing different issues at the client but often with the same client contacts. The mix of teams was good fortune. Some partners volunteered because they were intrigued by what they'd heard about our original experiments. Others volunteered because they had been struggling with unpredictability and/or high travel demands and thought being involved might help their teams (and the partners' upward feedback scores). Some of the original ten teams signed up because they were already convinced about the experiment's potential, having participated in either one of our original experiments or one of the very earliest BCG-facilitated experiments.

To explore how PTO was enacted on these ten teams, Melissa Mazmanian, at the time a graduate student at Sloan School at MIT in organization studies, joined me and Jessica to help with a set of interviews with all the people who were involved. Because we had been involved in the conceptualization of the initiative, we wanted to bring in someone more removed from it in terms of the questions asked, the ways she listened to the answers, and how she was perceived by those with whom she was speaking. Melissa introduced herself as a graduate student from MIT (thus immediately disconnecting her from us, the "Harvard Business School research team") who had been brought onto the team to provide a more neutral point of view of the experiment. She asked people to explain their experiences and to feel free to be critical about what had worked and what had not, making clear she was not personally or professionally invested in the results.

A total of fifty-two individuals were staffed on these ten teams, eight of whom were on multiple of the ten teams. Of those eight, four were partners who signed on to be a PTO team again after the conclusion of the first one. Two of these partners did so because after their first experience with the initiative, they were convinced that the PTO process had value; the other two had a more mixed experience their first time around but wanted to try it again. The remaining four people who were on multiple teams comprised three consultants and one associate. We interviewed each participant on these ten teams for thirty to ninety minutes. We did not repeat the interviews with partners who participated in multiple teams but chose instead to interview them one time about their multiple PTO projects. The two consultants who were involved on multiple teams were interviewed twice, one for each case, while the other two individuals who were involved in PTO on two cases were interviewed only once. We also attended five of the ten kickoff meetings for these ten teams.

The PTO Rollout Team helped facilitate these ten teams. At the time, the Rollout Team consisted of George Martin, Paul Schwartz, Rachel

TABLE A-1

The first ten PTO teams

Team	Type of project	Size of team	Travel/local	# of offices	Length of experiment	Length of case	Industry of client
Healthcare Lean I	Strategy	2 partners, 1 principal, 1 project leader, 3 consultants, 1 associate	Travel	2 offices (Boston and DC)	7 weeks	12 weeks	Pharma
Healthcare Lean II	Implementation	2 partners, 1 principal, 3 consultants	Travel	2 offices (Boston and DC)	16 weeks	16 weeks	Pharma
Healthcare HR	Implementation	2 partners, 1 project leader, 2 consultants, 1 associate	Travel	All Boston (except 1 partner)	14 weeks	14 weeks	Pharma
Insurance	Implementation	1 partner, 1 principal, 1 consultant (acting as project leader), 1 associate	Travel for some, local for some	2 offices (Boston and New York)	14 weeks	16 weeks	Financial services
Hospital	Implementation	2 partners, 2 project leaders, 2 consultants, 2 associates	Travel	2 offices (Boston and Dallas)	16 weeks	16 weeks	Healthcare
Retail	Strategy	1 partner, 1 principal, 1 project leader, 2 consultants, 2 associates	Travel for some, local for some	3 offices (Boston, DC, Philadelphia)	9 weeks	12 weeks	Retail

Project	Staffing	Type	Travel/Local	Location	Duration	Duration	IT
Tech Operations A ("Tech")	2 partners, 1 project leader, 2 consultants, 1 associate	Strategy	Travel	All Boston (except 1 partner)	10 weeks	10 weeks	IT systems
Tech Operations B	2 partners, 1 principal, 2 consultants, 1 associate	Strategy	Travel	All Boston (except 1 partner)	8 weeks	8 weeks	IT systems
Tech Efficiency	2 partners, 1 project leader, 1 consultant, 1 associate	Strategy	Local	All Boston (except 1 partner)	7 weeks	7 weeks	IT systems
Tech Global	2 partners, 1 principal, 1 project leader, 2 consultants, 2 associates	Implementation	Travel	4 offices (Boston, Chicago, DC, New York)	8 weeks	12 weeks	IT systems

Levine, and two top-performing consultants who had been pulled from client facing work to help launch the initiative, along with my Research Associate, Jessica Porter, and myself as advisers. The team met weekly with Rachel, who played the role of "executing partner." These weekly meetings lasted 1.5 to 2 hours and occurred without the senior partners—George and Paul—who further held monthly leadership team meetings of 1 to 1.5 hours to get updates. We attended all of these meetings—both to observe them but also to share our knowledge.

During this period, we attended all twenty-four weekly PTO Rollout Team meetings, five leadership meetings, and several other meetings that included partners from other offices—a half day spent with the Chicago partners and a half-hour presentation to the firm's Worldwide Officer Group.

Another way we collected data during this phase was through surveys. With our input, BCG conducted a baseline survey before the initiative's all-staff, all-day kickoff. We also conducted our own monthly surveys of the Boston office so we could compare teams that were involved in PTO with those that were not, asking questions about perceived client value, job satisfaction, work-life balance, and comfort raising work and personal issues. We also surveyed PTO team members on a weekly basis to get more in-depth data on their experiences—our questions probed about their time-off goals and whether they had rescheduled or canceled their night off or had done any work on their nights off. They were further asked to assess how the team was doing in terms of working together to support each other and comfort raising issues. To corroborate this information, we asked the facilitators to fill out weekly updates on each team, evaluating progress regarding talking openly and supporting the time off.[5]

Phase 4—Beyond the Ten Teams—Toward a Global Initiative

For the remainder of the first year, we continued to attend weekly case team meetings of the PTO Rollout Team, the monthly leadership meetings, and to administer monthly surveys to the entire Boston office. At the end of the first year, we also conducted a Boston office survey to compare with our baseline survey from the previous year.

We have subsequently conducted an annual survey at the conclusion of years 2 and 3. The New York/New Jersey offices were included in the survey starting at the end of year 2, and we further added the Washington, DC/Philadelphia office in year 3.

We use the year 3 survey data to analyze teams that *embrace, partially engage* ("partial"), or *dismiss* PTO, (as reported in full in chapter 2 and mentioned in the introduction and chapter 12). We created those three categories by categorizing people as committed to a rule as long as there was some indication that they were engaged (3 or above on a 7-point scale) in the practices associated with the rule. Thirty-seven percent were engaging in both rules ("embrace"); 49 percent were engaging in one of the two rules ("partial"). The remaining 14 percent were not engaging—some because they don't employ the rules of engagement at all (11 percent "reject" PTO), and others because they say they are participating but demonstrate little commitment to make it work (3 percent participate "in name only"). We further explored the breakdown within dismiss (14 percent) and found no significant differences between the 11 percent who reject PTO outright and the 3 percent who participate in PTO in name only, and therefore present only the data from the aggregated category of dismiss PTO, along with partial PTO and embrace PTO.

We further looked at how these categories break down for each measure by level. Of particular note is the difference between principals and project leaders on embrace and dismiss on some of our key outcome measures—especially that the embrace group is much more likely to see themselves at BCG for the long term (73 percent versus 25 percent) as reported in chapter 9.

We had planned to further compare our annual surveys to track changes over time. However, as we were finishing this book, BCG gave us access to results from their HR survey (ISR) conducted by an external vendor, Towers Watson, which enabled us to get a pure premeasure of consultants' experiences working at BCG before we began any experiments and also a way to compare BCG Boston with other BCG offices around the world. This proved invaluable to rule out the alternative hypotheses that the changes we were observing over time were an artifact of larger organizational, industry, or economic changes. We therefore use BCG's ISR data for the longitudinal comparisons presented in chapter 6, whenever measures exist. We continue to use data from our survey to explore work process measures, as the ISR has no measures of work process but rather focuses only on the experience of doing the work.

Beyond the surveys, in year 3 we engaged in another intense data collection effort, this time with the added issue that one of the team's members was trying to work part-time. For a twelve-week case, we co-facilitated a team with a BCG facilitator, and again conducted thirty- to ninety-minute interviews with each of the seven team members before and after the case. We also interviewed four of them on a weekly basis for fifteen to thirty minutes to debrief them about their nights off, and spent twenty to thirty minutes every other week with the team's principal. We spent one day on site with the team, six days in the New York office for in-person meetings and observations, and an additional twelve hours attending meetings by phone (where other team members were attending by phone as well).

Regarding the larger organization expansion of the PTO process, we have continued to attend the weekly PTO Rollout Team meetings, as well as the increasingly frequent gathering of facilitators. By the end of year 3, the PTO Rollout Team consisted of nineteen facilitators from around the globe who would convene in Boston every three to four months, primarily to learn how to best be facilitators, to continually refine what PTO should look like, and to contribute to the larger expansion of PTO around the globe.

Over the past three years we have observed, in total:

- 141 weekly PTO Rollout Team meetings (out of a total 148 weekly meetings that occurred)

- All 15 leadership meetings of the PTO Rollout Team that have occurred

- 5 day-long gatherings of the worldwide facilitators

We have been in contact with fifty-four of the fifty-five facilitators who have been a part of this initiative at this point—most having been involved as part of a three- to six-month rotation.

Beyond BCG

In addition to our research at BCG, I conducted interviews with professionals in various client-service industries—law, accounting, consulting, public relations, investment banking, and hedge fund management—and conducted surveys of professionals and managers from around the globe. There were twenty-one one- to two-hour interviews conducted after our phase 1 research at BCG and before we started to experiment. The unpredictable nature of work had emerged as an important theme at BCG, and the purpose of those interviews was to better understand how unpredictability played out in other professions—both within the workday and around the boundary of when one was working.

I conducted an additional forty-eight interviews lasting one to two hours during phase 4 of our research, to better understand whether and how PTO might be applied in other settings.

In the academic arena, I taught the Harvard Business School case *George Martin at BCG* to over one thousand students in Executive Education at HBS, probing about the students' own experiences as part of the classroom discussion, and following up with many of them outside of class.

We also have survey responses from managers and professionals who were alumni of a set of HBS executive education programs over the past thirteen years. We wanted to survey managers across a range of levels, so we included three of HBS's comprehensive leadership programs at junior, mid, and senior levels in organizations. We also included professionals involved in a leading professional service firm course. In total, we sent out surveys to 2,916 people and received 1,606 responses—an overall response rate of 59 percent. The breakdown among the leadership programs is as follows:

- 14 percent of the total sample were professionals involved in leading professional service firms (LPSF) (response rate = 84 percent).

- 27 percent of the total sample had attended a leadership program for junior level managers (PLD) (response rate = 78 percent).

- 22 percent of the total sample had attended a leadership program for mid-level managers (GMP) (response rate = 60 percent).

- 37 percent of the total sample had attended a leadership program for senior managers (AMP) (response rate = 45 percent).

As this book went to press, I had begun to launch PTO initiatives in new organizations and different industries. I hope you will join me in this process and together we can continue the quest to create teams and organizations where work is conducted in ways that best suits individuals' needs without ever undermining—and ideally improving—the work process itself. As you adapt PTO to your own setting, please keep me abreast of what you discover.

GLOSSARY:
CONSULTING TERMINOLOGY

Associate. Associates at the Boston Consulting Group are generally hired directly after finishing their undergraduate degrees at top colleges and universities. They do analysis, modeling, interviews, and client support. After two to three years at the firm, associates typically leave to explore other opportunities or go to graduate school. BCG often sponsors associates who agree to return to the firm for a set number of years after finishing their graduate degrees.

Billing. BCG bills clients by the week. BCG and the client negotiate the price and timeline of the project as well as the composition of the team and their deliverables.

Boston Consulting Group (BCG). BCG was founded in 1963 and is considered to be one of the three most elite management consulting firms in the world. The firm is made up of 71 offices in 40 countries with approximately 5,000 members of the consulting staff.

Business services team (BST). About one-third of BCG employees compose the Business Service Team. The BST is not directly involved in client-service work, administering the firm's internal processes, including staffing, human resources, recruiting, finance, and administrative support.

Career development committee (CDC). Composed of partners, principals, and members of the Business Service Team, the CDC is tasked with developing the firm's talent. Each associate and consultant is assigned a member of the CDC, known as his or her CDC representative, who serves as a mentor to help guide that person through the annual review and promotion process. CDC reps gather reviews and feedback on their mentees and meet with them yearly to discuss reviews and promotion timing. Some CDC reps take a larger role, checking in more often and advising on the types of projects their mentee should look for. As a group, the CDC meets periodically to provide input into bonuses and the timing of specific promotions.

Career path. The trajectory is "up or out" at each stage of the hierarchy. After approximately two years, consultants are promoted to project leader or asked to leave the firm. After approximately two years as a project leader, consultants are promoted to principal or asked to leave the firm. Typically, principals stay in that position for two-and-a-half to four years before being promoted to partner or being asked to leave. The partner level is divided between partner and senior partner. After seven to nine years, partners are evaluated, and only the most success-ful are promoted to senior partner, and the others must leave the firm. (See figure G-1.)

Case. BCG's name for a client engagement or most any project under-taken as a team is a case. A case's length of time, team membership, and deliverables are all determined in advance, but may be renegotiated once the work begins.

Case assignment. Consultants are assigned to work on a particular case. However, they will often stay with the same client for multiple cases. Partners (and sometimes principals) tend to stay involved for the

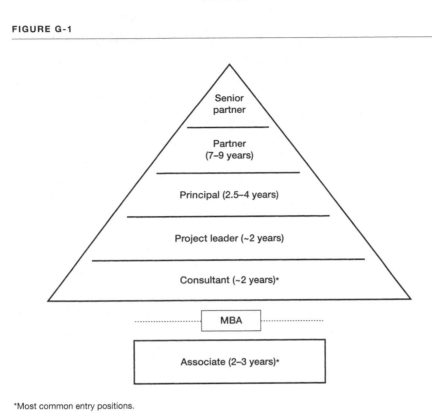

*Most common entry positions.

duration of the client relationship. Associates and consultants may stay on for more than one case but rarely for more than six to nine months, because of the firm's goal of exposing junior people to a multitude of learning and development opportunities.

Case duration. BCG cases tend to take twelve to sixteen weeks to complete, though some are much shorter or longer. Due diligence cases, for instance, known for their intensity, run for just two to four weeks. An implementation case usually takes between six and twelve months to complete.

Case team. Consultants generally work in teams of three to five people, led by a project leader and/or principal reporting to one or more executing partners. Most cases also have one or more senior partners involved. At any given time, several case teams might be working for the same client, often led by the same partner(s).

CEO selection. BCG's CEO is chosen by the partners in the firm every three years. Hans-Paul Bürkner became CEO in 2003 and was re-elected in 2006 and 2009.

Client. BCG's clients include *Fortune* 500 companies, as well as midsize businesses, nonprofit organizations, and government agencies seeking help in developing and/or refining strategies, implementing strategic changes, and/or designing and implementing other improvement programs.

Client relationships. BCG's business model relies on cultivating long-term relationships with clients, ideally comprising a sequence of cases helping the client across a variety of areas. These relationships are usually "owned" by one or more partners, who are involved in overseeing the work for "their" clients.

Consultant. Consultants do the core analysis, modeling, interviews, and client support on cases. As consultants become more senior, they are often given management responsibility for pieces of the work. BCG recruits the vast majority of its consultants from top business schools, but also recruits a handful of new PhD and MD graduates each year. The standard stint is two years; consultants not promoted within twenty-seven to thirty months are asked to leave. More consultants join the firm each year than any other position.

Consulting staff. All members of the firm who are client-facing—associates, consultants, project leaders, principals, and partners. The term *consultant* is also used in some contexts to refer to all members of the consulting staff, not just those holding the position of consultant.

Cross-office staffing. Many BCG case teams are staffed with consulting staff from offices in other cities. Often this is done for strategic reasons to better serve the client, such as putting a Boston-based consultant who is trained as a doctor on a healthcare case that the New York office is working on. Likewise, when teams are led by partners from different offices, the team is often staffed with consultants from each of those offices. Or a team might be cross-staffed because an office is oversold and does not have enough staff available and therefore must recruit staff from other BCG offices to fill a team.

Deck. The PowerPoint slides that pull together the consultants' analyses and research into a central location, often with sophisticated graphics and charts. Decks are presented to clients as interim deliverables and clients receive a final deck at the end of the engagement summarizing the team's findings and recommendations.

Due diligence case. BCG is sometimes hired to evaluate potential acquisition targets for their clients, which they refer to as a due diligence case. These cases are often quite intense with a short duration, between two and four weeks.

Executing partner. The partner with the primary responsibility for guiding the team and managing the senior clients for a given project. The executing partner is usually a partner, but may also be a senior partner.

Executive committee (EC). The firm's governing body, along with the CEO. Composed of leaders from around the world, including regional chairs, heads of the practice areas, the head of the "People Team," and the CFO, the EC functions similarly to a board of directors, setting the agenda for the firm, making decisions about global and regional initiatives, and making recommendations for issues the partner group needs to address. Certain roles represented on the executive committee are chosen by the CEO, while others are elected by the partnership.

Follow-on work. Engagement that evolves directly out of existing work. For instance, a company might hire BCG to help it develop an acquisition strategy. Once that strategy is developed, there's a high likelihood that BCG would then be hired to help identify potential acquisition targets, and so on. Also, by spending months working with a client, BCGers often detect additional problems and propose to the client additional ways BCG might be involved, which results in further cases.

Governing structure. BCG is governed by both geographic and practice area leadership, who sit on the executive committee and report to the CEO.

Implementation cases. A case that helps the client put something into action—whether an isolated new process or a large-scale change effort. Often what is being implemented is a strategy that BCGers created with the client in an earlier (most likely strategy) case. Implementation cases tend to involve broad client interaction and a significant amount of travel.

Lateral hires. Individuals without previous experience at BCG as either a consultant or associate who are hired into the firm directly as project leaders, principals, or partners.

Magic time. While consulting staff are likely to be allocated to a specific case(s) for 100 percent of their working time, BCG further expects them to help with additional firm-related activities such as recruiting, training, and writing proposals. Since they are already fully staffed to casework, BCGers have come to describe, with some irony, this extra work as taking place in "*magic time*"—a period that exists beyond the commitment to their primary case assignment(s).

Management consulting. An industry based on helping other companies improve their performance. Consultancies vary in both breadth and depth, ranging from very small boutique firms, which are highly specialized according to geography or expertise, to global firms, which serve virtually every industry in every geographical market. With approximately 5,000 members of the consulting staff in 71 offices around the world, BCG is a global player typically ranked among the world's top three management consulting firms.

Module. Cases are divided up to enable associates and consultants to have discrete pieces of work for which only they are responsible. The principal or project leader is usually responsible for integrating the results from these modules into a comprehensive deliverable (or deck) for the client.

Northeast Award. Each year, BCG recognizes those partners who excel both commercially and in their mentorship of teams, based on the amount of revenue they generate and their upward feedback scores. Those partners who perform at the top on both dimensions receive the Northeast Award, a prestigious honor that goes to approximately 10 to 12 percent of partners each year.

Office administrator (OA). Each BCG office has a managing partner responsible for leading that office's partner group and representing the office regionally. The OA is chosen by the regional head with input from all of the partners in the office.

Partner. Partners and senior partners (see "Career path"). Most BCG partners come from within the firm, though lateral hires into the partner ranks do occur, particularly at times when the firm is trying to grow quickly to meet the demand for its services. All partners are equity partners, with equal voting rights. Each partner takes responsibility for client relationships—nurturing existing relationships and cultivating new ones. Partners also oversee the case team, providing guidance and input on the team's work. Partners tend to work together in teams, with one or more designated as the *executing partner* tasked to work more closely with both the team and the clients than the other partners involved.

People team. An oversight body made up of senior partners who guide how the firm recruits, develops, and retains its consulting staff. The head of the People Team sits on the EC.

Post-merger integration (PMI). Cases assisting with mergers or acquisitions in which there are a number of systems that need to be integrated between the various companies involved. PMIs tend to be very intense cases because there are so many levels of coordination; they typically require large teams to support the integration.

Practice area. BCG encourages senior talent to develop expertise in particular industries—healthcare, financial institutions, consumer, industrial goods, energy, insurance, public sector, technology, and media and telecommunications, as well as specific functions, such as corporate development, organization, marketing and sales, operations, global advantage, information technology, and strategy. Each of these areas is considered a *practice area*.

Principal. The position in the BCG hierarchy that follows project leader and precedes partner. Principals take a significant leadership role on the team. Most teams have either a project leader or principal, but when both are on the same team, the principal is in charge. The principal holds the responsibility of integrating the various modules into the final client deliverables. At the principal level, individuals begin to have increasing responsibility outside of their individual cases, as well. They are expected to help with writing proposals and selling work. Most principals are promoted from within but some are hired laterally. Principals who want to become partner try to align themselves with a group of partners who will be able to sponsor them when the decision time comes, generally after two and a half to four years in the position of principal.

Program management office (PMO). The people assigned to actively manage timelines, goals, communication, metrics, and whatever other processes are necessary for the integration of the work on particularly complex projects.

Project leader. The person assigned to a case team to supervise the team members and maintain relationships with the client day to day, while keeping in close contact with the partners involved in the case. The project leader manages individual consultants as they complete their deliverables, overseeing their content through frequent iterations. The project leader is also responsible for integrating the various modules into the final client presentation. Most project leaders are promoted from within, though a small percentage are also hired from industry or other management consulting firms. After two years in the job, project leaders are considered for promotion to principal.

Proposal process. New cases are generated in a number of ways. Sometimes it is a very formal process, in which the firm receives an RFP (request for proposal) and assigns a partner and/or principal to develop a pitch outlining how they would approach the project, including project duration, size of team, and total cost. In circumstances like this, BCG is often competing with several other firms. Other projects are sold much less formally. A current or former client, for example, might approach a partner about an issue, and the partner will pull together a proposal to deal with it, usually with the help of a principal or project leader. Still other projects evolve directly out of existing work. For instance, a company might hire BCG to help them develop a sales force effectiveness strategy. Once that strategy is developed, there's a high likelihood that BCG would then be hired to help implement it.

Red zone report. A document that several BCG offices use to keep track of consultants' hours and flag individuals and teams working in the red zone—more than sixty-five hours per week for several consecutive weeks. Being in the red zone triggers inquiry by the office leaders into what is going on in the case and what needs to change to get the hours under control.

Region/regional chairs. BCG is broken into three regions: the Americas, EMEA (Europe, Middle East, and Africa), and Asia Pacific. Each region has a regional chair, usually a successful partner who is chosen by the CEO to lead that region. Regional chairs sit on the EC and also convene regular meetings of office administrators (OAs) and practice area leaders within their regions.

Regrettable losses. High performers who leave the firm. Consulting firms expect some voluntary attrition, but they have a goal of retaining the high performers.

Reviews. The consulting staff undergoes frequent reviews, generally at least four a year. Reviews are held at the end of each case and every three months on long cases. Reviews for associates and consultants are generally written by the project leader or principal with input from the partner. Project leaders and principals are reviewed by the executing partner, sometimes with input from the senior partner(s). The review process is standardized. All BCG offices worldwide use the same forms and categories for reviewing the consulting staff.

Scope. The parameters of the project—length, team composition, and deliverables—are set at the proposal stage. It's not uncommon for the scope to grow as the project progresses because of client requests, challenges with the work, or a desire to impress the client. Consultants sometimes refer to a case as having *scope creep* to indicate that they believe the scope has grown to the point of becoming problematic for the current team to deliver the promised deliverables in the set time.

Senior partner. Senior partners are charged with supervising multiple cases often overseeing broader client relationships and taking on larger practice area and other internal responsibilities. Promotion to senior partner does not impact compensation or guarantee job security.

Slides. PowerPoint slides are the preferred method among BCG consultants for presenting analyses and findings, both internally and to clients (see "Deck").

Staffing. The criterion for assigning staff to projects at BCG is balancing the needs of the particular case with those of the firm, which includes developing talent and accommodating the personal preferences of the people themselves.

Staffing coordinator. Every BCG office has at least one person who is in charge of staffing case teams. The staffing coordinator works to meet the needs of the office, the firm, the case as well as the individuals. A staffing coordinator can suddenly become quite popular (or unpopular) in the eyes of partners eager to get the best consultants assigned to their teams.

Steering committee. The key client contacts—the main stakeholders that BCG needs to report to and engage within a given case—assembled into a group. The case is then often designed around a timeline of steering committee meetings to discuss progress and issues. These meetings tend to be one of the main drivers of a case team's work, since each steering committee meeting usually requires its own deck. The final presentation is also usually made to the steering committee and possibly additional stakeholders.

Strategy cases. The original type of case that BCG launched its business to handle in 1963. Strategy cases remain a central focus. Some might be very specific, such as designing a strategy for how a client might offshore a certain department; others are very broad, like generating a strategy for increasing shareholder return. Consultants often covet strategy cases for the intellectual challenge. These cases also tend to require less travel to the client site. However, due to the amount of uncertainty involved in coming up with the answer, the work schedules can be particularly unpredictable.

Team room. In most consulting projects, the client provides a workspace for the consultants, usually a small windowless conference room or vacant office(s).

Tier 1. Internal projects in which consultants are convened to utilize their expertise on projects to help improve BCG itself—rather than advising a client. Sometimes these in-house projects are knowledge-based, such as gaining a better understanding of the future of telecommunications to help BCG teams better serve their clients. Others are designed more to improve BCG's internal systems, such as rethinking the firm's marketing strategy or reviewing training programs. Tier 1s are funded by the CEO, practice area, or region that engages them.

Training. BCG has an elaborate set of training programs. On entry, newcomers—whether associate, consultant, or lateral senior hire—undergo multiple trainings at the office level. There are also regional trainings for those at promotion points to project leader and principal, as well as global trainings for experienced consultants, project leaders, principals, and new partners. Additionally, many offices hold periodic officewide trainings to help staff develop specific skills.

"Up-or-out" system. If an individual is not promoted to the next level within a predefined range of time, they are counseled out of the firm. (See "Career path.")

Upward feedback. Junior team members are encouraged to provide formal reports to team leaders after each case. Partners receive this *upward feedback* from associates, consultants, and the project leader and/or principal. Project leaders and principals receive feedback from associates and consultants on their teams. The review process is standardized such that each BCG office uses the same forms and review categories. The firm also uses upward feedback results for determining certain annual awards, compensation, and promotion recommendations.

World wide officer meeting (WWOM). Twice each year, BCG partners from the firm's offices around the world attend a weeklong retreat called the WWOM. The meeting consists of plenary sessions and breakout groups designed to help partners share knowledge and expertise with each other, network, and vote on measures impacting the firm, including new candidates for partner.

NOTES

Introduction

1. This quote is from Melissa Mazmanian, Wanda Orlikowski, and JoAnne Yates, "The Autonomy Paradox: The Implications of Wireless Email Devices for Knowledge Professionals," MIT Sloan working paper no. 4884-11, June 2011.

2. Amazon lists more than thirteen thousand books in the category of "business self-help." Their message, for the most part, is about how by making such changes as organizing oneself better, managing e-mail better, and managing one's boss better, one can be more efficient and in turn do more in less time, and as a result—hopefully—have time for a richer fuller life outside work. Some authors take a specialized approach, with a focus on one particular lever for increasing productivity, while others take the broader view, with recommendations for almost a complete personal transformation.

David Allen, for instance, helps people establish a system for organizing their workspaces, their to-do lists, and their e-mails. Allen argues that in order to be truly productive and creative, one must be relaxed, and he offers actionable steps for removing real and figurative clutter in order to achieve this relaxed state (David Allen, *Getting Things Done: The Art of Stress-Free Productivity* [New York: Viking Penguin, 2001]).

Other authors aim to help readers focus and prioritize by understanding the *Pareto Principle*—the theory that in almost any arena 80 percent of outcome comes from 20 percent of the work. By understanding 80/20, these authors propose, people can be more productive at work and have more time for leisure by eliminating the work that is low value. Richard Koch is one author who urges personal application of 80/20 to maximize personal productivity in *The 80/20 Principle: The Secret to Achieving More with Less* (New York: Doubleday, 1998, 2008) and *Living the 80/20 Way: Work Less, Worry Less, Succeed More, Enjoy More* (Boston: Nicholas Brealey Publishing, 2004). In *The 4-Hour Workweek: Escape 9–5, Live Anywhere and Join the New Rich* (New York: Crown Publishing, 2007), Tim Ferriss takes this even further, with a strategy for readers to increase their productivity through 80/20 and other techniques, with a goal of negotiating more flexible arrangements that allow individuals to work remotely and, ultimately, less. Ferriss argues that by freeing oneself from conventions around where, when, and how they work, people can eliminate a substantial amount of waste from their jobs in exchange for more autonomy and physical and temporal freedom.

Other books focus on better understanding how the brain works in order for the individual to work more productively. David Rock (*Your Brain at Work: Strategies for*

Overcoming Distraction, Regaining Focus, and Working Smarter All Day Long [New York: Harper Collins, 2009]) and John Medina (*Brain Rules: 12 Principles for Surviving and Thriving at Work, Home, and School* [Seattle: Pear Press, 2008]) both use research in neurology to demonstrate that people are more effective when they focus on one task at a time. This subgenre offers readers ways to focus more, pay attention and avoid distraction.

There are others who take a more holistic approach to personal effectiveness, such as Stephen R. Covey's classic *The 7 Habits of Highly Effective People: Powerful Lessons in Personal Change* (1989; New York: Free Press, 2004) or, more recently, Tony Schwartz's *The Way We're Working Isn't Working: The Four Forgotten Needs That Energize Great Performance* (New York: Free Press, 2010). These books aim to help people become more effective in all spheres of their lives by rethinking fundamentally how they live and act day to day, at home and at work. Both Covey and Schwartz offer exercises to help people become more reflective, live in alignment with their values, and ultimately care for themselves physically, emotionally, and spiritually in order to reach their full potential personally and professionally.

There is also a quickly growing field that focuses on helping people better manage their technological connectivity. Noelle Chesley finds that communications technology results in negative "spillover" between work and family—namely that increasing use of cell phones and pagers causes family dissatisfaction as work spills into family time (Noelle Chesley, "Blurring Boundaries? Linking Technology Use, Spillover, Individual Distress, and Family Satisfaction," *Journal of Marriage and Family* 67 [December 2005]: 1237–1248). This blurring has only increased with the adoption of BlackBerrys and smartphones, which allow for constant connectivity via e-mail and text messaging. Melissa Mazmanian and her colleagues note that individuals often love their BlackBerrys and handheld devices because the constant connectivity allows for (perceived) autonomy and flexibility, as well as control over how they receive and respond to information. Yet she found that individuals quickly develop a compulsion to check messages at all times and that ubiquitous e-mail communication becomes a shared organizational norm rather than an individual choice (Melissa Mazmanian, Wanda Orlikowski, and JoAnne Yates, "CrackBerries: The Social Implications of Ubiquitous Wireless E-Mail Devices," in *Designing Ubiquitous Information Environments: Socio-Technical Issues and Challenges*, eds. Carsten Sorensen, Youngjin Yoo, Kalle Lyytinen, and Janice DeGross [New York: Springer, 2005], 337–343).

Sherry Turkle describes how technology is providing new opportunities to connect anywhere, anytime, and that this is coming at large—and often unrecognized—costs to ourselves and our relationships with others (Sherry Turkle, *Alone Together: Why We Expect More from Technology and Less from Each Other* [New York: Basic Books, 2011]). She points to parents stressed to keep up with e-mail and children who complain of their parents' distraction, despite their own constant communication with friends through Facebook, texting, and instant messaging.

Some of these books specifically address what to do about the increased demands of technology, again focusing on what individuals can do to better accommodate the pressures they face. Gil Gordon (*Turn It Off: How to Unplug from the Anytime-Anywhere Office Without Disconnecting Your Career* [New York: Three Rivers Press, 2001]) and William Powers (*Hamlet's BlackBerry: A Practical Philosophy for Building a Good Life in the Digital Age* [New York: Harper Collins, 2010]) both offer strategies for individuals to protect their own time and space away from work and technology, helping balance the demands of work and family but also to be more productive when they're working.

3. For information on the consulting industry, see: Jack W. Plunkett, *Plunkett's Consulting Industry Almanac 2011* (Houston: Plunkett Research, 2011); also Naomi Newman, *Vault Guide to the Top 50 Management and Strategy Consulting Firms* (New York: Vault Inc. 2010). For a historical account of the consulting industry, see James McKenna, *The World's Newest Profession: Management Consulting in the Twentieth Century* (New York: Cambridge University Press, 2006). Data on MBA students at the fifty top U.S. business schools is provided by http://money.cnn.com/news/economy/mba100/2010/industries/all/.

4. Details about our survey are provided in the appendix. Other recent studies also show people to be *on* a great deal. A 2008 phone study of fifteen hundred U.S. professionals who use a BlackBerry or other mobile device (and make more than $50,000 per year and take two or more business trips each year) found that 84 percent said they check these devices just before going to bed and again as soon as they wake up (http://www.prweb.com/releases/2008/09/prweb1330304.htm, accessed 8/16/11). In a Pew study of full-time and part-time adult workers, 48 percent of BlackBerry/PDA users reported being required to read and respond to e-mail while away from work (Mary Madden and Sydney Jones, "Networked Workers Study," Pew Research Center's Internet & American Life Project, September 2008, http://www.pewinternet.org/Reports/2008/Networked-Workers/1-Summary-of-Findings.aspx). A 2008 AOL survey of U.S. e-mail users found that 78 percent of those with a handheld device checked e-mail while on vacation; 41 percent kept their handheld device near them while sleeping so they could hear if an e-mail came through; and 62 percent checked work e-mail over the weekend (AOL study: http://corp.aol.com/press-releases/2008/07/it-s-3-am-are-you-checking-your-e-mail-again, accessed 7/7/2009).

5. In his 1979 study of doctors, Evitar Zerubavel observed how the beeper was intruding on the private lives of doctors. He noted that beepers were expanding the range of time during which it was socially acceptable to reach someone. It has always been socially unacceptable to call someone at 3:30 a.m., as that was a violation of that person's private time. But he noted how it had become acceptable to beep a doctor, wherever, whenever (Evitar Zerubavel, *Patterns of Time in Hospital Life: A Sociological Perspective* [Chicago: University of Chicago Press, 1979]).

Chapter 2

1. Lotte Bailyn and her colleagues have written about achieving the *dual agenda* of work effectiveness and work- and personal-life integration. They use a collective goal to encourage groups to raise assumptions about work that make it difficult to have a personal life and then work together to explore alternative ways of working. Organizations wishing to enact a dual agenda go through an exploratory audit to understand assumptions and norms in the organization. They examine what types of behavior are valued, both formally and informally, and the consequences of that behavior on employees' lives outside of work. With that understanding, they then strive to create new practices that aim to improve gender equity and/or employees' work-life balance by addressing the work issues that were problematic. Bailyn notes that this approach can be quite powerful, since by bringing in work-life and/or gender equity as a personal incentive, employees are more motivated to reflect on how the organization could work better.

In many ways PTO adds to how to achieve a dual agenda. The core addition is combining the collective goal with *structured dialogue*. Both PTO and CIAR (collaborative interactive action research—the method proposed by Bailyn and her colleagues to achieve the dual agenda) use a collective goal to motivate the desired changes in the work that in turn will enhance work-life. By adding structured dialogue, PTO makes the resulting process both self-sustaining and generative. At BCG, PTO began about a predictable night off, but over time on a team it came to be about whatever issues— work or personal—were undermining the team's work process and individual members' work-lives. While the discovery process in both CIAR and PTO utilizes personal issues as a catalyst for reflection on organizational practices, with PTO people end up engaged in a process of ongoing improvement—raising whatever issues are problematic for them, whether or not these issues had anything to do with achieving the collective goal, and be they work or personal. See Lotte Bailyn, Joyce K. Fletcher, and Deborah Kolb, "Unexpected Connections: Considering Employees' Personal Lives Can Revitalize Your Business," *Sloan Management Review*, 38, no. 4 (1997): 11–20; and Rhona Rapoport, Lotte Bailyn, Joyce Fletcher, and Bettye Pruitt, *Beyond Work-Family Balance: Advancing Gender Equity and Workplace Performance* (San Francisco: Jossey-Bass, 2002).

2. In my earlier work, I focused on a group of software engineers who were frustrated that the constant interruptions of the normal workday forced them to come in early, stay late, and work weekends in search of what they called the *quiet time* they needed to do the creative thinking for their design work. After watching them work, I wondered what the effect would be of the group working together to set aside the morning hours several days a week for them to get some of that precious quiet time.

After four months of experimenting with quiet time three mornings a week, the engineers not only launched their new product on time—a true victory for this team— but they also concluded that they had been more productive than ever. Almost as gratifying was the fact that their success had transformed their project manager into a major advocate of the change process. Still, when the experiment ended and the engineers moved on to new teams, they quickly reverted to their old work habits, and I got my first lesson in the power of organizational culture to stifle change, even when it clearly made employees happier and more productive. I described my findings in my doctoral dissertation, which evolved into my first book, *Finding Time* (Leslie A. Perlow, *Finding Time: How Corporations, Individuals and Families Can Benefit from New Work Practices* [Ithaca, NY: Cornell University Press, 1997]).

3. A wide range of approaches on how to create openness exist. Some take the broad goal of helping leaders create organizations characterized by openness, such as Warren G. Bennis, Daniel Goleman, and James O'Toole's *Transparency: How Leaders Create a Culture of Candor* (San Francisco: Jossey-Bass, 2008). Similarly, Herb Blaum offers advice on creating a culture of openness and inclusion (Herb Blaum, *The Transparent Leader: How to Build a Great Company Through Straight Talk, Openness, and Accountability* [New York: Harper Collins, 2004]).

Others strive for openness as a key element toward creating a desired type of organization; for example, Peter Senge (*The Fifth Discipline: The Art and Practice of the Learning Organization* [New York: Currency Doubleday, 1990]) advises that openness is important to create a learning organization—both openness to speaking honestly about issues and an openness to listening to others and challenging one's own thinking.

Another school of thought focuses on helping individuals communicate more effectively. Patterson et al. give advice for handling conversations where the stakes are high and emotions can run strong, whether in one-on-one or group settings (Kerry Patterson, Joseph Grenny, Ron McMillan, and Al Switzler, *Crucial Conversations: Tools for Talking When Stakes Are High* [New York: McGraw Hill, 2002, 2009]). Similarly, Douglas Stone and his colleagues from the Harvard Negotiation Project help people identify the underlying structure of any conversation so that they can communicate more effectively in both challenging and everyday situations (Douglas Stone, Bruce Patton, Sheila Heen, and Roger Fisher, *Difficult Conversations: How to Discuss What Matters Most* [New York: Penguin, 2010]).

Another subgenre focuses on team communication. Thomas Harris and John Sherblom offer practical advice on how to best navigate typical stages in group process; see, for example, Thomas Harris and John Sherblom, *Small Group and Team Communication* 5th ed., (Boston: Allyn and Bacon, 2010).

4. Amy Edmondson and James Detert addressed the link between open dialogue and work-life balance in a chapter entitled "The Role of Speaking Up in Work-Life Balancing." They raised the importance of engaging in open dialogue "for dealing with the complexities of negotiating the multiple needs and offerings that together constitute a healthy work-life balancing act." They, like the rest of us, however, did not further recognize the value of combining open dialogue with a change agenda, such as the collective goal of personal time off provides (Amy Edmondson and James Detert, "The Role of Speaking Up in Work-life Balancing," in *Work and Life Integration: Organizational, Cultural, and Individual Perspectives*, eds. Ellen Ernst Kossek and Susan J. Lambert [New Jersey: Lawrence Erlbaum Associates, 2005, p. 397]).

5. The study about the self-scheduling of nurses was conducted by Lotte Bailyn and her colleagues (Lotte Bailyn, Robin Collins, and Yang Song, "Self-Scheduling for Hospital Nurses: An Attempt and Its Difficulties," *Journal of Nursing Management* 15 [2007]: 72–77).

6. See Roger Martin, *The Opposable Mind: Winning Through Integrative Thinking* (Boston: Harvard Business School Publishing, 2009), 6. Or as the novelist F. Scott Fitzgerald famously put it: "The test of a first-rate intelligence is the ability to hold two opposed ideas in mind at the same time, and still retain the ability to function" (F. Scott Fitzgerald, *The Crack-up,* ed. Edmund Wilson [1945; New York: New Directions, 1993], 69). Wendy Smith and Marianne Lewis refer to this as a *paradox lens* and further review the literature on paradox to support their claim that effectively managing paradoxes is at the core of organizational sustainability (Wendy K. Smith and Marianne Lewis, "Toward a Theory of Paradox: A Dynamic Equilibrium Theory of Organizing," *Academy of Management Review* 36, no. 2 [2011]: 381–403).

7. I intentionally use the word *dialogue* because of its particular meaning that has to do with a group setting aside assumptions, finding common meaning, creating mutual trust, and thinking together; see David Bohm, *On Dialogue* (London: Routledge, 1996); Peter Senge, *The Fifth Discipline;* and Edgar H. Schein, "On Dialogue, Culture, and Organizational Learning," *Organizational Dynamics*, 22, no. 2 (Fall 1993): 40–51. William Isaacs defines dialogue as "shared inquiry, a way of thinking and reflecting together" (William Isaacs, *Dialogue: The Art of Thinking Together* [New York: Doubleday, 1999], 9). Edgar Schein further notes, "An important goal of dialogue is to enable the group to reach a higher level of consciousness and creativity through the gradual creation of a shared set of meanings and a 'common' thinking process . . . Dialogue aims to build a group that can think generatively, creatively, and most important, together . . . Dialogue is thus a vehicle for creative problem identification and problem solving" (Schein, "On Dialogue, Culture, and Organizational Learning").

8. As a result of embracing the two rules of engagement at the center of PTO, a process of continual learning, adaption and improvement emerges. Amy Edmondson

describes such learning behaviors as "activities carried out by team members through which a team obtains and processes data that allow it to adapt and improve. Examples of learning behavior include seeking feedback, sharing information, asking for help, talking about efforts, and experimenting. It is through these activities that teams can detect changes in the environment, learn about customers' requirements, improve members' collective understanding of a situation, or discover unexpected consequences of their previous actions" (Amy Edmondson, "Psychological Safety and Learning Behavior in Work Teams," *Administrative Science Quarterly* 44, no. 2 [1999]: 350–383). She writes elsewhere that learning teams are about "recognizing a need for change, evaluating new possibilities, and implementing a new course of action" (Amy Edmondson, "The Local and Variegated Nature of Learning in Organizations: A Group-Level Perspective," *Organization Science* 13, no. 2 [2002]: 128–146).

9. Peter Senge defines a *learning organization* as "an organization that is continually expanding its capacity to create its own future" (Senge, *The Fifth Discipline,* 14). More generally, organization development (OD) is an attempt to influence the members of an organization to increase their candor with each other about their views of the organization and their experience in it and to take greater responsibility for their own actions as organization members. The assumption behind OD is that when people pursue both of these objectives (candor and responsibility) simultaneously, they are likely to discover new ways of working together that they experience as more effective for achieving their own and their shared goals (Eric Neilsen, *Becoming an OD Practitioner* [Englewood Cliffs, New Jersey: Prentice-Hall, 1984]).

Creating a team where there is continual learning, adaptation and improvement is a highly sought after goal. According to David Garvin and colleagues, "In the face of intensifying competition, advances in technology, and shifts in customer preferences . . . organizations need to learn more than ever . . . Each company must become a *learning organization*" (David Garvin, Amy Edmondson, and Francesca Gino, "Is Yours a Learning Organization?" *Harvard Business Review,* March 2008, 109–116). Edmondson has gone farther, asserting, "Today's central managerial challenge is to inspire knowledge workers to solve, day in and day out, problems that cannot be anticipated," and this, she posits, requires a shift from the traditional focus on "execution-as-efficiency" to a new focus on "execution-as-learning." She explains: "The best organizations have figured out how to learn quickly while maintaining high quality standards" (Amy Edmondson, "The Competitive Imperative of Learning," *Harvard Business Review,* July–August 2008, 60–67).

Despite the desirability of creating a learning organization, it has been difficult to realize this ideal. Indeed, Garvin, Edmonson, and Gino note, "The ideal of the learning organization has not yet been realized" (Garvin, Edmondson, and Gino, "Is Yours a Learning Organization?"). It is a challenge to get people to engage in a process of assessing and rethinking the way they work, week in and week out. People tend to get stuck in what Chris Argyris, known for his groundbreaking work regarding learning organizations, describes as "defensive routines, creating undiscussables and then making the undiscussability undiscussable—a protective shell is formed around our deepest assumptions, defending us against pain but also keeping us from learning the causes of that pain." According to Argyris, transparency is limited and asking for transparency is dangerous (Chris Argyris, "Learning in Organizations," in *Handbook of Organization Development*, ed. Thomas Cummings [Thousand Oaks, CA: Sage Publications, 2008]: 53–67). Peter Senge and coauthors further point out: "Skills involving fundamental new ways of thinking and interacting take years to master . . . Deep

beliefs and assumptions are not like light switches that can be turned on and off"
(Peter Senge, Art Kleiner, Charlotte Roberts, Richard Ross, and Bryan Smith, *The Fifth
Discipline Fieldbook: Strategies and Tools for Building a Learning Organization* [New York:
Currency, 1994], 22).

Chapter 3

1. Four of the original ten teams were from the "Tech Company"—Tech Global,
Tech Efficiency, Tech Operations A, and Tech Operations B. The case from Tech that
we predominantly focus on in the text is Tech Operations A, but for simplicity we refer
to it simply as the *Tech* team.

2. The original kickoff of the Tech Operations A team also included members of
Tech Global, which had the same two partners and launched at the same time.

3. Despite a recognition that openness is desirable, it has been difficult to create. Indeed, there continues to be widespread silencing of differences in organizations. One study interviewed professionals from a range of industries and found that
85 percent had opted not to speak up in the past about serious concerns they had
in their organization, and only half felt comfortable speaking up generally at work
(Francis Milliken, Elizabeth Morrison, and Patricia Hewlin, "An Exploratory Study of
Employee Silence: Issues That Employees Don't Communicate Upward and Why,"
Journal of Management Studies 40, no. 6 [2003]: 1453–1476). And while the costs of
silence can be high, it is difficult to address (Michael Beer and Russell Eisenstat, "The
Silent Killers of Strategy Implementation and Learning," *Sloan Management Review* 41
[2000]: 29 40). Organizational culture, group/team culture, hierarchy, and individual
disposition can each influence whether individuals feel safe to speak up at work (Elizabeth Morrison, Sara Wheeler-Smith, and Dishan Kamdar, "Speaking Up in Groups: A
Cross-level Study of Group Voice Climate and Voice," *Journal of Applied Psychology* 96,
no. 1 [2001]: 183–191). My own research suggests that it can be even more challenging
to create openness in situations of intense time pressure, when people can be inclined
to bite their tongues and silence differences in order to focus on short-term deadlines
(Leslie Perlow, *When You Say Yes but Mean No: How Silencing Conflict Wrecks Relationships
and Companies* [New York: Crown Business, 2003]).

In my work with Nelson Repenning, we further found that silence can beget
silence—each act of silence exacerbating perceptions of difference in a group and
resulting in a self-sustaining cycle. We also found there was a tipping point at which
an additional act of silence could generate an organizational norm of persistent silence
(Leslie Perlow and Nelson Repenning, "The Dynamics of Silencing Conflict," *Research
in Organizational Behavior* 29 [2009]: 163–193).

4. Healthcare Lean I was also one of the original ten PTO teams, and will be discussed further in chapter 7.

5. As discussed in note 3, silence and a lack of openness are prevalent in organizations, with individuals often concerned that there will be negative repercussions for
speaking up. It's not surprising, then, that researchers have also explored the role of
trust in organizations in shaping people's tendency to take risks, including the risk of
speaking up. Researchers have described a process by which one trusts enough to take
a risk and is met with a favorable outcome, which in turn increases trust and results in
more willingness to take risks; see Roger Mayer, James Davis, and F. David Schorman,
"An Integrative Model of Organizational Trust," *Academy of Management Review* 20,
no. 3 (1995): 709–734; and Gareth Jones and Jennifer George, "The Experience and

Evolution of Trust: Implications for Cooperation and Teamwork," *Academy of Management Review* 23, no. 3 (1998): 531–546.

Amy Edmondson suggests a similar cycle exists with the related concept of *psychological safety*—"a shared belief that the team is safe for interpersonal risk taking" (p. 350). Edmondson argues that team psychological safety encourages team members to take risks that, if not punished by the team, build more psychological safety (Amy Edmondson, "Psychological Safety and Learning Behavior in Work Teams," *Administrative Science Quarterly* 44, no. 2 [1999]: 350–383).

6. Twenty-five years ago, John Gabarro wrote a now-classic chapter on working relationships, describing how they are developed through a four-stage process—orientation, exploration, testing, and stabilization. *Orientation* describes the brief initial stage in which the parties have general impressions of each other's capabilities and trustworthiness and set general expectations for one another. This quickly evolves into *exploration*, a longer period in which the individual parties start to assert themselves and determine how open they can be. In this stage, initial impressions are either confirmed or rejected, trust builds or does not, and, if the interactions are positive, they move onto the next stage of the relationship, *testing*. During the testing stage, the parties test the boundaries and mutuality of trust, expectations, and influence. Through this process, the limits of the relationship become defined and *stabilized*, at which point trust and expectations are less likely to change. Gabarro notes that when people go through all of the stages productively, they can develop effective working relationships with a basis of mutual expectations and trust through which they can work through differences and adapt as the needs of either party change (John Gabarro, "The Development of Working Relationships," in *The Handbook of Organizational Behavior*, ed. Jay W. Lorsch [Englewood Cliffs, NJ: Prentice-Hall, 1987]: 172–189).

Chapter 4

1. We found that, with PTO, a shift occurred from an individualistic focus on one's own work and self-interest to a more collective focus where team members cared about the team's work goals and team members as people with rich full lives beyond work. Jennifer Croker and Amy Canevello capture this difference between focusing on the self and caring for the others in their research on "self-image" versus "compassionate" goals. Similar to what is happening in our experiments, they are capturing the difference between people who are focused on their own individual performance and well-being and those who are focused on others and the well-being and ongoing improvement of the team (Jennifer Crocker and Amy Canevello, "Creating and Undermining Social Support in Communal Relationships: The Role of Compassionate and Self-image Goals," *Journal of Personality and Social Psychology* 95 [2008]: 555–575).

2. Sidney Jourard first showed the relationship between self-disclosure and personal relationships (Sidney Jourard, "Self-Disclosure and Other-Cathexis," *Journal of Abnormal and Social Psychology* 59, no. 3 [1959]: 428–431). A core intermediary variable is getting to like a colleague personally (not just as a competent fellow worker): when someone discloses aspects of his or her personal life, it increases the possibility of liking that person, which, in turn, strengthens the group's interpersonal relationships (Nancy Collins and Lynn Carol Miller, "Self-Disclosure and Liking: A Meta-Analytic Review," *Psychological Bulletin* 116, no. 3 [1994]: 457–475).

3. Jane Dutton argues that high-quality connections—"marked by mutual positive regard, trust, and active engagement on both sides"—create energy for improving the world in which we live and work (Jane Dutton, *Energize Your Workplace: How to Cre-*

ate and Sustain High-Quality Connections at Work [San Francisco: Jossey-Bass, 2003], 2). Dutton makes the point that any connection has the potential to be a high-quality connection—it need not be a deep or intimate relationship. Dutton and Emily Heaphy further describe the experience of being in a high-quality connection and the mutual empathy, mutual empowerment, and new shared understanding that emerges (Jane Dutton and Emily Heaphy, "The Power of High-Quality Connections," in *Positive Organizational Scholarship: Foundations of a New Discipline*, eds. Kim Cameron, Jane Dutton, and Robert Quinn [San Francisco: Berrett-Koehler Publishers, 2003], 263–278). David Cooperider and Leslie Sekerka elaborate on how the shared understanding leads individuals to work together to seek out the best in the system. They further describe how the positive emotion emanating from the shared discovery creates a surge of energy that gives people the courage to push forward and make changes when circumstances might otherwise have inhibited them (David Cooperider and Leslie Sekerka, "Toward a Theory of Positive Organizational Change," in *Positive Organizational Scholarship: Foundations of a New Discipline*, 225–240). More recently, Ryan Quinn focuses on the specific energy that is created through high-quality connections and the positive, reinforcing dynamic between connections and energy (Ryan Quinn, "Energizing Others in Work Connections," in *Exploring Positive Relationships at Work: Building a Theoretical and Research Foundation*, eds. Jane E. Dutton and Belle Rose Ragins [Mahwah, NJ: Lawrence Erlbaum Associates, 2007], 73–90).

4. A collective action orientation has long been shown to result from feeling part of a collective. More than twenty years ago, Alberto Melucci (1989) suggested that the construction of a collective identity is the most central task of "new" social movements. In other words, at the core of creating collective action is the creation of a shared or collective identity, a sense that "we" are in it together, attempting to address a shared goal or, in particular, in the social movements literature, a shared injustice (Alberto Melucci, *Nomads of the Present: Social Movements and Individual Needs in Contemporary Society*, eds. John Keane and Paul Mier [London: Century Hutchinson, 1989]).

According to social movement theorists, the source of motivation to take collective action is created through a shared sense of injustice—a sense that there is something wrong in one's world that the group, working together has the possibility to address. Both the sense of injustice and the sense of optimism are believed to be critical. As Doug McAdam, John McCarthy, and Mayer Zald have documented, "At a minimum people need to feel both aggrieved about some aspect of their lives and optimistic that acting collectively they can redress the problem" (Doug McAdam, John McCarthy, and Mayer Zald, eds., *Comparative Perspectives on Social Movements: Political Opportunities, Mobilizing Structures, and Cultural Framings* [New York: Cambridge University Press, 1996], introduction, 5).

There is not a pervasive sense among the participants in our experiments that the world is unfair—that there is something wrong. Indeed, people legitimate the way it is, thinking that the work requires this behavior and if they cannot cope, they must leave the firm (and even industry). Individuals are convinced that any need for change is their own problem, to be dealt with by them on their own. They reason that in client-service work there is no alternative. Hence, there is neither a sense of being aggrieved or an optimism that their actions could somehow make it any different.

We find insight into this difference between our experiments and traditional social movement theories in positive psychology. Until recently, psychology (and medical science) focused on helping overcome deviance, or gaps. It was about making people normal. Positive psychology, in contrast, is about helping normal people become better. Rather than being about overcoming gaps, it is about making the ordinary extraordinary (Marcus Buckingham and Donald O. Clifton, *Now Discover Your Strengths* [New York: The Free Press, 2001]). Similarly, what our experiments are doing is enabling a way for collective action to improve the workplace in which people exist. It is not so much about helping solve a problem as it is helping provide new opportunities in a context where the possibility of improvement has never been considered.

Also distinct from research on social movements, the collective action orientation itself is created through mobilizing structures put in place by the organization. Social movement theory revolves around groups of individuals taking action to combat authority; in our case, in contrast, the organization (or authority) is putting in place structures to legitimate collective action and the challenging of the status quo. It is not an us-versus-them mentality where the worker is taking on the organization; rather, the organization is helping to create the collective movement to the benefit of the workers and the organization.

5. The positive dynamic that we observed on PTO teams as a result of working collectively toward a goal of personal interest is predicted by Marcial Losada and Emily Heaphy's nonlinear dynamic model showing the liberating and creative power of positivity. They note: "We need to have organizations where the polarity of other and self, of you and I, is integrated into a sense of we; where the polarity of inquiry and advocacy, of questions and answers, can drive a productive and ongoing dialogue; where the abundance of positivity, grounded in constructive negative feedback, can generate the state of realistic enthusiasm that can propel organizations to reach and uphold the heights of excellence." Losada and Heaphy further observed how "by showing appreciation and encouragement to other members of the team, they created emotional spaces that were expansive and opened possibilities for action and creativity" (Marcial Losada and Emily Heaphy, "The Role of Positivity and Connectivity in the Performance of Business Teams: A Nonlinear Dynamics," *American Behavioral Scientist* 47 [2004]: 740–765).

Chapter 5

1. Pfeffer and Sutton argue that implementation is at least as important as developing knowledge and describe methods several successful companies have used to turn knowledge into action, including driving out fear and creating an atmosphere of respect and trust (Jeffrey Pfeffer and Robert Sutton, *The Knowing-Doing Gap: How Smart Companies Turn Knowledge into Action* [Boston: Harvard Business School Press, 2000]).

2. The notion of experimentation as a micro adjustment of the work process comes from Stefan Thomke's *Experimentation Matters: Unlocking the Potential of New Technologies for Innovation* (Boston: Harvard Business School Publishing, 2003). Thomke further outlines how organizations can establish both a culture that encourages experimentation and learning (by rewarding failure and engaging customers, for instance) and an infrastructure that supports it in order to achieve a competitive edge. The quotation comes from Thomke's quote of Thomas Peters and Robert Waterman's *In Search of Excellence* (New York: Harper Business, 2004).

Chapter 6

1. The data depicted in figure 6–1—except the portion on how well a team was collaborating—was gathered for BCG through annual employee surveys administered

each year by Towers Watson, an independent talent management consulting firm. These external surveys, which were not linked in any way to PTO, have allowed us to compare trends in Boston over time with a true baseline before PTO, as well as to compare Boston trends with other BCG offices. It was important to confirm that other factors were not driving the improvements, such as economic, industry, or even firmwide changes. What we found is that the longer an office had been doing PTO, the greater the degree of change. The Boston office, where PTO started and almost every team is now doing PTO, has seen the most dramatic increases over time of any of BCG's North American offices. In the rest of the Northeast region (Boston, New York, New Jersey, Washington, DC, and Philadelphia), there have also been increases during the time period that PTO has been rolled out, though not as dramatic as the increases in Boston. In BCG offices in the rest of the United States, where there has been substantially less PTO penetration (because many offices started implementing PTO one to two years after the Boston office), there has been essentially no change over the same time period. For example, after three years of PTO in Boston, the number of people who felt their office had a culture in which it was safe to speak up increased by 37 percent, compared with an increase of 11 percent in the Northeast and 2 percent in the rest of the United States. The number of people who felt a sense of personal accomplishment in their work increased by 14 percent in Boston, compared with a 7 percent increase in the Northeast and a 1 percent increase in the rest of the United States during the same period. In Boston, the number of people who felt they had control over their work schedule after three years of PTO increased by 39 percent, compared with an increase of 19 percent in the Northeast and no increase in the rest of the United States over the same time period. The number of people who felt colleagues were considerate of their personal lives increased by 29 percent in Boston, compared with 16 percent in the Northeast and no increase in the rest of the United States. Boston also saw a 10 percent increase in those who identified their work as adding value to their clients, compared with a 4 percent increase in both the Northeast and the rest of the United States. This pattern leads us to believe that firm level, industry, or global economic factors were not driving the improved responses in Boston and (to a lesser extent) the Northeast.

We also grouped respondents based on their answers to the question about their sense of personal accomplishment and their sense of control over their work schedule to analyze the effects of living the Dream versus being caught in the Grind. We define someone as living the Dream if they are high on personal accomplishment and control (1 or 2 on a 5-point scale) and caught in the Grind if they are low on both measures (3 or higher).

2. In the 1970s, Mihaly Csikszentmihalyi coined the term *flow* to describe a deep engagement in work or activities. The pianist who loses herself in her music, the surgeon who tunes out distraction to focus on a procedure, the athlete who is "in the zone." According to Csikszentmihalyi, activities which induce flow have clear goals, opportunities for frequent feedback, and a balance between the challenge and one's skills to meet it (Mihaly Csikszentmihalyi, *Finding Flow: The Psychology of Engagement with Everyday Life* [New York: Penquin: 1997], 30).

One enters a state of flow by exercising control rather than passively accepting circumstances. Csikszentmihalyi explains that by constantly questioning whether something needs to be done or how to do it better, people can create more value, exercise more control, and find more meaning in their work, even if the work itself is dull or routine.

Living the Dream is very much like being in *flow*. A person in flow at work is energized by their work—they can embrace a challenge knowing they are focused on the
right activities and are confident in their skills, and in doing so they actually feel more
powerful and more connected to their work. Their work becomes personally meaningful and rewarding, and their enthusiasm spills into their personal lives, where they are
also motivated to create opportunities for flow activities. Living the Dream denotes the
same kind of flow for managers working in an office, conference room, or coffee shop:
the opportunity to experience the exhilaration of an extremely demanding job, and
to do so with control over one's schedule.

3. Our notion of *Junkie* is similar to the type of person Hewlett and Luce refer to
as having an *extreme job*, where they work long hours under conditions of high pressure and unpredictability, but coupled with high compensation and a fair amount of
exhilaration from the work (Sylvia Hewlett and Carolyn Buck Luce, "Extreme Jobs:
The Dangerous Allure of the 70-Hour Workweek," *Harvard Business Review*, December
2006, 49–59).

4. The idea of *continuous improvement* (CI) was popularized by W. Edwards Deming, a statistician and consultant who is credited for inspiring companies to focus on
quality as their biggest priority. Deming posited that when companies focus on cutting
costs quality actually suffers, but when they focus on improving quality, they identify
waste and are able to cut costs (W. Edwards Deming, *Out of the Crisis* [Cambridge:
MIT, 1982]). Deming popularized his philosophy first in Japan and later in the United
States. CI has become an overarching goal for many organizations, with the objective
of creating a culture which values ongoing innovation to reduce waste and improve
processes at all levels. A key element of Deming's philosophy was that treating workers as commodities was contrary to the goal of continual improvement; he viewed
employees as a critical partner for any management serious about diagnosing waste
and improving quality.

Several methods of continual improvement have been introduced in the years since
Deming first published *Out of the Crisis* in 1982. One of the best known is Lean, based
on the Toyota Production System. Introduced in *The Machine That Changed the World*
written by James Womack, Daniel Jones, and Daniel Roos (New York: Simon & Schus-
ter, 1990), Lean methodology aims to use less time, less space, less effort, and less in-
ventory, and therefore requires the organization to learn continuously as it cuts waste.
A key concept in Lean is to envision the product from the perspective of the customers,
cutting any cost/process that they do not directly pay for, which is likely to provide a
true advantage over competitors.

Six Sigma is another form of CI. Originally introduced by Motorola in 1986, this
method looks to improve quality through the use of statistical process control to reduce
variation in processes. Centered around a model called DMAIC—define opportunities, measure performance, analyze opportunities, improve performance, and control
performance. *Sigma* refers to the percentage of defect-free products created by a given
process. A Six Sigma process would produce 99.99966 percent of products without
defects. Companies use Six Sigma for the same reason others use Lean: as a way to
establish competitive advantage by producing high quality products as efficiently as
possible. (See Peter Pande, Robert Neuman, and Roland Cavanagh, *The Six Sigma Way:
How GE, Motorola, and Other Top Companies Are Honing Their Performance* [New York:
McGraw Hill, 2000].)

Kaizen is the Japanese word best translated "improvement." Closely associated with
Lean, *kaizen*'s philosophical underpinnings are generally understood to be an empha-

sis on constant, though sometimes incremental, change, plus the belief that improvement is participative—valuing the intelligence of workers and in turn improving their experience of work. While the specific mechanics of how *kaizen* is enacted varies widely from organization to organization, the common thread is a deep commitment to this philosophy at all levels of the organization (Adam Brunet and Steve New, "Kaizen in Japan: An Empirical Study," *International Journal of Operations and Production Management* 23, no. 11–12 [2003]: 1426–1446).

5. Organization learning is another approach aimed at helping companies remain competitive by understanding how to vest learning at the organization rather than the individual level. Those striving to create learning organizations wish to enable "double-loop" learning, by which people not only learn to do specific tasks and processes, but also to question and refine them as they go (see Chris Argyris and Donald A. Schon, *Organizational Learning: A Theory of Action Perspective* [Boston: Addison Wesley, 1978]). The idea of creating learning organizations was popularized by Peter Senge, who described the five disciplines of a learning organization: personal mastery, mental models, shared vision, team learning, and systems thinking. Senge contends that continual study and practice of each discipline at the individual and group level enables the creation of learning organizations: high-performance organizations that are better able to manage change and competitive forces with an energized and committed workforce (Peter Senge, *The Fifth Discipline: The Art and Practice of the Learning Organization* [New York: Currency Doubleday, 1990]).

The concept of team learning has been embraced as a way to take the goals of organization learning to a more local level. Senge stresses that team learning is critical for organizations since the team is a key unit of decision-making and action (Senge, *The Fifth Discipline*, 219). A number of other researchers, notably Amy Edmondson, have explored how best to foster and enable team learning and then leverage team learning into organizational learning. This emphasis on team learning recognizes that it is the ability of individuals to learn from one another that can help the organization reach a state of continuous learning and improvement (Amy Edmondson, "Speaking Up in the Operating Room: How Team Leaders Promote Learning in Interdisciplinary Action Teams," *Journal of Management Studies* 40, no. 6 [2003]: 1419–1452).

6. Both the streams of research on the dual agenda and ROWE (results-only work environment), like PTO, are motivated by a focus on personal time off. The dual agenda, as described in footnote 1 in chapter 2, uses a process for change (CIAR) that has, like PTO, originated from the research team working in collaboration with the firm to identify ways of working that inhibit work-life balance or undermine gender equity and seek to find small collective goals around which to rally the team and empower them to rethink their work in ways that benefit the work process and individuals' work-lives. ROWE, in contrast, originated from managers (Cali Ressler and Jody Thompson) within an organization who brought change about at BestBuy by emphasizing that as long as people are meeting their objectives, it should not matter where or when they work. They have since gone out to try to create the same sort of change in other organizations (through their consulting firm, CultureRx). In the meantime, researchers from the University of Minnesota, led by Phyllis Moen and Erin Kelly, have focused on studying ROWE at Best Buy from an academic perspective.

In all three cases—PTO, CIAR, and ROWE—there is the same overarching intent to use a collective goal of personal interest to motivate change in the work that will benefit both individuals and the work process itself. CIAR and PTO both use a small goal that is meant to rally people around a particular issue of importance to them.

CIAR focuses predominantly on creating ongoing change in the work that remains focused on that goal, or adding additional goals and repeating the process. PTO focuses on using the goal as more of a catalyst to create ongoing change that expands far beyond the initial goal. The core difference between PTO and CIAR is PTO's addition of the structured dialogue, which has had the effect of making the whole process more generative as people build trust and commitment and start to raise additional issues—both work and personal—and work together to address those as well.

ROWE, in contrast to both PTO and CIAR, begins with a much more ambitious goal. In many ways, PTO and ROWE strive for the same end point—a culture where people are free to rearrange and rethink their work process to meet personal as well as work needs, and where increased efficiency can benefit not only the organization, but also the individual. The fundamental difference is that ROWE asks people to buy into this ambitious goal from the start. PTO, in contrast, puts out a small, seemingly doable, much less threatening, first step and builds over time to this broader cultural effect of instilling continuous improvement in the work process to the benefit of both individuals and the organization.

Another key difference between PTO and ROWE is the emphasis of the goal itself. PTO focuses on people starting with the goal of team members breaking the cycle of responsiveness and being able to turn off. ROWE, in contrast, is more focused on individual preferences and autonomy to work where or when they want. See Rhona Rapoport, Lotte Bailyn, Joyce Fletcher, and Bettye Pruitt, *Beyond Work-Family Balance: Advancing Gender Equity and Workplace Performance* (San Francisco: Jossey-Bass, 2002); Cali Ressler and Jody Thompson, *Why Work Sucks and How to Fix It: No Schedules, No Meetings, No Joke—the Simple Change That Can Make Your Job Terrific* (New York: Penguin, 2008); and Erin Kelly, Phyllis Moen, and Eric Tranby, "Changing Workplaces to Reduce Work-Family Conflict: Schedule Control in a White-Collar Organization," *American Sociological Review* 76, no. 2 (2011): 265–290.

7. The ultimate spirit of openness, passion, and collective experimentation on PTO teams provides a stark contrast to the way teams that were not participating in PTO operated. The behavior of the non-PTO teams was symptomatic of *performance oriented-cultures,* where everyone is focused on proving how competent they are at their jobs and avoiding revealing any evidence to the contrary (see Amy Edmondson, "Framing for Learning: Lessons in Successful Technology Implementation," *California Management Review* 45, no. 2 [2003]: 34–54; and Amy Edmondson and Josephine Mogelof, "Explaining Psychological Safety in Innovation Teams," in *Creativity and Innovation in Organizational Teams,* eds. Leigh Thompson and Hoon-Seok Choi [Hillsdale, NJ: Lawrence Erlbaum Associates, 2006], 109–136). On effective PTO teams, the culture shifts from trying to impress superiors to continual experimentation, learning about the flaws in the work process and improving them; the experiment transformed the day-to-day work from a performance-oriented to a learning-oriented culture—and moreover, a learning-oriented culture that is not limited to improving only the work but the work-lives of the teammates as well.

Chapter 7

1. The importance of leadership support is well documented in the literature on learning and change. In *The Fifth Discipline,* Peter Senge writes:

> When all is said and done, learning organizations will remain a "good idea," an intriguing but distant vision until people take a stand for building such organiza-

tions. Taking this stand is the first leadership act, the start of inspiring (literally "to breathe life into") the vision of learning organizations. In the absence of this stand, the learning disciplines remain mere collections of tools and technique—means of solving problems rather than creating something genuinely new (Peter Senge, *The Fifth Discipline: The Art and Practice of the Learning Organization* [New York: Currency Doubleday, 1990], 304).

Ingrid Nembhard and Amy Edmondson have further focused on the importance of leadership in particular in creating the psychological safety that facilitates taking the risk to speak up to offer ideas, raise concerns, or ask questions. They talk specifically about the importance of "words and deeds by a leader or leaders that indicate an invitation and appreciation for others' contributions." They note, "Without a recognizable invitation, impressions derived from the historic lack of invitation will prevail. And without appreciation (i.e., a positive, constructive response), the initial positive impact of being invited to provide input will be insufficient to overcome the subsequent hurdle presented by status boundaries" (Ingrid Nembhard and Amy Edmondson, "Making It Safe: The Effects of Leader Inclusiveness and Professional Status on Psychological Safety and Improvement Efforts in Health Care Teams," Special Issue on Healthcare: The Problems Are Organizational, Not Clinical. *Journal of Organizational Behavior* 27, 7 [2006]: 941–966).

2. We were introduced to the notion of a *teamlet* by a BCG principal who brought to our attention an article in the *New England Journal of Medicine*. The notion of teamlet is "a two-person team for patients . . . because some practices have larger teams, the teamlet model recognizes that the two-person dyad is part but not all of the larger team" (Thomas Bodenheimer, "Coordinating Care—a Perilous Journey Through the Health Care System," *New England Journal of Medicine* 358 [2008]: 1064–1071). The notion of teamlet nicely captures the coverage partners within the larger team that are established to ensure coverage for nights off.

3. See John Gabarro and John Kotter, "Managing Your Boss," *Harvard Business Review* 58, 1 (1980): 92–100.

Chapter 8

1. I studied three groups of software engineers—in India, China, and Hungary—working for the same U.S.-based company, and discovered that though they were equally productive, they accomplished their work in different ways that had more or less versatility and flexibility, and these differences seemed to be culturally influenced. For instance, the Hungarian engineers who greatly valued time for art and leisure had found a way of being more versatile at work that enabled shorter, more flexible hours than the Indian engineers, who valued their personal time less and found the work conditions at the office, which had modern plumbing and air-conditioning, significantly more appealing than their modest homes. What was most fascinating to me was that each group was absolutely convinced that its way of doing the work was the only way to be competitive in the global marketplace—and was surprised to find out that there were other equally productive ways of working (Leslie Perlow, Jody Hoffer Gittell, and Nancy R. Katz, "Contextualizing Patterns of Work Group Interaction: Toward a Nested Theory of Structuration," *Organization Science* 15, 5 [2004]: 520–536; Leslie Perlow, "Time to Coordinate: Toward an Understanding of Work-Time Standards and Norms in a Multi-Country Study of Software Engineers," *Work and Occupations* 28, no. 1 [2001] pp. 91–111).

2. John Child suggests that the establishment of structural forms, manipulation of environmental features, and choice of relevant performance standards are not imposed by contextual factors but a matter of "strategic choice" (John Child, "Organizational Structure, Environment and Performance: The Role of Strategic Choice," *Sociology* 6, no. 1 [1972]: 1–22). What we find with the nature of how the work is done—the task design—is conceptually the same. It is not the case that tasks are designed by some set of factors determined by the work itself. Rather, the ways tasks are performed is a matter of "strategic choice." Teams are "choosing" to do the work in certain ways and then coming to believe that their way is the way it has to be. In actuality, their way need not be the only way and, moreover, there are tangible benefits from doing the work in certain ways rather than others.

3. The idea that some level of dissatisfaction is necessary to bring about change is widely accepted in the organization development and organization change literature. Richard Beckhard noted, "An essential condition of any effective change program is that somebody in a *strategic position* really *feels the need* for change" (author's emphasis) (Richard Beckhard, *Organization Development: Strategies and Models* [Reading, MA: Addison-Wesley, 1969], 10). John Kotter describes this as "creating a sense of urgency," the first step of his eight-step process for leading change. According to Kotter, a sense of urgency is a necessary condition to counteract the complacency that leads many people to accept the status quo, even when change is truly needed (John Kotter, *Leading Change* [Boston: Harvard Business School Press, 1996]; John Kotter, *A Sense of Urgency* [Boston: Harvard Business School Press, 2008]).

Michael Beer suggests that dissatisfaction with the status quo must be felt by those who will need to adapt their behavior as part of the change, and it must be deep enough to create a lack of confidence in the organization and even in the individuals themselves. It is necessary, according to Beer, because that dissatisfaction with the status quo becomes a source of energy and motivation for change (Michael Beer, *Leading Change* [Boston: Harvard Business School Publishing, 1988]; and Michael Beer, "Sustain Organizational Performance Through Continuous Learning, Change, and Realignment," in *Handbook of Principles of Organizational Behavior: Indispensable Knowledge for Evidence-Based Management*, 2009 edition, ed. E. Locke [West Sussex, UK: John Wiley and Sons, 2009]).

4. Quotation from Karl E. Weick, "Small Wins: Redefining the Scale of Social Problems," *American Psychologist* 39, no. 1 (1984): 40–49. More recently, Weick and Frances Westley have written a review article on organization learning and again highlighted the value of small wins. They recognize that there are others who hold that resistance to change can only be countered by dramatic, revolutionary, transformational change. Weick and Westley suggest, however, that small wins have three important characteristics that should not be overlooked. First, small wins can occur in parallel and sequence and can amount to much more than a single win and ultimately can approximate more radical change. Second, small wins can precede and pave the way for more radical change. And third, often in retrospect, what really was a series of small wins, seems like more radical change than it was (Karl E. Weick and Frances Westley, "Organizational Learning: Affirming an Oxymoron," *Handbook of Organization Studies* 2, no. 10 [1996]: 440–458).

Chapter 10

1. Paul Schwartz was involved for the first nine months of the PTO rollout, although he was most active in the initial three to four months. He played the role of the skeptic on the PTO Rollout Team. That was quite useful in the early months in help-

ing George and Rachel refine the message and anticipate areas of resistance. As the effort expanded, the emphasis turned to the practicalities of facilitation and rollout, and this coincided with Paul becoming very busy commercially. Paul receded into the background and eventually removed himself entirely from the team. But he never lost his enthusiasm for how much PTO benefited him personally as well as his teams. He credited PTO with providing him the ongoing commitment to make time at least twice a week for his two-hour run, which meant not starting work until 9:30 or 10 a.m.

Chapter 11

1. Given the long history of organization development (OD) and the value that facilitation has been found to play in the effort to change deeply held assumptions, the fact that facilitators would be of such value should not have been such a surprise. In 1969, Wendell French defined OD as "a long-range effort to improve an organization's problem solving capabilities and its ability to cope with change in its external environment with the help of external or internal behavioral-scientist consultants, or change agents," a definition that is still used today (Wendell French, "Organization Development, Objectives, Assumptions and Strategies," *California Management Review* 12, no. 2 [1969]: 23–34; David Jamieson and Christopher Worley, "The Practice of Organization Development," in *Handbook of Organization Development*, ed. Thomas Cummings [Thousand Oaks, CA: Sage Publications, 2008]: 99–121). Edgar Schein has written extensively on the role of process consultation as a key tool for OD. Schein posits that all organizational issues can be distilled to issues involving human interactions and processes, noting then that an understanding of human processes is required to aid organizational improvements. The process consultant brings knowledge of group process, communication, and behavioral science to bear as she helps the client (internal or external) self-identify organizational problems and potential solutions. Schein stresses that the role of the process consultant is not to provide specific advice so much as to help the client better perceive and understand his environment such that he can act on that understanding (Edgar Schein, *Process Consultation Vol I: Its Role in Organization Development*, 2nd ed. [Reading, MA: Addison-Wesley, 1988]; and Edgar Schein, *Process Consultation Revisited: Building the Helping Relationship* [Reading, MA: Addison-Wesley, 1999]). While BCG facilitators were not specifically trained in group process, and certainly did not have the skills or training reflected in Schein's concept of process consultation, the facilitator's role still shared much in common with that described in OD. PTO facilitators helped teams reflect and change their team dynamics.

2. As academics, being so actively engaged in our own experiment would have made us uncomfortable—if we were only trying to document what happened during the experiment. But we were trying to document what was *possible* as a result of the experiment: could an elite firm staffed with ambitious, competitive employees willing to work sixty-plus hours a week change its reigning 24/7 culture? And so our role in trying to maximize PTO's success was consistent with our experiment's objective.

3. William Shakepeare, *As You Like It*, Act II, Scene VII, 139 ff.

4. Erving Goffman, *The Presentation of Self in Everyday Life* (New York: Doubleday, 1959).

Chapter 12

1. To change the definition of *good work* requires altering what people perceive matters—which ultimately involves changing both the formal organization rewards

but also the informal norms and expectations. Many have noted that without this change, work done differently will not be considered good work. Amy Wharton and Mary Blair-Loy describe the pressures to work long hours and reluctance to work part-time, especially among American finance professionals in a global company, suggesting strong cultural pressures (Amy Wharton and Mary Blair-Loy, "The 'Overtime Culture' in a Global Corporation: A Cross-National Study of Finance Professionals' Interest in Working Part-Time," *Work and Occupation* 29 [2002]: 32–63). Cynthia Fuchs Epstein et al. further describe the expectations of top firms, especially in the legal world, and the costs of deviating—being stigmatized, marginalized, and often penalized (Cynthia Fuchs Epstein, Carroll Seron, Bonnie Oglensky, and Robert Sauté, *The Part-Time Paradox: Time Norms, Professional Lives, Family, and Gender* [New York: Routledge, 1999]). Hewlett and Luce suggest that company culture is not just about what the firm values but the people it is hoping to attract; they write about organizations' desire to reward this hard-driving, always-on, always-committed, long-hours mentality because otherwise they will create an environment that is unattractive to "A players" (Sylvia Hewlett and Carolyn Luce, "Extreme Jobs: The Dangerous Allure of the 70-Hour Workweek," *Harvard Business Review,* December 2006, 49–59). Their view suggests that individuals' work identity drives work culture rather than the other ways around—that workers' identity is socially constructed (see note 2 below).

2. A rich stream of research on social, occupational, and organizational identities highlights the role of social environments in shaping not only people's actions, but also their sense of self, legitimacy, and possibility for action.

Much of this scholarship builds on George Mead's fundamental insight that individual identity is intricately related to social interaction and projections of self that emerge from and are reproduced within situated social worlds. See George Mead, *Mind, Self & Society from the Standpoint of a Social Behaviorist* (1934; Chicago: University of Chicago Press, 1967); Peter Berger and Thomas Luckman, *The Social Construction of Reality: A Treatise in the Sociology of Knowledge* (New York: Anchor Books, 1966); John Van Maanen, "The Self, the Situation and the Rules of Interpersonal Relations," in *Essays in Interpersonal Dynamics,* eds. Warren Bennis, John Van Maanen, Edgar Schein, and Fred Steele (Greenwich, CT: JAI Press, 1979); and Dorothy Holland, William Lachicotte Jr., Debra Skinner, and Carole Cain, *Identity and Agency in Cultural Worlds* (Cambridge, MA: Harvard University Press, 2001). Theodore Schatzki notes that a person's identity "is tied to the practices in which he or she participates" (Theodore Schatzki, *The Site of the Social: A Philosophical Account of the Constitution of Social Life and Change* [University Park, PA: Pennsylvania State University Press, 2002], 82). In other words, identity is "constructed in and through conduct rather than as *pre-existing* conduct" (Damian Hodgson, "Management Putting on a Professional Performance," *Organization* 12 [2005]: 51–68). Or, specific to our case, people's sense of identity (and addiction) is tied up with how much they are on, as a social construction rather than a psychological factor.

Mary Blair-Loy further documents the deeply contextual nature of individuals' commitment or in Blair-Loy's word, "devotion," to their work. (Mary Blair-Loy, "Work Devotion and Work Time," *Fighting for Time: Shifting Boundaries of Work and Social Life,* eds. Cynthia Fuchs Epstein and Arne Kalleberg [New York: Russell Sage, 2004]). Dan Kärreman and Mats Alvesson draw on the notion of social identity to further explain how organizational action and individuals' sense of self are related (Dan Kärreman and Mats Alvesson, "Cages in Tandem: Management Control, Social Identity, and Identification in a Knowledge-Intensive Firm," *Organization* 11, no. 1 [2004]: 149–

175). Timothy Kuhn documents the link between discourse and identity, suggesting that workplace time commitments are conditioned by conceptions of the self available in social and organizational discourses. He notes that "identity regulation is an outcome of the set of discursive resources deployed in members' talk as they account for their uses of time" (Timothy Kuhn, "A 'Demented Work Ethic' and a 'Lifestyle Firm': Discourse, Identity, and Workplace Time Commitments," *Organization Studies* 27, no. 9 [2006]: 1339–1358). Put differently, individuals make sense of who they are based on how they act, itself deeply contextual. Melissa Mazmanian was very helpful in making the connections to the above literature.

3. David Nadler and Michael Tushman, *Competing by Design: The Power of Organizational Architecture* (New York: Oxford University Press, 1997).

4. Michael Tushman and Elaine Romanelli, "Organizational Evolution: A Metamorphosis Model of Convergence and Reorientation," *Research in Organizational Behavior* 7 (1985): 171–222. Tushman and Romanelli present what has become a prominent theoretical framework for characterizing fundamental organization change as happening through relatively long periods of stability that are punctuated with short bursts of fundamental change.

5. Ultimately, if doing good work and being a good worker are cultural constructions, as we believe, each plays an important role in shaping the other. Hence the informal norms and expectations and formal rewards as well as individuals' identity are tightly linked, and change requires changing this interdependent system. That is exactly the nature of David Nadler and Michael Tushman's congruence model, which suggests that organizational change requires changing all four elements of the system—the formal rewards, informal norms and expectations, workers' identity as well as the work practices themselves (Nadler and Tushman, *Competing by Design*).

6. According to Michael Beer, successful change is "planned at the top but led in subunits" (Michael Beer, *High Commitment, High Performance: How to Build a Resilient Organization for Sustained Advantage* [San Francisco: Jossey-Bass: 2009], 311). His research has shown that efforts for change pushed only from the top are unlikely to last: "They can result in compliance and cynicism rather than real learning and commitment to change . . . [they undermine] experimentation—the essence of successful change" (ibid., 312). In contrast, changes driven from the bottom "enable spontaneous experimentation and learning . . . This makes change more relevant, valid, and feasible" (ibid., 312). Such changes, he notes, are often not captured, reinforced, and disseminated. According to Beer, the most effective change comes from both ends of the organization, with senior leaders providing support and direction but allowing change to emerge from within the organization. Almost a decade earlier, Dexter Dunphy tried to reconcile the two conflicting views—top down leadership change and participative management—and advocated for embracing the paradox. Dunphy suggested that the role of leadership was to encourage participation by systematic investment in key personal, professional, and corporate capabilities that support meaningful participation (Dexter Dunphy, "Embracing Paradox: Top-Down Versus Participative Management of Organizational Change," in *Breaking the Code of Change,* 134). In our case, leadership didn't support the exploration or innovation apriori. In contrast, the vision was one team's vision to achieve a collective goal and include structured dialogue, to enable that to happen. However, after the change proved successful, leadership did invest in ways aimed at further generating "meaningful participation." After three years, at the Executive Committee meeting, the senior leadership made its first indication of its plan to become more top down, beginning to impose its expectation on others that they would embrace the process.

7. In an award-winning scholarly paper, Donde Ashmos Plowman and her colleagues describe how the idea of a group of parishioners at the Mission Church (in the downtown area of a large city in the Southwest) to offer the homeless breakfast on Sunday mornings resulted in a series of more small but remarkable changes. The breakfast idea emerged more out of boredom than generosity, but others joined the breakfast group, which, in a short time, was offering the homeless medical, dental, and eye clinics along with legal assistance, job training, laundry services, and shower facilities. Beneficiaries of those programs began joining the church and significantly altering the mix of the congregation. Before long, the mission of Mission Church had been fundamentally altered. A modest gesture generated partly out of desire to find some way to liven up a Sunday morning led to a radical change in the church (Donde Ashmos Plowman, Lakami Baker, Tammy Beck, Mukta Kulkarni, Stephanie Thomas Solansky, and Deandra Villarreal Travis, "Radical Change Accidentally: The Emergence and Amplification of Small Change," *Academy of Management Journal* 50, no. 3 [2007]: 515–543). Much like in our case, senior leadership at Mission Church had not been involved in triggering the original change, but rather only got involved later to provide legitimacy and marshal resources. Our change was also based on the aggregation of small wins that were viral. Our effort, however, was more strategic on the part of the change agents themselves.

8. The fact that there are cultural, structural, and individual barriers to effective implementation of work-life policies and practices is not new. Lee et al. identified four barriers to reduced work load arrangements: (1) organizational culture that emphasized face time; (2) jobs that were hard to contain; (3) pressure to return to full-time work; and (4) inexperienced or unsupportive senior managers. They further scrutinized arrangements that worked and found it was about both the person and the context: "The success of reduced work load arrangements is not assured by simply choosing the right person or the right job. Rather, success appeared to be a result of many factors, and establishing arrangements seemed to be the beginning, not the end, of ensuring success" (Mary Dean Lee, Shelley MacDermid, Margaret L. Williams, Michelle Buck, and Sharon Leiba-O'Sullivan, "Contextual Factors in the Success of Reduced-Load Work Arrangements Among Managers and Professionals," *Human Resource Management* 41, no. 2 [2002]: 209–223). Thomas Lawrence and Vivien Corwin further theorize that part-time work is at odds with the full-time (and greater) commitment of time required of professionals to be successful in organizations today (Thomas Lawrence and Vivien Corwin, "Being There: The Acceptance and Marginalization of Part-Time Professional Employees," *Journal of Organizational Behavior* 24 [2003]: 923–943); a point that was made a few years earlier by Epstein et al., that the stigma associated with working part-time arises because part-timers are "de facto deviants from established guidelines for work time" (Epstein et al., *The Part Time Paradox*, 25). What PTO provides is a way to address these deep cultural and structural issues—creating a new system aligned around a new definition of what it means to do good work and be a good worker.

Appendix

1. *Action research* is core to the practice of organization development—applying research in organizations as a way to improve the organization, and learning from the results of that action to refine the research itself (definition from W. Warner Burke, "A Contemporary View of Organization Development," in *Handbook of Organization*

Development, ed. Thomas Cummings [Thousand Oaks: Sage Publications, 2008], 13–38). The term was originally coined by Kurt Lewin in 1946 to refer to research that would lead to social action, which was related to Lewin's interest in bridging the concrete and the abstract (Kurt Lewin, "Action Research and Minority Problems," *Journal of Social Issues* 2, no. 4 [1946]: 34–46; Michael Peters and Viviane Robinson "The Origins and Status of Action Research, *Journal of Applied Behavioral Science* 20, no. 2 [1984]: 113–124). A key part of action research is that the process is collaborative—the organization, or subjects, are an active part of the process and engaged in learning along with the researchers (Peters and Robinson, "The Origins and Status of Action Research"). Generally, an action research project follows a pattern of action, analysis, and reflection, which results in feedback that is incorporated into the ongoing action. This was the natural progression in our research at BCG. BCG teams continued to experiment while we analyzed data, fed it back, and observed as they in turn adapted their behavior. The iterative nature of this ongoing process of data collection, analysis, and reflection—leading to them trying out new behaviors and us observing what happened—provided us a marvelous opportunity to gain a deep, rich understanding of the PTO process and what it takes to make it work most effectively.

2. Spela Trefalt, a doctoral student at HBS at the time, helped conduct some of these early interviews.

3. After completing the day-off-a-week experiment on a local client, we decided that the next study should be to repeat the day-off experiment with a client with whom the team had to travel. While we searched for a travel case with which to conduct a predictable-time-off experiment, we began two additional experiments. One had a collective goal that focused on "virtual days" (working away from the client site or office), and another with the goal of reducing travel. Neither included the important insight that came later about combining time for structured dialogue with the collective goal. And while both yielded valuable insights—about teaming and the possibility of altering a goal midstream—neither were completed with our full investment in making the experiment work. Rather, when we finally found a travel team who would experiment with taking time off, we shifted our primary attention there. As a result, these two experiments with teams working "virtually" and "reducing travel" left many unanswered questions that can be more confusing than useful; therefore, I have chosen to omit any further discussion of them.

4. These ten teams were all based in the Unites States; the rollout described in phase 4 was global.

5. During this phase we were paid for the time we spent helping George Martin, Rachel Levine, and the PTO Rollout Team strategize and implement plans for expanding the experiments. We also devoted a significant amount of our own time for research purposes, observing and interviewing team members, attending meetings of the PTO Rollout Team and teams engaging in PTO, and administering surveys.

INDEX

ACKNOWLEDGMENTS

Sleeping with Your Smartphone is the result of a team effort. Jessica Porter was my research associate, collaborator, and project manager through it all—from the earliest days at BCG until the index was complete. She immersed herself in BCG, conducting interviews, traveling extensively with teams, administering surveys, analyzing and reanalyzing data, facilitating teams, and helping make sense of thousands of pages of notes. I could not have seen the project through without her enduring support, her endless patience, and her unwavering commitment to getting it right.

Also invaluable was Melissa Mazmanian, who helped write surveys, conducted interviews, and spent countless hours coding, categorizing, and synthesizing data. Spela Trefalt, Kristina Reeder, Yana Gilbert, Elizabeth Hansen, Christine Rivera, and George Baker were also important contributors in different phases of the project. My assistant Daria Wright was always there, ready to provide whatever was needed—whether proofreading, designing figures, addressing technical issues, or tracking down references.

This book would never have been written without our many partners at BCG, who not only welcomed us into their lives and generously shared their experiences but also became champions of PTO, spreading the word throughout their firm. The members of the initial experiment teams deserve special recognition, both for taking the risks associated with being involved but also for providing the endless feedback that helped shape what this effort would become. For reasons of confidentiality I cannot name individuals—but you know who you are.

Also central to the effort behind this book are the more than fifty PTO facilitators who helped me understand how the process I devised *really* works. At every one of our meetings, I would try out my current thinking, they would voice their critiques, and I would walk away with a deeper, richer understanding of what I was trying to conceptualize. The managing partner then leading the Boston office, George Martin (a pseudonym), had the vision to expand the experiments into a BCG initiative; time and again, he inspired us to push further and to accomplish things we never dreamed possible.

My key contact at BCG, Rachel Levine (also a pseudonym), supported and promoted our research from the beginning. She led one of the earliest experiment teams, read draft after draft of the manuscript, and offered detailed feedback while appreciating my need to preserve my academic integrity. Her partnership throughout the project—especially leading the PTO Rollout Team—helped me to truly appreciate the synergy that is possible between research and practice. I am convinced that neither BCG's PTO initiative nor this book would be where they are today if Rachel and I had not been working side by side.

I also want to thank my mentors from the various institutions I am honored to be affiliated with—from MIT, where I did my graduate work, to my early years as a faculty member at the University of Michigan, to my current position at Harvard Business School. These people provided key intellectual insights that pervade this book: Lotte Bailyn, John Van Maanen, Jane Dutton, Robert Quinn, Jack Gabarro, Mike Tushman, and Nitin Nohria. Harvard Business School's Division of Research and Faculty Development also generously supported this project.

As I researched and wrote this book, many colleagues and students helped me to better understand what I was seeing and how to frame it, particularly: Michael Beer, Julie Battilana, Robert Eccles, Robin Ely, Jody Hoffer Gittell, Boris Groysberg, Melissa Hayes, Rakesh Khurana,

Deborah Kolb, members of QUIET group, and my students in many HBS executive education programs.

Sleeping with Your Smartphone has also benefited greatly from many insightful and diligent readers: Rory Altman, Daisy Dowling, Jack Gabarro, Sharon Meers, Nancy Rothbard, Edward Schein, Michael Shenkman, Michael Tushman, John Van Maanen, Joy Perlow, Jon Perlow, and Joshua Coval. Each read the manuscript from start to finish—often multiple times—and provided frank, constructive, and detailed feedback. Thank you all for helping shape so much of what this book has become.

Two people deserve to be singled out for opening doors and making things happen at critical moments. When Jill Altshuler, a friend from my own early days in management consulting at Corporate Decisions, learned that I was seeking a professional service firm that would permit me to do an in-depth study of how they worked, she introduced me to George and Rachel at BCG. When I asked Robert Sutton to endorse my book, he immediately called into question the proposed title—and then with incredible generosity coached me through a last-minute effort to come up with a better one.

My literary agent Jim Levine had faith in this book from the beginning and patiently helped me every step of the way, from the proposal to the final marketing plan. His friend Edward Tivnan, a gifted writer, guided me magically through endless revisions—and joined Jim in providing me with guidance, support, and the inspiration to keep making the book better.

Also pushing me in that direction was my editor Melinda Merino, who worked with me up to the final deadline. Her vision did not always align with my own, but slowly and persistently (and diplomatically), Melinda persuaded me to make some important changes. As a result of her commitment and perseverance, *Sleeping with Your Smartphone* is a far better book.

Many authors give perfunctory thanks to their parents. But my parents, Joy and Jon Perlow, really did go far beyond the call of duty. They each read the manuscript several times and were not shy in offering their own—often conflicting—perspectives. Both were also there for me at the other end of the phone during my precious windows of "free time"—listening to my doubts, giving me confidence, and helping me bring some balance to my own busy life. (And when her helping hand was needed, my mom never hesitated to travel the more than two hundred miles that separate our homes. Thank you, Mom!)

My family continually reminds me of the importance of turning off. Whenever I get too absorbed in my work, my husband Joshua Coval, who is my chief adviser, critic, and champion, never fails to refocus me on what is really important by asking: "When you're eighty years old, would you prefer to have put in those extra hours working or have spent the time as a family?"

I had my first conversation with BCG to propose this project the same day I learned I was pregnant with my oldest daughter, now finishing kindergarten. I complete this book having given birth to three amazing daughters who are the true joy of my life. They inspire me every day to do whatever I can to help create a world where they will be able to have fulfilling careers and personal lives.

ABOUT THE AUTHOR

Leslie Perlow is the Konosuke Matsushita Professor of Leadership at Harvard Business School. Her goal is to identify ways organizations can alter their work practices to benefit both productivity and employees' well-being. She works closely with organizations to implement these changes—and study their impact. Trained as an ethnographer, she is a keen observer of the microdynamics of work—how people spend their time and with whom they interact—and the consequences for organizations and individuals.

Perlow is the author of two previous books, *Finding Time: How Corporations, Individuals, and Families Can Benefit from New Work Practices* (1997) and *When You Say Yes But Mean No: How Silencing Conflict Wrecks Relationships and Companies . . . and What You Can Do About It* (2003). She has also published numerous articles in journals, including *Administrative Science Quarterly, Organization Science,* and *Harvard Business Review.* Prior to her academic career, Perlow worked as a management consultant with Corporate Decisions, Inc. She graduated from Princeton University with a degree in economics and received her PhD in Organization Studies from MIT. Perlow lives in Newton, Massachusetts, with her husband and their three young daughters, who serve as a daily reminder of all that is involved in successfully integrating work and family.